Mexico and the
Spanish Civil War

Mexico and the Spanish Civil War

T. G. Powell

University of New Mexico Press
Albuquerque

Library of Congress Cataloging in Publication Data

Powell, Thomas G.   1936–
    Mexico and the Spanish Civil War.

    Bibliography: p.
    Includes index.
    1. Mexico—Foreign relations—Spain. 2. Spain—Foreign relations—Mexico. 3. Mexico—
Foreign relations—1910–1946. 4. Spain—Foreign relations—1931–1939. 5. Spain—History—
Civil War, 1936–1939.   I. Title.
F1225.5.S7P68   946.081   80-52280
ISBN 0-8263-0546-6

This book is for my mother, Elizabeth Powell

Contents

Acknowledgments

The author expresses profound gratitude for assistance received in preparing this book to: Fredrick B. Pike, Mark Falcoff, Robert E. Quirk, Ana Staples, and Albert L. Michaels. Financial help from State University of New York Research Foundation and State University College at Buffalo made the study possible. Additional aid came from Sarah Emery and other staff members at Buffalo State's Butler Library and from Carol Julian of its History Department. José Héctor Ibarra and María Lourdes de Urbina at the Archives of the Mexican Secretariat of Foreign Relations assisted the author in various ways. Thanks are also extended to Francesca Linares de Vidarte, Juan Vidarte, María Luisa Tejeda Chardí, Donald and Coralia Hetzner, and to helpful staff members at the following libraries in Mexico City: Biblioteca Nacional, Hemeroteca Nacional, Biblioteca Daniel Cosío Villegas, and Benjamin Franklin Library.

Preface

By describing and interpreting Mexico's response to the Spanish
Civil War, the following study fills a gap in Mexican historiogra-
phy. The Spanish war years, despite being a crucial period in
Mexico's political and diplomatic history, have attracted minimal
scholarly attention. Those few exceptions to general academic
neglect of the topic concentrate on Republican refugees who
settled in Mexico after the war. For the most part, though,
assessments of Mexico's role in Spain's tragic conflict still come
from partisan sources: either supporters of Mexican aid to the
Spanish Republic or admirers of General Francisco Franco. These
emotional versions of the story have been of little use to serious
students of Mexican history. One ideological faction, loyal to the
ruling Revolutionary Party, portrays the Mexican government's
Spanish policy as an altruistic defense of various noble principles;
among these democracy, international justice, and anti-imperialism
are most frequently cited. The other group, largely composed of
traditional Catholic Hispanists, sees Mexican assistance to Republican Spain in terms of a worldwide conspiracy to destroy Christianity, the old Spanish heritage, and even Western civilization itself.
For these people, Mexican support of the "Communist" Spanish
Republic constitutes clear evidence of the "Bolshevism" of Mexican political leaders in the 1930s.

Over the years, the Revolutionary version of the story has been
accepted by most Mexicans. They find an enduring source of
national self-esteem in the patriotic myth, for it depicts their
country as courageously giving a number of moral lessons to the

rest of the world. Although scholarship necessarily contradicts
many obvious fictions, its intent here is not to assault a popular
Mexican legend; instead it seeks to narrate events accurately and to
interpret them fairly. Such an account of Mexico and the Spanish
Civil War can illuminate both Mexican foreign policy and the
nation's social and political dynamics at a critical moment in its
history.

The book begins with an introductory chapter on Mexico's
Revolutionary legacy that relates major issues and conflicts in
Mexican life to the situation in Republican Spain, which had
certain parallels to Mexico. It is argued that because Mexico
remained so divided politically and so prone to violence in the
1930s only consistent army loyalty to the Revolutionary regimes
prevented a full-fledged *Mexican* civil war. Sporadic, domestic
clashes characterized the entire decade, with the inflammatory
religious controversy being especially troublesome. Mexicans were
conditioned by their own circumstances to respond emotionally to
the conflict in Spain, yet many of them remained apathetic. This
indifference appears to have stemmed from several factors: ignorance and illiteracy; preoccupation with the struggle against
poverty; and the country's historic depreciation of Spaniards and
things Spanish.

This theme of attitudes toward Hispanism and members of the
Spanish colony in Mexico is taken up in Chapter 2. Also explored
are official relations between the Revolutionary governments in
Mexico and Spanish Republican administrations from 1931 until
the beginning of the civil war in July 1936. It will be seen that
during the 1920s and early 1930s increasing numbers of educated,
urban Mexicans became aware of "the other Spain," that is, the
liberal reformist element in peninsular life. To a large extent this
new sensitivity was communicated by two celebrated Mexican
writers, José Vasconcelos and Alfonso Reyes, both of whom later
entered the civil war debate with their customary vigor. Despite
these contacts, few Mexicans prior to July 1936 gained much
awareness of the radical, totalitarian strain in Spanish leftist
politics; when it came to dominate the Republic at the outset of
the war, however, many so-called dedicated Revolutionaries were
unpleasantly surprised.

Liberal-left Republicans and their Revolutionary counterparts in
Mexico established an affectionate, harmonious relationship in

1931. Mexican politicians of the 1930s appreciated that the Spanish Republic constituted a rare source of moral support for what they regarded as their ongoing Revolution; and they joyfully perceived the Republicans as following their example in regard to "social renovation." For the Republicans, the Mexicans were welcome companions at all times. Both countries had few diplomatic friends during the decade. Also argued in Chapter 2 is that the Spanish Republic began with a considerable degree of goodwill even among conservative-traditionalist Mexicans. Many of them used its originally democratic character as a polemical weapon against their own authoritarian government. By praising Spanish liberty, they hoped to gain some concessions of political freedom for themselves. This conservative estimation soon turned sour: Republican attacks on the Spanish Church, the regime's inability to control extremists, and its open admiration for anticlerical General Plutarco E. Calles—Mexico's military strongman—all rather quickly turned this initial approval into bitter hostility.

The military and diplomatic assistance rendered to Loyalist Spain by the Mexican government under President Lázaro Cárdenas, and the rationale for that aid, are described in detail in Chapter 3. Despite encountering many serious foreign policy problems as a result of its pro-Republican stand, the Cárdenas administration took every feasible action to save its increasingly dependent friend. This was logical since support of the Republic before the world furthered a major Mexican objective: to get the United States and other powers committed to the principles of nonaggression and anti-imperialism. Yet, bungling by Mexican and Spanish politicians frustrated much of what Cárdenas wanted to do for the Republic, and Mexico made no converts abroad to its position on the Civil War. In regard to international aspects of the question, special attention is given to the Spanish American countries, most of whom viewed Mexico with suspicious hostility even before Cárdenas began to champion Republican Spain.

Also discussed in the chapter is the Mexican army's consistent endorsement of the president's Spanish diplomacy through all the turbulence of the civil war years. Some of the most enthusiastic supporters of the Republic in Mexico were field-grade officers with a Revolutionary background. Several junior officers obtained leaves of absence to fight in Spain. Yet the Spanish Civil War had a decidedly sobering effect on the Mexican military establishment, old revolutionaries included. Mexican soldiers tended to be appalled by the Republican Terror and by the disorderly condition of the Loyalist army due to the meddling of powerful, left-wing labor unions and political parties. They concluded that such a situation must never develop in Mexico; when labor leader Vicente Lombardo Toledano called for armed workers militias "to defend the Revolution against fascism," the army took action immediately to prevent Cárdenas from accepting his proposal.

Pro-Republican and pro-Franco activities by Mexican nationals are examined in Chapter 4. It contains accounts of Mexican military volunteers who fought on the Republican side, analysis of the debate on Spain at home, and a summary of the role played by Mexico's press during the Civil War. Just as there were several basic and very different reasons why Mexicans supported the Republic, pro-Franco sentiment came from a wide range of positions on the Mexican right. It will be seen that Mexican supporters of the Nationalist rebellion were less enthusiastic about fascism or totalitarian politics in general than their opponents have claimed. Moreover, the brunt of ideological and public relations support for the Loyalists was borne by members of the Revolutionary Party, who stressed democracy and legality, and by such leftists as members of the Mexican Communist Party, officers of the fellow-traveling Mexican Workers Confederation, and Marxists without party affiliation. Left-wing propaganda emphasized the need to protect the Spanish workers and their revolution from domestic class enemies and foreign fascists abroad who had imperialistic designs on Spain. President Cárdenas himself used both arguments selectively, his audience determining the nature of his appeal. Those Mexican liberals who had accepted the Revolution (many did not) also acted on behalf of the Republic; but like their counterparts in Spain, they had no real choice once the battle lines had been drawn. Privately, many Revolutionary liberals deplored the bloodshed and totalitarianism that rapidly came to characterize the Republic. In the book's final chapter, Mexico's remarkable, unique role in rescuing countless Spanish Republicans from certain death after the civil war had ended is described. This operation is viewed from the perspectives of both international diplomacy and domestic politics. In addition, evolution of Mexico's Spanish war myth is traced.

Whenever possible, *Mexico and the Spanish Civil War* has been based on unpublished documents filed at the Archives of the Mexican Secretariat of Foreign Relations. Published documents have been used extensively as have the memoirs and other writings of contemporary officials, politicians, and polemicists. For primary sources of opinion, Mexican newspapers and journals have been consulted. Included among the periodicals are publications of the Church, army, labor unions, and other important institutions and organizations. The book also draws on such valuable sources of information as scholarly monographs, unpublished doctoral dissertations, and published collections of interviews with major Mexican political and intellectual figures. The civil war reminiscences of several Mexicans and Spaniards who kindly granted interviews to the author have also provided valuable material. Any errors of fact or misguided interpretations, of course, are the author's sole responsibility.

1

Obstacles to Stability in Revolutionary Mexico, 1910-40

Modernization and Revolution in Mexico

Mexico experienced a modernization process in the nineteenth century that satisfied relatively few people. Begun by liberal politicians who dreamed of a secular, capitalist society run by themselves in pseudodemocratic fashion, the process had been carried forward by General Porfirio Díaz, dictatorial ruler of the country from the 1870s until his overthrow in 1911. Several major flaws accounted for the unhappy outcome of Mexican moderniza-tion. Departure from time-honored Spanish social and economic traditions in favor of foreign development models destroyed Mexico's ever-precarious societal balance. New legislation and more efficient business practices by landowners deprived peasants of their lands and removed customary paternalistic protection from sharecroppers and laborers on large estates. Despite the appear-ance of a secure peace, maintained by army and police terror, the sufferings and hence revolutionary potential of rural Mexicans increased each year.[1]

As in various European countries, Mexican modernization also victimized and alienated urban artisans, who were hard pressed by new economic conditions and unwilling to descend into Mexico's expanding industrial proletariat. This latter group began to show signs of organizational ability and militancy in the early 1900s when several major strikes against textile and mining companies had to be suppressed by massive government violence against the workers.[2] Many middle-sector Mexicans had also chafed at President Díaz's formula for modernization, since its many concessions to foreign capitalists and corporations allowed them to take virtual control of the national economy. The dictator, moreover, kept his political circle restricted to a small clique, its members monopolizing fees, commissions, and bribes exacted from foreign investors. By the early 1900s bourgeois malcontents excluded from the system's benefits had found the courage to challenge it.[3] Finally, Mexico's Church and many Catholics remained intransigent foes of modernization itself. Although coddled by Díaz, who astutely avoided the mistakes of his liberal predecessors by refusing to persecute Catholicism and to despoil ecclesiastical wealth, the Mexican Church would not even offer compromise on such issues as societal secularization and proscription of clerical incursions into politics.[4]

Mexico's Revolution of 1910 began ironically under the auspices of bourgeois liberal leadership in the person of Francisco Madero, a wealthy eccentric. Not the least of Madero's oddities was his belief that return to the pseudodemocracy of the 1850s would calm social tensions inflamed by modernization. Since modernizing liberals themselves had provoked a long period of constant domestic turbulence in Mexico, Madero's political vision had an especially quixotic character. Tragic events soon changed the Revolution's course. Lower-class victims of modernization joined the upheaval and trapped President Madero between themselves on the left and conservative, clerical defenders of Spanish colonial traditions on the right. Allied with the latter group were surviving supporters of Díaz. The incompetent Madero perished in February 1913, murdered during a military coup headed by rightist General Victoriano Huerta, the famous *cucaracha* (cockroach) that Revolutionaries immortalized in a popular song. General Huerta's coup immediately revived the Revolution, which came to be spearheaded by an uneasy coalition of liberals, led by gray-bearded Venustiano Carranza, and ragtag radical movements directed by two picturesque but controversial chieftains: Emiliano Zapata and Francisco "Pancho" Villa.[5]

Backed by United States President Woodrow Wilson, who did not like Huerta, the Revolutionaries toppled the hated tyrant in 1914. After Huerta's flight into exile, the rebels themselves split into warring factions. Carranza battled Zapata and Villa. By 1916 Carranza had triumphed, only to be robbed of his liberal victory by ideological reverses at the Revolutionary constituent congress of 1917. Dominated by politicians who realized that Mexico's old modernization formula no longer had validity, the congress superimposed on basic liberal principles constitutional provisions exalting state power over virtually every facet of life. Subsequent Revolutionary regimes could then create a post-modern political system to deal effectively with such momentous problems as foreign imperialism, economic reconstruction, the cultural gap between Indians and other Mexicans, poverty and illiteracy, and continuing Church resistance to modernity itself.[6]

Mexico's Constitution of 1917 did not, however, automatically provide practical solutions to these problems. President Álvaro Obregón (1920–24) made a modestly successful start at problem solving, but his administration was followed by a largely destructive period of bigoted tyranny and corruption under General Plutarco E. Calles, president from 1924 to 1928 and "boss" of Mexico from 1929 to 1934.[7] Amid ongoing violence, President Lázaro Cárdenas (1934–40), another Revolutionary general, finally worked out a feasible plan for ruling Mexico and for making its socioeconomic structure reasonably functional. Cárdenas's program, despite its employment of Marxist rhetoric, had a strongly traditional bias: it preserved the dominant-dependent, two-culture society of the Spanish colonial period and put an authoritarian, corporatist stamp on Mexican politics and social relations.[8] Cardenista Mexico thus had much in common with General Franco's Nationalist government in Spain, a regime that the Mexican president despised, and which he tried valiantly to defeat during the Civil War by rendering unceasing aid to the Spanish Republic. Although he would have angrily denied it, Cárdenas himself even resembled Franco in presiding over what was essentially a military dictatorship.

The terms *conservative* or *reactionary* are used periodically in this study to indicate individuals or groups hostile to Mexico's

Revolutionary regimes, yet ideologically diverse elements made up this opposition. Some of the ruling party's sharpest critics were old liberals who had been associated with Madero and Carranza. As has been noted, even Cárdenas embodied a rather traditional approach to Mexico's modernization crisis, and the president preserved far more Mexican institutions and customs than he altered. Conservatives separated themselves from the Revolution in the 1930s through defense of the Catholic Church and its historic prerogatives, a concomitant resistance to secularism, pronounced Hispanist sentiments (shared by some Revolutionaries, however), antagonism to United States economic and cultural influences, and fear of organized labor. Some of the more prominent conservatives also had the misfortune to be members of the displaced ex-elite that had ruled Mexico prior to the 1910 upheaval. It is striking how many major antagonists of Calles, Cárdenas, and the Spanish Republic had been associated officially with Huerta's counter-revolutionary regime of 1913–14.

Taking an overall view of Mexican conservatives in the 1930s, one notes that some of them opposed modernization itself; some had reconciled themselves to a measure of modernity; and others proposed post modern totalitarian solutions to national problems. Finally, certain defenders of the old liberal order, prestigious veterans of a Revolution that they thought had been fought to restore the modernizing process by purging it of political tyranny, grew disillusioned and repudiated the Revolutionary regimes. They simply could not accept post modern rejections of laissez-faire capitalism and liberal pseudodemocracy that had come in the wake of the 1917 Constitution. Moreover, they found the demagogy and brutality of the ruling party repulsive. These ideological positions are treated more extensively at several places in the book.

Republican Spain shared many characteristics with Revolutionary Mexico in the 1930s. Still economically underdeveloped, both countries afforded low standards of living to most of their people. Predominantly illiterate and landless rural majorities subsisted wretchedly on the margin of civilization. Urban laborers received poor wages and faced high unemployment rates year after year. National unity did not exist. Large sections of the population remained alienated from their government. The middle sectors were small; democratic institutions were weak. Military praetorianism frustrated the few champions of representative civilian government. Bitter conflicts between anticlericals and Catholics reflected continuing societal division on such issues as religious toleration, religious instruction in the schools, state regulation of ecclesiastical finances and of Church activity in general, and the social and political authority of the hierarchy. Although each country lacked strong military defenses, prior to 1936 Mexico rather than Spain seemed the most likely victim of possible foreign aggression.

Antimodern forces had been repeatedly defeated in Mexico since the mid-nineteenth century. Their prospects in the 1930s seemed almost hopeless. But in Spain traditionalists had retained considerable strength. Liberal Spanish Republicans, nominally in control of the government (1931–33; 1936), belatedly tried to make capitalistic modernization work in the context of a multiparty parliamentary system. They lacked political ability, however, and their radical allies gave them more trouble than cooperation. Against the determined resistance of traditionalists and totalitarians, they labored without any assurance of army loyalty. Indeed only recently (1923–30) General Miguel Primo de Rivera had maintained a conservative military dictatorship on behalf of the defunct Bourbon monarchy. In 1932 there was an abortive army revolt, and in 1936 a military uprising precipitated the Civil War.[9]

Here, a brief description of the politics and political figures of Republican Spain will be useful, as it can serve as a basis for understanding some of the allusions to peninsular affairs and figures later in the book. The first Republican government of 1931–33 was a Left-Center coalition of liberals, socialists, and even some politicians of conservative views. Its figurehead president was Niceto Alcalá-Zamora, a practicing Catholic and an ex-monarchist. Yet the tone of this Republican administration was set by the anticlerical left Republican, Manuel Azaña, who led the Republican Action Party. Azaña served both as prime minister and later as president during the Civil War. He came to symbolize Republican Spain for many people in the peninsula and abroad, even though he eventually became merely a "prisoner" of the Communists and their fellow-traveling instrument, Prime Minister Juan Negrín.

Supporting this regime, as well as the Popular Front government ushered in with the elections of February 1936, was the Spanish Socialist Party, which had long been fragmented into moderate and radical factions. Indalecio Prieto led the moderate Socialists. He served as War Minister for part of the Civil War. Among the moderates were party theoretician Julián Besteiro, Julio Álvarez del Vayo, and Juan Negrín. Álvarez del Vayo served as ambassador to Mexico in the early 1930s and was Minister of State during the war; Negrín became prime minister in the spring of 1937. Both men proved to be tools of the Spanish Communists. Special envoy to Mexico, Juan-Simeón Vidarte, was also a moderate Socialist. The radical wing of the party was led by Francisco Largo Caballero. Largo Caballero served as prime minister for the first part of the war, but eventually fell from power due to Communist pressure. He had resisted Communist attempts to dominate him. Additional, nominal socialists belonged to the Radical Socialist Party (not to be confused with the radical Socialists), a small group ideologically close to Clemenceau's Radicals of the Third French Republic. Marcelino Domingo led this faction, which included the Republic's ambassador to Mexico, Félix Gordón Ordás. Both men were in Mexico for much of the civil war, Domingo as an energetic propagandist. Also on the left were a large anarchist group, committed to the violent overthrow of bourgeois capitalism and hence scornful of electoral politics, and the Spanish Communist Party, Stalinist in orientation and accustomed to taking orders from Moscow.

An equally disparate coalition of mainly ideological parties characterized the Spanish right, which was in power from November 1933 to February 1936, and which almost universally supported General Franco's rebellion. Conservative Alejandro Lerroux led the misleadingly named Radical Party. He served as prime minister from 1933 to 1936. Several other conservative parties or alliances of factions stood to the right of Lerroux's Radicals: the Confederation of Autonomous Right Parties (CEDA) represented Catholic interests and was led by José María Gil Robles; the Carlist Party, dating from the early nineteenth century, sought restoration of a highly traditional, intensely pro-Catholic monarchy; other monarchist parties existed, one of them led by José Calvo Sotelo; and finally, the Falange Española, led by José Antonio Primo de Rivera, sought a post modern, totalitarian solution to Spain's modernity crisis. As Stanley G. Payne has observed, Spanish Falangists wanted their country "to make a great historical leap, vaulting feudal backwardness and liberal capitalism at the same time." The Falangists were far from traditional in that they scorned the old defunct monarchy and displayed open contempt for such proclerical leaders as Gil Robles of the CEDA.[10]

The Mexican political situation, although not conducive to stability, at least favored the government's survival. Mexico's revolutionaries had created the National Revolutionary Party (PNR) in 1928, an authoritarian instrument with which they confidently ruled. Dominated by a loyal if factionalized military establishment, the PNR had been controlled since its inception by General Calles. Of humble social origins, Calles made the most of his political success. Corruption and *nouveau riche* vulgarity characterized his administration. The general himself had a huge belly, oversize ears, and a big nose. He had once worked as a bartender, and he looked more like a veteran prizefighter than a chief of state. Cartoonists found him an ideal subject, regularly producing hilarious caricatures of his ungainly face.[11] Calles maintained his authority by combining demagogy, bribery, and selective terror with modest economic and social reforms, and by espousing crowd-pleasing nationalism. In 1935, however, he lost control of the PNR and of the country to President Lázaro Cárdenas, a skilled politician who refused to follow his orders.[12] Army loyalty gave PNR governments a distinct advantage over the Spanish Republic's liberal-left administration. Both Calles and Cárdenas faced heavy opposition from alienated rightist groups and even from elements within the Revolution, but each could depend on the army. Had it not been for this military loyalty to the government and its programs, Mexico like Spain would probably have been torn apart by a full-scale civil war in the 1930s.[13]

The PNR and Its Critics

Formation of the PNR followed several years of bloody strife between General Calles and militant Catholics encouraged by a Church hierarchy that had never reconciled itself to the Revolution's secularism and anticlericalism. In certain rural areas the conflict had been marked by guerrilla warfare known as the Cristero Rebellion (1926–29). During the turmoil, a Catholic assassinated PNR President-elect Álvaro Obregón in 1928. Although Church and state agreed to a truce in 1929, mutual hatreds and fanaticism continued to spark violence.[14] In this poisoned atmosphere another presidential election took place. Angered by military tyranny, graft, and statism, José Vasconcelos, a prominent liberal writer and former secretary of Public Education, challenged PNR candidate General Pascual Ortiz Rubio, an obvious tool of Calles. When Vasconcelos attracted mass support, the PNR disrupted his campaign by assaulting his followers. After the regime announced a clearly fictitious landslide victory for Ortiz Rubio, Vasconcelos bitterly went into exile—to be tormented by Callista phantasms for the rest of his life. Some of his backers revolted and were killed. Having passed its initial test, the PNR stood ready to help General Calles enforce his particular approach to the Revolution.[15]

Despite being an authoritarian party that suppressed all serious political opposition and persecuted Mexican Catholics, the PNR in power had a surprisingly tolerant attitude toward criticism, even when it was scurrilous.[16] Calles never shut off free speech, never eliminated press freedom. He did close temporarily a few especially annoying newspapers, and occasionally he tried to silence a major critic, but neither he nor Cárdenas later ever forced cloture of debate on any issue. Mexicans thus remained free to discuss such controversial questions as the Spanish Civil War; and even so called fascists enjoyed virtually unlimited opportunities to publicize their views.[17]

The Vasconcelos campaign demonstrated that not only conservatives opposed the PNR. A number of moderates, equally upset by Calles's exaltation of the state and arbitrary rule, repeated the call for a return to the Revolution's original liberal principles as expounded by Madero. Luis Cabrera, a prominent writer and former Treasury secretary under Carranza, courageously advocated this position. He and many other libertarian intellectuals could not support the PNR's Leviathan state and so fell out of fashion in official circles. As government power expanded even more under Cárdenas their alienation deepened, and leftists unfairly dubbed them reactionaries. Cabrera's pungent criticisms had been especially nettlesome to Calles, who exiled him in 1931. The general, Cabrera had pointed out, suppressed liberty in the name of social justice for peasants and workers, yet still had not delivered promised reforms.[18]

When Calles moved somewhat leftward in 1933–34, and thus unleashed several of the PNR's more radical tendencies, other middle-class moderates voiced their anxieties. It seems clear that they feared social upheaval as well as excessive state power. In one of the decade's most celebrated books, *Profile of Man and Culture in Mexico* (1934), scholar Samuel Ramos unhappily observed:

> The dominant tone in Mexican politics in recent years has been radicalism. Demogoguery has taken upon itself the propagation among the masses of extremist social doctrines that lack roots in Mexico, and which, given our national circumstances, are simply utopian.[19]

In 1936, after over a year of Cardenism, Cabrera published a summary of his reflections on recent political trends. It was a classic statement of Mexican liberalism's objections to the Revolution's post-1917 course, which seemed to old liberals to be taking the country toward "Sovietization." Mexico's society and its constitutional government, Cabrera wrote, were distintegrating under the onslaught of Cárdenas and his supporters, who "want to revoke the 1917 Constitution, which they call antiquated and useless, in order to establish a dictatorship of the proletariat based on a classless society."[20] Mexican conservatives shared these same fears. They, too, charged the PNR and an "irresponsible" labor movement with wrecking the nation's economy, oppressing the middle and upper classes, and generally setting the stage for full-fledged Bolshevism.[21]

Many Mexican rightists, like the Franquistas in Spain, contrasted their own nationalistic patriotism with the PNR's alleged internationalism. Cárdenas, they said, threatened to destroy the country's sovereignty by subjecting it to foreign domination. For Mexico to survive as a nation it had to return to its historic traditions, all intimately connected to the Catholic faith, and thus avoid becoming a Communist satellite. Speaking to a convention of the rightist Mexican Social Democratic Party in 1937, Diego Arenas Guzmán reiterated this thesis in terms that echoed what Franco's publicists had been claiming as a major justification for the army rebellion against the Republican government.

> Only paranoids, traitors, or other irresponsible people, it seems to me, attack the concepts which sustain Mexican nationality: family, religion, property, patriotism. Wicked are the clenched fists that prepare to strike the fatherland. Wicked are the arms that raise the red and black flag, for

rather than being a symbol of proletarian redemption as claimed, it is really the symbol of Jewish imperialist penetration throughout the world. Wicked are the voices that sing the *Internationale* as a substitute for our national anthem. It is not necessary to be a rightist, a fascist, a conservative, a clerical, or a reactionary to curse these abominable attacks. It is only necessary to be Mexican.[22]

Mexico Under the PNR

From 1924 to 1934 Calles kept Mexico in an uproar by failing to restore the social equilibrium disturbed by modernization, the Revolution, and his encouragement of virulent anticlericalism. He did at least conciliate a United States government worried about nationalization of American oil companies, but this achievement won him few friends among his xenophobic countrymen. Professing to view the masses paternalistically, Calles actually treated them with contempt. Rather than offer tangible material benefits from his administration to Mexican workers, he tried to distract them with warfare against the Church. One of his closest political associates, corrupt labor leader Luis Morones, inhibited rather than advanced the working man's cause. The last of Calles's three puppet presidents, wealthy General Abelardo Rodríguez (1932–34), took the position that strikes were unpatriotic. Under Calles, then, Mexico's modernity crisis, aggravated by the Depression, grew steadily worse.[23]

For years the clumsy despot did nothing to ameliorate this situation. The PNR continued to persecute Catholics, obstruct ecclesiastical functions, and attack religious beliefs. Such policies perpetuated the danger of renewed civil strife and gave to the Calles administration a striking ideological similarity, on one point at least, to the anticlerical Spanish Republican government of 1931–33.[24] Laws granting federal and state governments power to restrict the number of clergy functioning in any particular area were used in some locations to eliminate completely the presence of priests. In Tabasco state PNR Governor Tomás Garrido Canabal closed all Catholic churches, exiled or killed all known priests, and created a large, paramilitary youth organization called the Red Shirts to intimidate Catholics. Armed bands of Red Shirts forcibly entered homes, seized religious materials, and destroyed them in public bonfires. Garrido himself issued a series of preposterous antireligious decrees, one of which ordered people to eat meat on Fridays.[25]

Catholics in neighboring Veracruz state suffered almost as much as the Tabascans. Governor Adalberto Tejeda (destined to play a major role in Cárdenas's civil war diplomacy) permitted only one priest to function for every 100,000 Catholics. At his direction, policemen and anticlerical mobs shot Catholics and their priests; bombed, burned, and sacked churches; and in general terrorized the faithful.[26] Exiled conservative writer Carlos Pereyra, later an apologist for Franco, compared Tejeda to Monsieur Homais, the anticlerical villain of *Madame Bovary,* and drew a grim picture of the PNR chieftain's state: "Priests kidnapped by Tejeda's police, pastors and children assassinated by his mobs, churches blown up or burned, such is the 'law' in Veracruz. Such is Tejeda. Sorrow. Panic. Viva Calles!"[27]

Some of the Mexican Church's trouble with the PNR stemmed from its rejection of secular solutions to the nation's pressing social and economic problems.[29] To a large extent this attitude had been imposed on Mexico's hierarchy by the papacy itself. Pius XI, for example, had taken a rather medieval stand in his 1931 encyclical *Quadragesimo anno.* The proper way to save the world from "amoral liberalism," he wrote, "is not to be found in class struggle and terror, nor in the autocratic abuse of state power; but rather in the spreading of social justice and Christian love throughout the socioeconomic order." True prosperity should be restored to the world "by means of the principles of a wise corporatism that respects the correct social hierarchy. . . ."[29] In March 1937 Pius XI sent an apostolic letter to the Mexican bishops in which he repeated this position: "In answer to frequent accusations that the Church either ignores social problems or is incapable of resolving them, you must not cease to assert that only the teachings and work of the Church, which are sustained by its Divine Founder, can provide a remedy for the grave ills that afflict humanity."[30] Following the Pope's lead, Mexican bishops fulminated against secular education, secular trade unions, and government interference with the rights of property. Such things, they once again told Mexican Catholics, had to be shunned as sinful.[31]

The PNR "socialist education" program of 1933–34, along with President Cárdenas's anticlericalism in 1935, produced new mili-

tancy among lay Catholics. This encouraged the hierarchy to reject
compromise with the government despite more religious persecution. Mexican bishops were determined to preserve the Catholic
bases of the good society.[32] In January 1936, a letter from the
hierarchy to clergy and laity once again ordered Catholics to
repudiate secularism and to avoid socialist education under pain of
mortal sin.[33] In June a collective pastoral instruction addressed to
"workers and peasants throughout the Republic" specifically
promoted corporatism and contained statements that seemed to
endorse fascism. "You should prepare," the bishops advised Mexican laborers, "to proceed decisively to the great work of organizing
our country on the basis of the Corporation. . . . The world is
presently disenchanted with liberalism; it will soon grow weary of
Communism; the Catholic idea begins to give life and strength to
social and economic organization which recognizes corporations as
its basis. The names of two illustrious Catholic statesmen already
stand out in the history of our era: Dolffus [sic] in Austria and
Oliveira Salazar in Portugal."[34] Intransigent conservatism, of
course, gave Mexico's Church a close resemblance to its counterpart in Spain.

Serious political difficulties had prompted the PNR's leftward
move that so upset Mexican Catholics. Despite antagonizing
conservatives and the Church, Calles had done little to attract
support from rank and file union members or landless agrarians.
With Mexico still mired in the Depression, many urban and rural
workers had begun open revolt. Critics effectively pilloried Callism's moral bankruptcy, and the government sensed mounting
danger.[35] Confronted by this crisis, Calles proclaimed the Revolution a failure. He called on the PNR to begin a new surge of social
reform to coincide with the presidential election coming up in
1934. At its 1933 convention the party adopted a six-year plan for
Mexico's economic and social development. It also selected
General Lázaro Cárdenas to be Mexico's next president. The
six-year plan projected greater state direction of the economy,
more agrarian reform, and full implementation of socialist education in Mexican schools.[36] Some sources indicate that Calles got his
idea for the six-year plan from Spanish Republican Ambassador
Julio Álvarez del Vayo, a socialist fellow-traveler who admired
Soviet programs and policies.[37]

Lázaro Cárdenas

Candidate Cárdenas was thirty-nine. He had fought in the Revolution as a teenager. Surviving factional strife, Cárdenas rapidly became a general in the Revolutionary army. Adept at politics, he grew friendly with strongman Calles, who trusted him enough to let him run the PNR. During the wave of anticlericalism in the 1920s Cárdenas was one of the country's leading church-baiters. He had the reputation of being a champion of proletarian causes, but Calles manifestly expected to prevent any serious movement to the left by his protégé. Despite the onset of middle age, Cárdenas remained physically strong, even rugged. He never seemed to tire. He had thick lips, dark skin, and a stern countenance that made him seem humorless. He felt a special affection for simple country folk, and he hated Mexico's urban intelligentsia. During his presidency, he would spend much of his time in rural areas rather than in Mexico City.[38] One of many ironies involved in Mexico's unshakable support for the Spanish Republic was that it forced the anti-intellectual, *macho* Cárdenas into alliance with cerebral, effeminate Manuel Azaña, a man whose type he heartily detested; in terms of temperament, Cárdenas had much more in common with General Franco than with the Republican chief of state. Azaña's widow (living in Mexico after the civil war) once expressed regret that her husband and Cárdenas never met, but another Spanish Republican woman present acutely rejoined: "If they *had* met, they would have *bitten* each other."[39]

Mexicans who had found the PNR state under Calles oppressively burdensome could take no comfort from Cárdenas's presidential campaign. In May 1934 he indicated that his administration would "intervene in all aspects of production and consumption, culture, and education."[40] He professed to believe that arbitrary exercise of government power on behalf of the working classes constituted democracy's purest form. Cárdenas thus shared the Hispanic world's general prejudice against Anglo-Saxon one-man, one-vote democratic theory, although it can and has been argued that many of the Republicans hoped to achieve electoral democracy in Spain itself.[41] Later as president, Cárdenas told the nation that by distributing wealth more equitably, elevating living standards, and providing equal cultural opportunities and access to power for "the working majorities," his government affirmed the basic principles of "true democracy."[42]

Catholics especially must have viewed Cárdenas's impending assumption of power with terrible anxiety. During his campaign travels, the candidate visited Tabasco where, after reviewing thousands of parading Red Shirts, he called the state a "laboratory of the Revolution." He described Governor Garrido's young henchmen as "truly idealistic because they think in a collective manner and because they advocate the well-being and happiness of everyone." Predicting that Red Shirt organizations would soon be found all over Mexico, Cárdenas expressed pleasure at the prospect. "The Mexican Revolution," he added, "has had a profound social interpretation in Tabasco, which we should [all] imitate with valor and sincerity."[43]

The Red Shirts took Cárdenas seriously. On May 10, 1934, a group of them recently arrived from Tabasco raided Mexico City's San Francisco Church, threw its religious images and other contents into the street, and burned them as policemen looked on without intervening.[44] Desecration of San Francisco came exactly three years after the initial church burnings and anticlerical mob violence in Republican Spain. At that time Spanish police had also watched indifferently or with approval. Many Mexican Catholics must have been reminded of Spain by the Red Shirts and driven to despair on election day in 1934 when Cárdenas gave additional stimulus to the Tabascan organization by announcing that he had cast *his* presidential vote for Garrido.

Cárdenas's inauguration on November 30, 1934, followed by less than two months Spain's "Red October," a bloody leftist-workers revolt against a constitutionally elected conservative government. Quickly suppressed by the Spanish army, the uprising nevertheless had disturbed many Mexicans. Now in their own country they witnessed labor agitation and strikes, which the new president openly encouraged. Socialist education began to be implemented in the public schools. Religious persecution went on. Cárdenas even brought the bizarre Tabascan governor into his cabinet as Secretary of Agriculture. Additional contingents of Garrido's Red Shirts came to the capital with him, thus turning the worst nightmares of Mexico City's Catholic middle class into chilling reality. Many Mexicans obviously believed that Cárdenas intended to unleash a leftist revolution similar to the one that had recently rocked Spain.[45]

On December 30, 1934, a month after Cárdenas's assumption of office, heavily armed Red Shirts fired on Catholics as they left a Church in Coyoacán, one of the capital's suburbs. They killed five people, and wounded thirty others. One Red Shirt died in the ensuing riot. Cárdenas appeared to approve of the murders, for he sent flowers to the fallen Tabascan's grave and in his New Year's message to the nation repeated his determination to enforce strictly all anticlerical legislation. Six months later the president pardoned all Red Shirts arrested in connection wtih the Coyoacán killings.[46]

Eventually Red Shirt activity was checked. Cárdenas exiled Garrido for his loyalty to Calles during a PNR power struggle in 1935, and the president finally realized how much harm Red Shirt violence was doing to his administration.[47] Still, the movement had inflicted serious public relations damage on Cárdenas, and before Garrido's organization passed into merited oblivion even PNR supporters fought among themselves over issues raised by the controversial Tabascan thugs.[48] In January 1935 a group of university students launched an assault on the Red Shirts operating in Mexico City. They had been inspired by David A. Siqueiros, a young artist and Communist agitator. (Two years later Siqueiros went to Spain, allegedly to fight for the Republic.) Calling the Tabascans "stooges" of the United Fruit Company and Yankee imperialism, Siqueiros led over a thousand youths to the National Palace to demand dissolution of Garrido's organization. He characterized it as more dangerous to the Revolution than extremist groups on the right. After the rally, Siqueiros's mob precipitated yet another political riot in the capital by attacking Red Shirt headquarters. Cárdenas then "encouraged" the Tabascan militants to return to their native state, apparently having changed his mind about the desirability of spreading Garrido's movement to every locale in Mexico. Unfortunately the president's action came somewhat late. Backers of the Revolutionary regime had begun to clash violently among themselves over ideological and political differences in a manner resembling the turbulence of Republican Spain. These battles increased restiveness in the country by adding to existing disorder.[49]

Despite curbing anticlerical excesses in Mexico City, neither Cárdenas nor the PNR backed away from their aggressive harassment of Catholicism. During 1935, nineteen of Mexico's thirty-two bishops remained in exile; and federal authorities allowed Red Shirt contingents to continue attacking religion in the provinces. The Tabascans joined local police in shooting at Catholics who demonstrated against socialist education, and their repeated assaults on villages caused numerous rural communities to arm themselves for self-defense.[50] Various state governors made new attempts to eliminate the Church completely, yet Cárdenas offered no criticism of their actions. The PNR daily newspaper, *El Nacional,* regularly attacked the Church and featured antireligious propaganda, as did PNR radio broadcasts. Ignacio García Téllez, secretary of Public Education, declared that he would "employ all efforts to destroy the Catholic Church," inaugurated the First Congress of the Proletarian Child, and energetically promoted the PNR socialist education program. In Feburary 1935 the government even prohibited the sending of religious materials and literature through the mails.[51]

Church desecrations and anti-Catholic violence continued, too. Throughout 1935 state governments confiscated religious buildings and used them for secular purposes. Governor Rafael Sánchez Tapia of Michoacán promoted a basketball game inside Morelia's cathedral during Easter week. The number of clergy permitted to function in certain areas continued to be very low. Police bullets killed six and wounded over one hundred Catholic demonstrators in Guadalajara. Renewed protests led to more bloodshed and many arrests, Archbishop Pascual Díaz himself going to jail. When Guanajuato's militant Catholics rioted against socialist education in 1936, the police killed or wounded many of them.[52] Still, Catholics refused to abandon their cause; in both cities and rural areas the bloody struggle went on.

Socialist Education and the Defense of Religion

Here, some background information on socialist education may be useful. At its presidential nominating convention in 1933, the PNR had decided to reform Article Three of the Mexican Constitution to provide for mandatory socialist education in public schools. This development followed a three-year campaign to remove priests, nuns, and religious instruction from the nation's *parochial* schools, a project of Education Secretary Narciso Bassols,

a Marxist. Determination to eliminate the Church's influence in
Spanish education, as an essential step toward building a laic
educational system, had been a major objective of Republican
Prime Minister Manuel Azaña since 1931. The Azaña regime's
legislation in this area had caused considerable Church antipathy
to the Republic. Thus the politics of education in Spain was a
source of bitter struggle, as it was in Mexico. As much of an
anticlerical as Azaña, Bassols later influenced Cárdenas's Spanish
policy during and immediately after the Civil War. Bald, frail, and
bespectacled, he looked more like a timorous clerk than the
aggressive politician and ideologue that he was. His actions in
Spain and France after 1936 gave rise to the belief that he had
become a Soviet agent, and Cárdenas did indeed eventually
remove Bassols from a diplomatic post in France in 1940 because of
his favoritism to Spanish Communists among the Republican
refugees awaiting passage to Mexico.[53]

The socialist education decision coincided with a general
leftward move by the PNR. Some party leaders hoped that it would
provide a Marxist ideological base for the impending revitalization
of Mexico's Revolution.[54] Throughout the country and within the
PNR, socialist education immediately became a divisive issue.
Catholics and middle-class people, conservatives and moderates,
students and teachers, all saw it as violating religious and academic
freedom. The government at one point estimated that sixty percent
of Mexico's teachers opposed the program. Many PNR luminaries,
outgoing President Rodríguez included, thought the idea ill advised. Rodríguez complained that replacing religious sectarianism
with socialist sectarianism in the schools would only end up by
"stifling individual initiative."[55]

In October 1934 the Mexican congress debated and approved
amendment of Article Three. As it did so, "Red October" raged in
Spain. Blood was shed at this time in Mexico, too, for widespread
violence accompanied the congressional action. In Mexico City
students at all levels took to the streets to make known their
hostility to socialist education. Even small children were recruited
by older students or by their parents to engage in demonstrations. A
protest strike at the National University had the support of all
schools and faculties and of the Federation of University Students.
Medical students exchanged shots with the police. From the
University, strikes spread to secondary schools. Students attacked

PNR headquarters; police and firemen battled with demonstrators and would-be marchers all over the city. At the state universities in Nuevo León, Zacatecas, Puebla, and Jalisco, students clashed with police and suffered many injuries. The disorders continued until Cárdenas obtained a truce with students by pledging to delay socialist education's implementation at the university level.[56]

In the Mexican congress angry leftists blamed the clergy for inciting the protest. Radical deputies belonging to the "National Revolutionary Bloc" discussed measures to counter what they saw as primarily Catholic-conservative resistance to socialist education. Luis E. Erro proposed that President Rodríguez deport all remaining bishops, and the Bloc supported him by urging Rodríguez, Calles, and President-elect Cárdenas "to end the clergy's lamentable power." Arnulfo Pérez suggested that newspapers with a "confessional character" be closed immediately by the government and that the two big Mexico City dailies, *Excelsior* and *El Universal*, be shut down eventually. Alejandro Gómez Maganda, later Mexican consul general in Barcelona during the civil war, recommended that the PNR form "assault groups" composed of workers and peasants "to keep in check the Revolution's enemies." The groups would attack conservative students and other people "being used by the clergy." Juan Manuel Carrillo wanted all "reactionaries" (practicing Catholics) purged from the bureaucracy and replaced by "true revolutionaries" who had been screened by a "Committee of Public Health." Luis I. Rodríguez, friend of Cárdenas and later a valuable ally of the Spanish Republicans, hoped that the Mexican hierarchy, once totally expelled, would be forever prohibited from reentering the country. Deputy Rodríguez had plans for the National University as well. Accusing rector Manuel Gómez Morín of betraying the University and the Revolution, Rodríguez vowed that the PNR would remove "Monsignor Gómez" and create a socialist university designed to educate proletarians rather than members of the privileged classes.[57]

Although neither the PNR nor President Cárdenas ever clearly defined socialist education, some of the Education Secretariat's guideline literature must have confirmed its opponents' fears that it represented part of a broad plan to destroy Roman Catholicism by introducing Communism in Mexico. In 1935 the Secretariat published *Detalles de la educación socialista implantables en México* by Luis G. Monzón, one of its many employees who belonged to the Mexican Communist Party (PCM). Monzón's handbook indicated that teachers must urge students to cooperate with the working class in establishing the "dictatorship of the proletariat" so that "extinction of the enemy may be a real and positive fact." By "enemy" Monzón presumably meant members of other social classes. Since socialism constituted a period of transition to Communism, the text continued, socialist education really amounted to Communist education. Mexico's principal pedagogical symbol henceforth would be the hammer and sickle and its hymn of combat the *Internationale.*[58]

In the provinces police and federal troops had their hands full containing socialist education's many opponents. On October 4, three thousand Catholics in Puebla, incensed by the state government's closing of a parochial high school, as well as by the new curriculum, rioted when they could not get a permit to march in protest. Police used tear gas to break up the melee. Fearing violence elsewhere, Puebla's state government banned any further demonstrations.[59] The next day students at Tampico's Preparatory School began a forty-eight hour strike to protest both socialist education and police attacks on demonstrators at several other institutions. They marched through city streets shouting "Death" to PNR educational policy. Parents also took action. So many of them kept their children home that Tampican schools remained virtually empty. Antigovernment rallies drew such crowds of parents that meetings had to be held outdoors, no building large enough to accommodate them being available. In Tampico, as in other communities, a rumor had circulated that authorities intended to brand children with hot irons to show that they now belonged to the socialist state.[60]

In Aguascalientes city, police and soldiers raided a meeting of several hundred parents on October 12 that had been called to plan a boycott of local schools. They jailed 150 opponents of socialist education for the "crime" of assembling to discuss a school boycott. About two hundred other people at the meeting escaped arrest.[61] In rural areas throughout Mexico, opposition to the new pedagogy frequently took the form of mob violence against school teachers who indicated approval of the government's program. Often incited by priests, these attacks had started even before Cárdenas ordered socialist education implemented. Between September 1934 and December 1936 villagers murdered thirty-seven teachers and wounded hundreds of others. By late 1936 an administration discouraged by such resistance began gradually and quietly to withdraw support from its own project as a prelude to forgetting about it altogether.[62]

Other determined defenses of religion characterized Mexico's countryside at this time. At the end of July 1936, with the Spanish war just underway, approximately five hundred women from villages near Vista Hermosa de Negrete, Michoacán, stoned the town hall and the homes of local anticlericals when the municipal president refused to allow the parish priest to exercise his religious functions. Peace returned to Vista Hermosa only when soldiers arrived to disperse the rioting women.[63] Taking heart from similar examples of popular conservatism in their own region, a group of young Catholic laymen from the state of Guanajuato organized the Sinarquista movement in May 1937 to defend the faith and to preserve Mexico's Hispanic traditions. Sinarquista ideology emphasized the need to end experiments with modernization and revolution, which allegedly had produced only alienation, injustice, class conflict, and increasing anarchy.[64] Like the Spanish Falangists whom they admired, Sinarquista ideologues favored authoritarian, corporate social organization; they also exhibited strong nationalist and Hispanist feelings. But here resemblance between the two groups ended, for the Mexicans were highly traditional and unequivocally Catholic. In this they seemed more like Spanish Carlists (enemies of modernity) than revolutionary Falangists, who thought that they had found the key to harmonious postmodern life and who, unlike the Sinarquistas, could accept an industrial, urban society. Despite their apparent similarity to the Falange, the Mexican millenarians hoped to resurrect a Spanish past that members of the peninsular movement regarded as hopelessly archaic.[65]

Sinarquista missionaries appealed mainly to discontented country folk, peasants, and peons who had not benefitted from the Revolution's agrarian reforms, who remained victims rather than beneficiaries of modernization, and who thus had little more than religion with which to confront their desperate misery.[66] Although Sinarquism grew rapidly during its first few years, in the early 1940s it rather abruptly lost much of its counterrevolutionary potential. With its messianic character and direct appeal to lower-class rural people, the movement simply was not part of the country's conservative mainstream. Even the newly founded Catholic party, *Acción Nacional* (PAN), found only limited bases for cooperation with Sinarquistas because of their authoritarian ideology and unorthodox operational methods.[67] After failing to restore colonial Mexico's "golden age" through experimental colonies in Sonora and Baja California, Sinarquistas lost considerable prestige and their leaders split into two factions, one of which began to advocate violence. President Manuel Avila Camacho (1940–46) took advantage of the favorable situation and outlawed Sinarquism. Its suppression proved to be relatively easy.[68]

Organized Labor and the Communists

Religious strife was but one of several obstacles to stability at this time in Mexico. Stimulated by Cárdenas, Mexican workers aggressively confronted management. Their principal leader was Vicente Lombardo Toledano, a Marxist academic who became a doctrinaire Stalinist in the mid-1930s. Always in the limelight, Lombardo came to symbolize everything about Cardenism that its opponents hated. *Excelsior* and other newspapers made him a favorite editorial target. Dapper, sad-eyed, and fond of expensive automobiles, Lombardo looked more like a movieland gangster than a prophet of proletarian revolt. His appearance belied his background, for he had been a brilliant student, then a professor at the National University. Even after entering labor politics, Lombardo remained active at this predominantly conservative institution, and students often hissed him loudly when he appeared at functions or spoke in meetings.[69]

In February 1936, the month of the Popular Front electoral victory in Spain, Lombardo and Cárdenas created the Mexican Workers Confederation (CTM), a powerful alliance of trade unions. Secretary General Lombardo worked closely with Cárdenas, on whom he depended, yet he always remained well to the left of the president. The CTM charter condemned bourgeois society as one which led to fascism, and Lombardo invited Communist Party members to take high positions within the organization.[70] On the basis of such behavior, and because of his adhesion to the Soviet line on international matters, many Mexicans concluded that Lombardo was a Russian agent.

Despite his tendency to annoy Cárdenas with demagogy that

often embarrassed the administration, Lombardo regularly received political and financial support from the PNR. Money from the Mexican Treasury paid for the CTM's Universidad Obrera (Workers University), and the CTM newspaper, *El Popular,* also had a federal subsidy.[71] Lombardo repaid this generosity by making the CTM an effective backer of the president's Spanish policy. Lombardo tried repeatedly during the 1930s to persuade Cárdenas to create an armed workers militia to defend Mexico and its Revolution from a Franco-type "fascist" attack, the imminence of which he never tired of announcing.[72] But Cárdenas refused to do this and so relieved many moderates and conservatives who nonetheless found other reasons for fearing the CTM. During a bakers' strike in January 1938, for example, union members stormed bakeries, shot at scabs, and surged through Mexico City's streets beating up anyone they found carrying bread.[73] Such actions paralleled union violence in Spain during the brief Popular Front regime in 1936. The turmoil had helped to bring on civil war there, and few Mexicans were likely to forget that as long as Lombardo remained on the scene.

Moderate and conservative Mexicans also had some reason to worry about the Mexican Communist Party, whose prospects brightened considerably after 1934. Prior to Cárdenas the PCM had gone through a bleak period of suppression at the hands of Calles, who resented its references to him as "an agent of the Pope" and its periodic armed rebellions. In retaliation Calles had broken diplomatic relations with the Soviet Union and had sent many party members to prison. He even ordered several of them shot. PCM Secretary General Hernán Laborde spurned President Cárdenas's conciliatory gestures toward the party until late 1935 when the Soviets ordered him to collaborate with the PNR. This was done to bring the Mexican party in line with the Comintern popular front strategy adopted by the Third International earlier in the year. Popular front strategy called for Communists to cooperate with other parties in order to defeat fascism. Welcomed by Cárdenas, the PCM came to have considerable influence in his administration, especially in the Education and Communications secretariats. Mexican Communists played a major role in implementing the president's pro-Republic policy during Spain's civil war. So did many fellow-travelers who were often identified with Communism in the popular mind. Cárdenas always maintained his independence of the PCM, and the party had inept leaders who were no match for him; yet few opponents of the Revolution perceived this. Consequently, they had an exaggerated yet real concern about a possible Communist takeover of Mexico.[74] For reasons of his own, former president Calles decided to encourage these fears.

Cárdenas Maintains His Authority

Alarmed by Cárdenas's policies and by his success at generating mass support among workers and agrarians, General Calles initiated a showdown with the president during the summer of 1935. His plans miscarried, and after a tense power struggle Cárdenas finally deported him to the United States early in 1936.[75] Diehard Callistas fought on; their activities, however, only added to Mexico's already turbulent atmosphere. Calles's deportation in April 1936 came two months after the Popular Front government took office in Spain, and the contrast between dealing with potential political disruption in the two countries is stark: the *madre patria* grew increasingly disorderly under a regime whose weak leaders could not even control the extremism of their own supporters, but in Mexico Cárdenas's deportation of Calles stiffled similar outbursts. Calles was not silenced, of course, and from Texas he accused Cárdenas of planning "to socialize the machinery of production, disregard property rights that guarantee our institutions, and establish a collective system of agriculture similar to the Soviet Union." Communism, he predicted, would not work in Mexico.[76]

Cárdenas was merely using leftists for his own more moderate purposes, however. Marxist rhetoric and Communist organizers enabled him to mobilize workers and country folk to "win their rights" and thus to keep them content with Mexico's historic economic and social structure. His genius was to give proletarians a sense of power while keeping them dependent on government paternalism. Left-wing action groups, such as the CTM and the Communists, by striking, propagandizing, and fighting in the streets, enabled the president to intimidate opponents while keeping his own direct involvement minimal. Despite appearances, his programs represented a strengthening of numerous societal structures and conventions that had their origins in the Spanish colonial period. Cárdenas simply reorganized them along postmodern, corporate lines.[77] Sensitive to the rising volume of protest, he answered it. The president told his critics in 1937 that his government represented a "democracy of workers" sustained by four main groups: teachers, peasants, industrial laborers, and "peacekeeping" soldiers. Mexicans need not fear "any type of dictatorship," nor would "events in Spain be repeated in New Spain."[78]

In 1937–38 wily Cárdenas let totalitarian leftists agitate for creation of a "Mexican Popular Front Government." Such a regime would have replaced the monopolistic PNR with an alliance of parties and labor organizations similar to the coalition that presided over Republican Spain.[79] It would have brought the CTM and the PCM directly into the administration. Blocking this, the president imposed his own sham version of a popular front on the Revolution: he reorganized the PNR along interest group lines and renamed it the Party of the Mexican Revolution (PRM). His move kept supporters of the government under firm presidential control. As Octavio Paz has noted in retrospect:

> Although its slogan was "for a democracy of workers," the Party of the Mexican Revolution was not democratic. . . . If no one remembers its debates, that is because there were none; its policies never were the product of public deliberation but rather of what was dictated by President Cárdenas. Even the inclusion in the party of the worker and peasant groups, far from strengthening them, contributed to their eventual servitude.[80]

Cárdenas also prevented any merger of peasant and industrial labor groups, thus assuring that Lombardo and his CTM never became strong enough to escape government tutelage.[81] Mexican agrarians had to join the National Peasant Confederation (CNC), another dependent instrument of the PRM.[82]

Upon nationalizing foreign oil companies in March 1938 and thus involving Mexico in its greatest diplomatic crisis in years, Cárdenas relaxed somewhat his pressure on Catholicism and began to make his political speeches more conciliatory. The president had picked up some tentative, limited support from many of his adversaries: Church, press, moderates, and conservatives lauded his "patriotic" oil expropriations. He further pleased them with an apparent espousal of compromise on religious issues. By backing away from some of his former excesses, Cárdenas also retained army loyalty. The president knew that many general officers hated the CTM and that they feared Lombardo's plan to create an armed workers militia. Now he went along with military demands that he permanently squelch the idea. This enabled him to keep at bay the extensive popular opposition that continued to be generated by the seemingly endless disorders and policy failures associated in many minds with leftism.[83] It also made it easier for him to go on helping the Spanish Republicans, a project that he had emotionally embraced but one that had brought with it domestic and foreign dangers for his regime.

2

Mexico and Spain Prior to the Military Rebellion of July 1936

Spaniards and Hispanism in Revolutionary Mexico

In the 1930s about 50,000 Spaniards lived in Mexico. They represented roughly 32 percent of the foreign population, and half of them lived in Mexico City. Approximately twice as many men as women made up the Spanish colony. The cities of Puebla, Veracruz, Tampico, and Mérida also had large concentrations of Spaniards. México, Coahuila, San Luis Potosí, Oaxaca, and Guanajuato states each had about one thousand resident Spaniards.[1] Mexico's Spaniards were generally affluent; many of them owned large rural estates. Spanish businessmen dominated textiles and several other Mexican industries; in the publishing field they enjoyed a virtual monopoly.[2] Spaniards made most real estate acquisitions by foreigners in Mexico, concentrating on urban properties. In some months in the 1930s they effected twice as many purchases as their closest rivals, the North Americans.[3] According to those Mexicans who did not like them, Spaniards also operated sleazy taverns, cabarets, and brothels, and peddled narcotics.[4] Mexican reformers accused Spanish landowners of exploiting and abusing their peons. Spanish writer Ramón del Valle-Inclán, who had lived in Mexico and loved the country, thought that most resident Spaniards played a harmful role and that the Mexican government should dispossess those who owned rural properties.[5]

Although often unpopular with Mexicans, Spaniards exercised influence far out of proportion to their relatively small numbers. In addition to land, factories, and publishing firms, they owned department stores, grocery stores, movie theaters, banks, and mines.[6] Despite the inroads United States culture had been making in Mexico, Spaniards in the 1930s still benefitted from prestige associated with the *madre patria*. Spanish writers and journalists resident in the country contributed regularly to the press, and Spanish academics found welcomes at institutions of higher learning, where they attracted considerable followings. Often wealthy members of the Spanish colony arranged and paid for these scholarly visits. Still, no chair of Spanish history existed at the National University until 1936.[7]

Many of Mexico's Spaniards had exceedingly conservative political views, and numerous outspoken monarchists joined discussions of peninsular affairs.[8] Describing the situation in 1924, when he returned to Mexico from Spain, Alfonso Reyes wrote:

> The Spanish colony in Mexico City was at the point of making a hostile demonstration against me . . . because in my declarations as a recent arrival I spoke of another Spain, different from the official one, and assured them that there were more than enough people in Spain who would want the advanced laws of Mexico.[9]

Liberal and radical Spaniards, however much overshadowed by their rightist countrymen in Mexico, were well organized. They maintained political organizations and published newspapers and journals. If the conservative Casino Español generally proscribed liberal or left-wing lectures, other Spanish social clubs such as the Orfeó Catalá welcomed them.[10]

Mexico's revolutionary regimes, despite giving Spanish and hispanophile Mexican traditionalists little comfort on the questions of secularism and North American influence, continued to express satisfaction about the Spanish colony's presence and to encourage additional Spanish immigration. PNR spokesman Juan de D. Bojórquez told a group of Asturians in 1932 that Spanish immigrants fit so nicely into Mexico that Mexicans had always regarded them as brothers. He added that Mexicans had "completely" derived their culture from Spain and that "the ideal immigration for Mexico . . . is Spanish immigration," because it tended to produce beneficial results for the country and led to "an increase in the production of wealth and ethnic unification." Mexican immigration law in the 1930s, moreover, gave preferential treatment to Spaniards, the only Europeans able to enter Mexico as immigrants in unlimited numbers.[11]

Popular attitudes toward Spain and Spaniards in the 1930s ranged from admiring love to scornful hatred. Prominent among those Mexicans who venerated Spain were upper- and middle-class Catholics who looked back fondly on Mexico's colonial past and who resented the increasingly visible United States, Protestant incursions into Mexican life. These people generally despised the Revolution's programs and ideals, and they had no desire to see Spain itself imitate Mexico politically and socially. They saw traditional Hispanic culture and values as bulwarks against North American imperialist influence and also against what they regarded as the Bolshevist radicalism and anticlericalism that threatened civilized life. For them preservation of a vigorous Spanish culture in Mexico was one of the best defenses against the imperialist menace presented by the United States. José Elguero, an editorial writer for *Excelsior,* published *España en los destinos de México* in 1929. In it he deplored the continued existence in Mexico of anti-Spanish sentiments because they "tended to deprive us of our own authentic Mexican personality, which has been formed under the influence of the Iberian culture that made of semi-barbarous Anáhuac a country of European civilization." He went on to argue that the nation's only culture worthy of being called by such a name was Hispanic, and an anti-Spanish Mexico would soon become thoroughly Yankee. Should Mexico lose what it had received from Spain, the country would become a satellite of the United States, "without ideals and without hopes."[12]

Jesús Guisa y Azevedo, publisher of a rightist journal called *Lectura,* and Fernando Robles, a Catholic militant, represented two other typically conservative Hispanist attitudes in the 1930s.

Guisa y Azevedo lamented the anti-Spanish, anti-Catholic deca-
dence that had always harmed the country.

> Those who deny Mexico deny the Spirit, deny Man, and deny
> traditional values. Lorenzo de Zavala, the radical liberals,
> Juárez, and today the "comrades" of rationalist thought . . .
> all have despaired of Mexico because they have not believed
> in it. They dedicated themselves to deny and to destroy it.
> That we should have done with Spain and Spanish influence,
> that the Anglo-Saxon should arrive, that Catholicism should
> give place to Protestantism, that the indigenous "civiliza-
> tions" should rise again, that Russian and proletarian ideals
> should inspire us; this is what has been said by those Mexicans
> who have not believed in Mexico.[13]

For Robles, too, the true essence of Mexico could only be found in
its Spanishness and in its Catholicism. Efforts to destroy either of
these qualities constituted attempts to ruin the country. In his
opinion, Spain was "the work of the miracle of the Christian faith,"
and Mexico represented a similar creation. Both countries were
children of "the sword and the cross." Mexicans reflected the pure
essence of that which was Spanish. To understand both countries
one had to "approach them along the road of Jesus." Mexico's
current "crisis" stemmed from assaults on its traditional values.

> Never before as now has the spiritual basis of that which is
> Mexican (which is to say, that which is Spanish), come under
> such severe attack. Marxism, of Jewish origin, is destroying
> that invisible stairway by which every Mexican ascends to the
> heavens. . . . And the Mexican, without his stairway, without
> any hope of reaching the heavens, ceases to be a Mexican and
> becomes mere potter's clay that any iron-handed strongman
> can shape. The religious question, therefore, is one of life or
> death for the patria. . . . The ruin of our Church represents
> the destruction of our very soul as a people.[14]

Liberals and radicals could also be found among Mexican
hispanophiles. They loved plebeian as opposed to oligarchic Spain,
and by 1931 far more Mexicans were aware of the "other Spain"
than had been the case formerly. According to José Vasconcelos,
this new awareness had been partly caused by periodic visits to
Mexico in the 1920s by famous Spanish intellectuals and politicians

of liberal or reformist persuasion: Marcelino Domingo, Ramón del Valle-Inclán, and Fernando de los Ríos. They won the hearts of many Mexicans and thus changed their attitudes toward Spain and Spaniards. Of Marcelino Domingo, Vasconcelos wrote that he

> . . . caused Spain to be applauded in Mexico, after so many years during which it had only been denigrated. . . . It is possible to say that Domingo, along with Valle-Inclán, reconciled Spain with Mexico in the minds of many whose only previous idea of Spain came from Protestant, Callista propaganda—the propaganda of an irredentist, clerical, and bullfighting Spain.[15]

One of Mexico's most prominent liberal Hispanists was Alfonso Reyes. A son of General Bernardo Reyes, Alfonso had lived in Spain for many years following his father's violent death in the military uprising against President Madero in 1913. Reyes found his cultural roots in the peninsula. "I consider myself," he wrote in 1932, "a Spaniard with nuance. . . . When I turn my eyes to my land I see it and I understand it as such a natural prolongation of Spain! Going to Spain was for me entering more into Mexico. The two loves are fused within me and nothing will be able to separate them."[16] Reyes, well before 1931, had concluded that Spain's many problems could best be solved by the moderate left. Rejecting both General Primo de Rivera's military praetorianism and Catalonia's anarchism and separatism, Reyes also found conventional Spanish conservatism unsatisfactory. The peninsular right, when in power, opposed social change, ignored the "necessities of the people," and thus provoked disturbances of national life. Reyes considered moderates such as the liberal monarchists to be "more disposed to negotiate with workers and seek solutions to the conflict between capital and labor."[17]

Many other Mexicans found it easy to reconcile their Revolutionary affiliation with strong Hispanist sentiments. Some of them did this by pointing to what they believed was a North American imperialist plot, which allegedly involved the "dehispanization" of Mexican culture as an essential step toward taking over the country. When an anonymous hispanophobe produced a pamphlet in 1919 calling for expulsion of Spaniards from Mexico and confiscation of their property, two Revolutionaries with impeccable credentials, José Vasconcelos and Miguel Alessio Robles, responded with a vigorous defense of Hispanism.[18] Vasconcelos is generally remembered as one of Mexico's archconservatives; prior to 1933, however, he had a consistently liberal-Revolutionary political and ideological record. Although challenging PNR leadership as an opposition candidate in the 1929 presidential election, he did so as a Revolutionary purist, promising to do away with military rule and corruption. Gradually, however, Vasconcelos became disillusioned with politics on the left and moved into reactionary ranks. Friendly attitudes of Spanish Republicans toward the Callista regime in Mexico influenced his political shift. He wanted nothing to do with Republicans and others if loyalty to the leftist cause required excusing what Vasconcelos regarded as the intolerable barbarisms of Calles.[19]

In 1919, before Vasconcelos was disillusioned with the left, he charged that the anti-Spanish pamphlet was part of imperialism's design to weaken Mexico. Spaniards remained Mexico's "natural allies" in the struggle against "North American capitalist absorption." Instead of persecuting Spaniards, Mexicans should remember how much their own anti-Spanish policies had benefited the United States in the past. Citing the Cuban example, Vasconcelos argued that large-scale Spanish immigration could be a very sordid barrier to imperialist penetration. Cuba, despite its present colonial status under the Platt Amendment, would never become another Texas or California, where the Hispanic influence was lost because of a "perverse" cultural default.[20]

Alessio agreed with Vasconcelos that the attack on Spaniards had been "deliberately timed to serve Yankee imperialist interests" by dividing Mexicans and Spaniards when Hispanic unity was both possible and urgently needed to offset powerful North American influence. He maintained that Mexico's many misfortunes should not be attributed to Spaniards; most of the damage had been done by the Americans. A strong Mexican nation could be formed with foreign help, but Spaniards rather than North Americans were more likely to provide truly beneficial assistance. This was partly because Spaniards "identify with our customs and our aspirations." Neither they nor Spain itself presented any threat to Mexico or other Latin American countries. Spaniards would help Mexicans "build a formidable dike to contain the restless North American expansionism that . . . seeks to extend its territorial domination all the way to the Panama Canal." Creation of such a barrier against

United States imperialism, Alessio said, had been one of the Revolution's goals. Mexicans should remember that Hispanism was an essential element in their patriotism and they should be proud of Spain's many contributions to their culture and well-being.[21]

Any account of Spaniards in Mexico in this era should at least take note of the activities of Spanish anarchists and their influence on the character of Mexican anarchism. In the 1920s and up to 1931, when Mexican anarchism went into an almost total eclipse, numerous Spanish anarchists were involved in organizational work on behalf of their Mexican counterparts; and leadership by Spaniards had much to do with giving the Mexican movement its violent character during the 1920s. No less a figure than Buenaventura Durruti visited Mexico at that time to stimulate more revolutionary activism by Mexican anarchists. Durruti's exploits, along with the violent militance of other Spanish anarchists, who persuaded the Mexican anarchist General Workers Confederation (CGT) to launch a general strike in 1923, produced stern reprisals by Mexico's Revolutionary regimes of Obregón and Calles. Unable to compete with the government-sponsored Regional Confederation of Mexican Workers (CROM), the Mexican anarchists lapsed into political insignificance at the very moment (1931) when the Spanish Republic appeared and gave to Spanish anarchists opportunities for growth and increasingly violent activism in the peninsula.[22]

Anti-Spanish Feeling

Hispanism and the emotions it evoked could arouse furious controversy in Mexico. A typical conflict occurred in October 1934 when Aída S. de Rodríguez, wife of President Abelardo Rodríguez, suggested that Mexico join other Spanish American countries in adopting a special flag to symbolize Hispanic American solidarity. The flag had been designed by an Uruguayan and was to be used in the October 12 *Día de la Raza* celebrations. It bore three Maltese crosses, replicas of those that had been on the sails of Columbus's ships. Anti-Spanish, anti-Catholic critics immediately attacked this proposal. The editor of *Redención*, an anticlerical newspaper in Tabasco, scorned Rodríguez's request that the flag be placed in Mexican schools, arguing that his paper represented labor organizations in the state, and that workers opposed such "religious fanaticism" as the display of flags with crosses on them. In Culiacán an irate leftist asked the state government of Sinaloa to oppose Mexico's adoption of the flag. Crosses, complained Augusto D. García, were antisocialist; a hammer and sickle would more appropriately symbolize Hispanic American fraternity. *Excelsior's* editorial staff, never reluctant to demonstrate their sympathy for traditional Spain, found García's comments outrageous. They accused him of showing "stupidity unworthy of a human being," and said that he would probably end up in a straitjacket "if the microbe of socialist demagogy continues to spread throughout his organism." Mexicans, they intoned, should remember that Spaniards had "left in these lands a superior culture and imparted an indelible character to the ideology of succeeding generations." Controversy over the flag, they added, showed that despite recent educational efforts ethnic prejudices still blocked Spanish American unity. Those who attacked the Spanish tradition perpetuated Spanish America's weakness by keeping its peoples divided. On October 12, 1934, the special flag was used throughout Mexico at various ceremonies, and on October 16 the Mexican congress voted to adopt the *Bandera de la Raza* as a symbol of Hispanic American fraternity. *Excelsior's* triumphant editors made this news their lead story on page one and topped it with a big headline.[23]

Pervasive anti-Spanish sentiments, evident among Mexicans since the independence era, remained very much present in the 1920s and 1930s. People manifested their hispanophobe feelings in various ways: hostility toward members of the Spanish colony (pejoratively called *gachupines*); demands to deport Spaniards and seize their property; depreciation of Spain, Spanish culture, and the Spanish colonial record in public schools. Not even a Hispanist secretary of public education, José Vasconcelos, had been able to remove such prejudices from the school system. Throughout the 1920s required textbooks in primary schools consistently denigrated Spanish culture and contrasted Spain unfavorably with the Anglo-Saxon countries—England and the United States. Mary K. Vaughn's study of required primary school books, *History Textbooks in Mexico in the 1920s*, indicates that even some Catholic pedagogues had an anti-Spanish bias.[24] Catholic author Longinos Cadena, for example, in his *Elementos de historia general y de historia patria*, required in grades five and six, blamed the colonial legacy of "backward Spain" for Mexico's present weakness. "The Anglo-

Saxon world," he wrote, "today heads the most active, most progressive, most inundating culture. What is the secret of such superiority in a race and their expansive power? We ought to study this to imitate it."[25]

From a Hispanist point of view, unfair treatment intensified during the 1930s as a Marxist-dominated Secretariat of Public Education stepped up attacks on the Spanish tradition. Public school teachers in 1935 received examination books containing several questions that Mexican hispanophiles and members of the Spanish colony regarded as deliberately insulting. One question stated that in forty years the Spaniards assassinated fifteen million Indians in Mexico and then asked students to calculate the average number of Indians killed each year. Another question required students to identify correct statements among the following possible answers: "During their rule of Mexico the Spaniards (a) encouraged drunkenness among the Indians; (b) built roads to facilitate communications; (c) encouraged robbery among the Indians; (d) utilized all sources of food production; (e) left the Indians in total ignorance." The teachers' exam books listed *a*, *c*, and *e* as the correct answers.[26]

Many Mexican leftists attached great importance to convincing the public, especially lower-class people and potentially liberal elements in the middle sectors, that traditional Spain and its socio-cultural legacy in Mexico stood for evil things: clericalism, obscurantism, oppressive political reaction, and aristocratic exploitation of the masses. They saw Spanish colonial tradition, Mexico's Spanish colony, and the hispanophile Catholic Church as obstructing their plans to create a "proletarian" society. CTM leader Lombardo denounced the Spanish record in Mexico again and again, his attacks keeping the controversial issue a predictable feature of newspaper commentary. Lombardo himself wrote regular columns in *El Universal*, a paper that he rather ungraciously labeled as "fascist" when addressing CTM audiences. Pro-Spanish *Excelsior* enjoyed answering Lombardo, and its columnists often exposed flaws in his logic or errors in his facts. In October 1934, *Excelsior's* Juan Franco responded to the labor leader's charge that Mexico's National University had never taught mathematics during the colonial period because it had been operated by obscurantist Spanish clerics. Franco pointed out that the university had established a chair of mathematics in 1637, and he suggested that

Lombardo "confine himself to such false, ignorant pronounce-ments" only in assemblies of workers and peasants to save himself from being embarrassed by people with more sophistication.[27]

Some of the most extreme attacks on Spaniards in the 1930s were launched by a small itinerant group of supernationalists who called themselves the Mexican Economic Reintegration Group. Led by Roberto D. Fernández, the Group accused Mexico's Spanish colony of being pernicious and harming the Mexican people through their domination of the national economy. (As has been noted, Mexican Hispanists claimed that the United States exercised this economic hegemony.) Pro-Spanish Mexicans, such as newspaper publisher Diego Arenas Guzmán, were denounced as "black *gachupines*" who had traitorously sold out to the Spaniards and their allies, the Roman Catholic clergy. The Group even accused General Calles and other PNR leaders of placing themselves at the disposition of resident Spaniards.[28] Such criticism of Calles, and the reprisals it invited, perhaps account for the organization's move from place to place: Mexico City, Durango, Veracruz. In January 1935, shortly after President Cárdenas had taken office, the Group sent him an open letter in the form of a printed flyer; they asked him to prohibit the planned opening of a new Spanish *colegio* on the grounds that the school would allegedly serve only conservative interests and thus be "a danger for the program of the Revolution . . . [and] an aggression against our national interests."[29] During the summer of that year the Group became even more belligerent, urging in propaganda leaflets a "war without quarter against the *gachupín* octopuses" that would result in their expulsion from Mexico and from all of "Indo-America."[30]

If the Revolution had generally heightened such anti-traditional, anti-Spanish feelings, it also had made widespread sympathy for Spain's new Republic possible in Mexico. Various Revolutionary sectors identified with their peninsular counterparts. All PNR supporters, moreover, could feel solidarity with the progressive Spain that was now emerging, especially with agrarian and educational reforms of 1931–1933. Mexican Revolutionaries saw the proverbial "other" Spain embodied in the Republic. PNR liberals in the 1930s admired and identified with Spanish libera-lism; Mexican radicals and totalitarians saw hope for a proletarian victory over bourgeois capitalism in Spanish extremism. After the civil war started, Revolutionaries could work together to help the

Republic battle what were regarded as its fascist enemies, domestic
and foreign. Mexico's industrial workers and even some peasants,
organized and directed mainly by Marxist leaders, took to heart
Republican Spain's struggle. This in itself was a rather extraordi-
nary development; in Mexico prejudice and ill will toward resident
Spaniards prevailed, and anti-Spanish sentiment ran strongest
among working-class people. In the past, poor Mexicans frequently
vented the hostility produced by their many frustrations and
deprivations upon local Spanish businessmen.

Mexico and the Spanish Republic: Official Relations and Reactions, 1931-33

Mexico suffered from a weak international position in 1930s
as a consequence of its revolutionary reputation. It had reason to
fear the major powers as enemies of the country's economic
nationalism, and relations with the United States were especially
strained. Among its Latin American neighbors, virtually all of
whom had highly traditional governments, Mexico had few friends.
These aristocratic regimes, supported by conservative newspapers,
reacted angrily to the PNR's leftist rhetoric and to its attacks on
Catholicism. Alejandro Gómez Maganda, a PNR politician with
some diplomatic experience in the hemisphere, blamed lack of
knowledge about Mexico and an unfriendly capitalistic press for
hostile Latin American attitudes toward his country.[31]

The Secretariat of Foreign Relations acknowledged the problem
early in 1933 and called for public relations campaigns to deal with
it. Foreign Secretary J. M. Puig Casauranc asked all Mexican
ambassadors and consuls to give regular speeches about their
country. These lectures "should tend to destroy prejudices by
establishing the truth about Mexico, since our social and political
convulsions of the past twenty-two years have led to erroneous
judgments abroad concerning all our affairs." As a result it had
become "urgently necessary to carry out methodically and constantly a systematic campaign in favor of our country." In 1933
Mexico did not even have diplomatic relations with Venezuela and
Peru. Its relations with Guatemala had deteriorated due to (among
other things) the murder of some Guatemalans in Campeche state
in 1930. Mexico had a "bad reputation" in Costa Rica that
Secretary Puig believed was due to "propaganda" spread by

intellectuals sympathetic to José Vasconcelos and consequently still angry about the Mexican presidential election of 1929.[32] Spain was the PNR's only diplomatic bright spot, just as Mexico was one of the few foreign friends of the Republic. Spanish Republicans had long admired the Mexican Revolution, and Ambassador Julio Álvarez del Vayo established a warm personal friendship with General Calles and various members of his regime. Álvarez del Vayo, largely a tool of the communists before and during the Civil War, later served as Republican minister of state.[33]

Mexico reacted quickly and with considerable jubilation to establishment of the Spanish Republic in April 1931. Mexican Minister Enrique González Martínez outraced Uruguay's diplomatic representative in Madrid and thus became the first foreign envoy to tell President Niceto Alcalá-Zamora that his country supported Spain's new government. On April 16 Mexico and Uruguay became the first two countries to recognize the Republican regime. When Spain raised the status of its diplomatic representation in Mexico from legation to embassy, Mexican President Pascual Ortiz Rubio responded by similarly elevating the status of Mexico's representation in Spain.[34] Perhaps more than any other Latin American government, Mexico's PNR found pleasure in contemplating new directions in Spanish politics. As one student of the period has observed, many Revolutionary leaders "regarded Spain as a 'little brother' in social development, taking the same path but lagging somewhat behind. Relations between the two nations were soon cordial. . . . [T]he parallelism of problems, and of means taken to solve them, strengthened the bonds between Spain and Mexico."[35]

Two official PNR views on Spain in the summer of 1931 came from President Ortiz, when he received the credentials of Ambassador Álvarez del Vayo, and from Mexico's new ambassador to Spain, Alberto J. Pani, when he presented his credentials in Madrid. Pani was a wealthy, experienced politician who had held several diplomatic and cabinet posts during the Carranza and Obregón administrations. President Ortiz remarked that he felt "special satisfaction" and genuine emotion in welcoming the Republic's envoy, sentiments rooted both in the "community of ideals" shared by Mexico and the Republic and in the certitude that the two countries were beginning a period of closer association and greater mutual understanding. Together they would try to solve common social problems and thus realize for their people "the purest and most reasonable norms of human well-being." In Madrid, Pani put even more emphasis on a common approach to similar social problems that endeared Republican Spain to Mexico and that "augured so well" for future relations.[36]

Just how sincerely some Callista politicians hoped for genuine social reforms in Spain remains an open question. Their real feelings may not have gone much beyond a desire to see Republicans deal decisively with the Spanish Church. President Ortiz was an exceedingly conservative front man for Calles's anticlerical but basically right-wing regime. And Pani had gained notoriety for his aristocratic pretensions. Sincere or not, PNR officials repeatedly expressed pleasure at the prospect of Spain becoming another "revolutionary" country like Mexico. During a festive ceremony at the Spanish embassy in 1933, Foreign Secretary Puig remarked that Mexico's "popular masses" appreciated the Republic's imitation of "the social movement initiated in Mexico in 1910." Spain's enactment of "laws similar to ours" proved that "we were right" in carrying out the Revolution.[37]

Most Mexicans were pleased also by the Republic's more forceful assertion of Spain's diplomatic presence in Latin America. Mexico finally gained admission to the League of Nations in September 1931, its entry facilitated by Republican Minister of State Alejandro Lerroux, who was as anticlerical as Calles and perhaps even more opportunistic and politically wily. His aid was important, though, and he received profuse thanks from the Mexican secretariat of Foreign Relations. In May 1933 Mexico and Peru reestablished diplomatic relations following successful mediation of their dispute by Spain. Mexicans again expressed their gratitude to the Republic. Several months later Mexican diplomat Francisco Castillo Nájera, serving as President of the League Council, lauded Spain for playing a "positive" role in Latin America. He mentioned the Mexico-Peru agreement as well as settlement of a controversy between Colombia and Peru, also mediated by the Republicans.[38]

Perhaps the most sincere official exchange of affectionate sentiments between Mexico and the Spanish Republic prior to the Civil War came during the summer of 1933 when two Spanish pilots, Capt. Mariano Barberán and Lt. Joaquín Collar, died in a plane crash at sea en route to Mexico from Havana on a goodwill mission. The sad incident touched the Mexicans, who made every possible effort to rescue the lost flyers; and Spaniards appreciated the concern shown by Mexico's government and its people. As Mexican pilots searched Caribbean waters for traces of the downed aviators, Ambassador Álvarez del Vayo remarked: "In the midst of the uncertainty which in these moments torments the Spanish people, our knowledge of the unrivaled solidarity with us on the part of all Mexicans . . . is for us [a tremendous] spiritual compensation." Somewhat later he added: "Today the Spanish embassy is a most eloquent respository of noble [Mexican] sentiments. We have received letters from students, messages from agrarian communities and workers organizations, and thousands of other letters from people deeply moved by the tragic disappearance of the two messengers of the new Spain."[39] The widespread outpouring of emotion transcended any latent anti-Spanish feeling and indicated the extent to which Mexicans were moved by a tragedy befalling Spaniards—an emotional disposition that proved important in 1936. On July 16, 1933, Spaniards in Madrid staged a big demonstration of gratitude to Mexico for its emotional response to the accident. At approximately the same time, members of Mexico City's Spanish colony marched to the National Palace to thank the Mexican government for trying so hard to rescue the pilots. They were addressed by Foreign Secretary Puig, who compared Barberán and Collar to Columbus, Cortés, and (somewhat incongruously) Cuauhtémoc, last of Mexico's native emperors. In September President Rodríguez awarded Mexico's highest official decoration posthumously to the two airmen.[40]

The Republic as an Intellectual and Political Issue in Mexico, 1931-33

Many Mexicans greeted the new Spanish Republic enthusiastically because its liberal-left government (1931–33) appeared committed to social programs similar to those of the Revolution, a point usually emphasized by those who have written about attitudes toward the *madre patria* in 1931.[41] This is a valid interpretation for those Mexicans who supported the PNR or who agreed with the political principles embodied in the 1917 Constitution.

Alfonso Reyes, a liberal writer whose acceptance of the Revolution had been rewarded with a diplomatic appointment in Spain in the 1920s, was one of countless Mexicans pleased by expectation of Mexican-style reforms in the peninsula. "As a believer in a regenerated Mexico," one of his biographers notes, "he could easily understand and be understood by the Spanish reformers." He had lived in Spain for over a decade, knew intimately many Spanish leaders, numbered himself among the authors of the Republican revolution, and claimed to be its principal prophet in America.[42] "Pedro Gringoire" (pseudonym for Gonzalo Báez Camargo, a Methodist minister and liberal journalist) also endorsed the "great transformation" of Spain begun by the Republicans. Gringoire found their projected agrarian reform and their intent to change Church-state relations by reducing ecclesiastical influence especially praiseworthy.[43]

Throughout 1932 and 1933 PNR supporters praised the record of Spain's liberal-left government. Interviewed by a journalist in 1932, former Mexican ambassador to Spain Enrique González Martínez credited the Spanish socialists' "responsible leadership" for making the Republic "a success." They had effectively prevented extremists from obstructing the administration's work. Because the country was being ruled by its "most conspicuous and most upright men," González remained optimistic about the future, even though he noted that at that time (April 1932) the regime prepared to enforce controversial new laws. The agrarian, labor, and religious questions would present the government with some very critical moments, but the Mexican diplomat thought that Alcalá-Zamora, Azaña, and other Republican leaders would pass through them safely.[44] In 1933 PNR Deputy Agustín Leñero returned from Spain extolling what he had seen.

> Many of our Mexican problems also exist in Spain, such as the agrarian, educational, and industrial problems. The Spanish government is making a great effort to dissolve the latifundia, which keep wealth from the hands of the people. Education and defanatization of the masses are major preoccupations there. . . . Spain is providing a great example of energy.[45]

Impressed by the Republic's educational effort and by the "culture" of its leaders, Leñero said that the "eminently spiritual and intellectual character" of the 1931 antimonarchy movement still existed among members of the administration.[46]

To focus just on the reception of the PNR, though, overlooks a large group who welcomed the Republic for very different reasons: conservative, Catholic opponents of the Revolutionary government. They tended to be more impressed by the seemingly democratic character that Spanish politics had assumed (excellent ideological ammunition to fire at Calles) or by the new opportunity for a genuine, effective Hispanism that would "unite" Spain with its former colonies, "revive" Spanish culture in Latin America, and thus provide new defenses against the encroachments of North American imperialism.

Some Mexicans looked favorably on the Republic, at least in the spring of 1931, simply because it appeared to represent so many noble ideals and to offer prospects for a more humanitarian government in Spain. Looking back from the vantage point of 1936, with the Civil War in progress, José Vasconcelos observed that from the mid-1920s to 1931 "throughout the world, all enlightened opinion sympathized with those who desired a Republic. . . . We were all ardent republicans in those placid days of conspiracies in Madrid cafes." According to Vasconcelos, optimistic Mexicans at that time invested many of their hopes for a brighter future for Mexico in the anticipated and eagerly awaited political changes in Spain.[47] This certainly emerges as the basic sentiment involved in several euphoric student celebrations in Mexico City following the collapse of Spain's monarchy. Interviewed by *Excelsior,* President Horacio Núñez of the National Student Confederation characterized the Spanish Republicans as having provided "a lesson" for Mexicans with respect to "the realization of great ideals." They were to be congratulated for shunning the "personalist" politics so lamentably prevalent in Latin America. Núñez's remark implied no great student enthusiasm for Calles and the PNR and consequently no desire to see the new Spanish government imitate Revolutionary Mexico.[48]

Rightist newspapers like *Excelsior* expressed editorial optimism and joy at the Republic's birth and extended its best wishes to the new Spanish leaders for success in grappling with such momentous problems as regionalism and social reform. The paper hoped for a smooth transition to effective popular government in Spain because "the Spanish case affects us Mexicans intimately." During the last two weeks of April 1931, *Excelsior* printed all points of view on the Republic: signed columns by Mexicans and Spaniards that ranged in attitude from liberal euphoria to ultraconservative resentment.

But when revolutionary violence erupted in Spain beginning in May with the burning of churches, antilabor and proclerical *Excelsior* was quick to express indignation. In addition to denouncing communists and anarchists for "initiating disorders," the paper's editors ran stories on political violence and slanted headlines to convey the worst possible impression of Spain's extreme left.[49]

Despite detailed and fundamentally correct news coverage of events and politics in Spain throughout the Republic's five years, many Mexicans had singularly distorted images of peninsular developments. Often it seemed that individuals saw only what they wanted to see; consequently, considerable fantasy characterized discussions of Republican Spain during these years. Difficulties arising from differing perceptions and false impressions had started during the Republic's earliest days. Mexican Hispanists José María Lozano and Miguel Alessio Robles drew strikingly different conclusions about which Spaniards had taken control of the new Republic when *Excelsior* interviewed them on April 16, 1931. Lozano thought that "socialists and trade unions" had come to power, and he expressed hope that no Lenins or Robespierres would emerge from their ranks. Alessio believed that "intellectuals and university students" headed Spain's "democratic" regime.[50] Mexicans also erroneously described the Spanish labor movement itself. Agustín Leñero, back from Spain in 1933 where he had found the Azaña government so "cultured," summarized Spain's labor situation for the press without even mentioning the anarchists; moreover, he called moderate socialist Julián Besteiro "chief of the Spanish labor movement," a far from accurate characterization.[51]

One of the major reasons that many conservative, Catholic Mexicans welcomed the Republic in 1931 was their hope that it could provide sufficient stimulation for a revival of what they termed democracy in Mexico. They saw Spain's example as possibly leading to resurgence of opposition to PNR "tyranny," and they also thought that Calles could be shamed into imitating the principles and procedures of Republican Spain, should Spaniards succeed in making their new political freedom work. Diego Arenas Guzmán's right-wing newspaper *El Hombre Libre* initially took this line. For some time the paper had been proclaiming in its headlines the PNR's "putrefaction," and its cartoonists mordantly satirized Calles and other Revolutionary politicians.[52] In mid-April a front-page article on the Republic was topped by the headline: "Here's Hoping That Spain Does Not Suffer the Sad Fate of Our Republics of Bosses and Puppets!" Next to the story a cartoon depicted King Alfonso XIII handing his crown to "the Spanish people" while to his right a heavily armed man ("PNR") clubbed a Mexican voter. A short text emphasized the difference in political behavior between "old monarchies consecrated by tradition and a glorious history" and under identical circumstances "improvised mobocracies of our republics that have remained on the margin of civilization."[53]

Luis Camarena, a regular *El Hombre Libre* contributor, pointed to the lessons that he thought Mexicans should draw from events in Spain after the first week of the Republic's triumph and noted differences that he perceived between Spanish politicians and the men who ruled Mexico.[54] Spain proved what could be achieved by people steadfastly determined to be free: "For us the important thing is the example that Spain has given to the whole world, with its beautiful gesture of democracy, of the value contained in popular efforts toward the realization of collective ideals." He hoped the Spanish example would inspire Mexicans to regain their faith in those same democratic ideals, put aside their fear of Calles, and demand their rights.[55]

Mexican opponents of the PNR also tended to be encouraged by what Spanish Republicans were doing and saying about Hispanism and relations with the Latin American countries. By the summer of 1931 the Republic had taken steps to reinforce Spain's political and cultural influence overseas. A new Constitution promulgated that year mandated the "cultural expansion of Spain," especially in Latin America; and the Republicans had committed themselves to full peninsular citizenship for all Spanish Americans. *El Sol's* pro-Republic editors in Madrid saw evidence that the largely rhetorical and "useless" Hispanic-Americanism of monarchical Spain had been abandoned, and that the Spanish people appreciated their government's innovations in foreign policy. Mediation of disputes in Latin America and assistance to Mexico in regard to membership in the League of Nations represented the type of diplomacy that could "unite all Spanish-speaking peoples in the achievement of common objectives." By conferring Spanish citizenship on the Americans "Spain will . . . crystallize the Bolivarian ideal; with this original juridical move, it will inaugu-

rate an era propitious for the future of the Hispanic spirit."[56] PNR
politicians also professed to see creation of a new "union of the
Iberian peoples" as a healthy development, but they remained
vague about its purposes, and their sentiments on the subject did
not approach the passionate intensity of such ardent hispanophiles
as Vasconcelos.[57]

Despite misgivings and disappointments about some prominent
Republican leaders because they openly praised Calles, Vasconcelos rejoiced over Spanish political developments. From Madrid in
1931 he urged Spanish Americans to join with Spain in forming an
Hispanic-American Federation. All Spanish-speaking peoples, he
said, had an obligation to "reintegrate the race" and thus to move
Latin America away from Pan-Americanism, a harmful misalliance
between imperialistic Yankees and unpatriotic military dictators.
The Republicans should lead in preserving Latin America's
threatened Hispanic culture, for Spain now enjoyed more liberty
than its former colonies: "For this reason we place our hope in the
new Spain. Madrid can become the center of an Empire more
important than that of Philip II, the moral Empire of nations that
have lost their way."[58]

Rodolfo Reyes (Alfonso's brother) was an ultraconservative
Hispanist who also lauded the new Republican government for its
promises to bring Spain and Latin America closer together.
Lecturing in November 1931 at Madrid's Ateneo, long the gathering place of liberal intellectuals, Reyes observed that "genuine
interhispanic life" could replace the past's "poetic Hispanic-
Americanism" now that the monarchy had disappeared. There
were several good omens for future relations between Spain and
America: the Republic's role in helping Mexico enter the League
of Nations, the high quality of many Republican diplomats assigned
to Latin American countries, and the Cortes' offer of peninsular
citizenship to all Spanish Americans. A fresh, aggressive Spanish
foreign policy in America, long urgently needed, would bolster the
"Hispanic American Nation" in its fight against Pan-Americanism
and United States imperialism. Many Spanish Americans had once
turned to the United States for cultural leadership because they
perceived monarchical Spain to be static and museumlike. Reyes
maintained, though, that those who saw North American culture as
more vital and dynamic than that of Spain became "dehispani-
cizers" and thus agents of Yankee imperialism. With the Republic's

birth, however, Spain had an opportunity to reestablish its cultural dominance in the region and so prevent destruction of its legacy.[59]

Those Mexican conservatives who welcomed the Republic in 1931 had hoped that Spanish politicians would *lead* Mexico into an orderly, more tolerant era, not *follow* its examples of social radicalism, religious persecution, and so-called anarchy. As a group of wealthy political scapegoats who felt oppressed, they yearned for freedom, respect for what they vaguely termed their rights, and an end to demagogic government by an official party composed of what they regarded as social upstarts. They were horrified by the PNR program, which threatened to destroy some of their most cherished institutions and values: the Church and Catholicism; traditional family life; upper class privileges; and Hispanic culture. But events in Spain and the conduct of Spanish diplomats in Mexico soon indicated that from the Republic their traditionalism and their plight in Callista Mexico would receive no support.

In mid-May 1931 *El Hombre Libre* was still lauding the Republican government for its "civilized" attitude toward the "antireligious barbarism" of Spanish extremists, and it still contrasted Republican leaders favorably to the "brutal caudillos" who ruled Mexico.[60] But subsequent political developments in Spain, which clearly established the anti-Catholicism of the liberal-left government, turned this paper's editors and many other Mexican conservatives against the Republic. As enemies of the PNR, they simply could not accept either the Republic's ever closer resemblance to Mexico or Ambassador Álvarez del Vayo's public adulation of Calles and the Revolution. The ambassador became friendly with Education Secretary Narciso Bassols, a man generally regarded by Catholics as one of their worst tormentors; the ambassador even ostentatiously accompanied him on some rural inspection trips. Always ready with generous words for PNR programs, Álvarez del Vayo once described the Mexican government as "a regime of lofty human values . . . , an example and a stimulus for today's Spain."[61] In Madrid, Justice Minister Fernando de los Ríos had also praised Mexico's Revolution, citing it as an example that Spanish Republicans would follow. He told a Mexican journalist: "There is a great similarity between your revolution and ours! We are facing identical problems—agrarian, social, religious, and economic. I think that the study I made of your laws will be very useful to me now."[62] Appalled by such statements, Mexican conservatives unhappily wondered why the Spaniards "were so thoroughly ignorant about Mexico," at first concluding that they had been misled by "official lies."[63]

Spanish Republicans, however, had always admired the Mexican Revolution, and they assumed that most Mexicans supported the PNR.[64] During his Mexican visit in the 1920s, Spanish writer Ramón del Valle-Inclán publicly supported agrarian reform and predicted that his new friend, President Obregón, would "do great things in America."[65] Yet for most Spaniards, Republicans included, Mexico was largely a myth; few of them had ever even seen the country. For many it remained the land of Benito Juárez and nineteenth-century liberalism. Calles was perceived as carrying on a liberal reform program.[66] The strength of popular conservatism in Mexico they underestimated as badly as they did similar feelings among their own people. It took a Civil War and exile in Mexico for the Republicans to realize their error. Mexican traditionalists lost their illusions about Spain much more rapidly.

Still a nominal Revolutionary, Vasconcelos continued to praise the Republic in 1931 and 1932. Events in Spain gave him many opportunities to promote Hispanism and to attack Calles. At times the Mexican writer overlooked shortcomings in the political performance of Republican leaders and of Spaniards generally so that he could contrast their wisdom and decency with the many vices of Callism and a Mexican public that tolerated it. In his journal *La Antorcha,* Vasconcelos emphasized Spain's new prestige under the Republic. The peaceful manner in which the Republic had been established would have a beneficial effect in Latin America, where ignorance and slander had created "an abyss" between Spain and the American republics. Reaffirming his faith in Republican leadership, Vasconcelos compared Indalecio Prieto's labor policies, which he found faultless, to the many "abuses" associated with an alliance between Calles and corrupt trade unions. He praised Manuel Azaña's moderate approach to the religious question, observing that the Spanish Church should be obliged to devote some of its wealth to "construction of the new Spain." Azaña, he wrote, was proceeding much more responsibly than the PNR's anticlerical "general-bandits."[67] Spanish public opinion, of course, took a far dimmer and more alarmist view of the policies of Prieto and Azaña. Conservatives and even many moderates were outraged by these examples of what they considered to be irresponsible leftism.

By 1936 Vasconcelos had altered profoundly his earlier opinions about the Republic and its leaders, many of whom he had known for years. These changes are readily seen in his major statement on the Spanish Civil War, *Que es el comunismo*. Vasconcelos had once praised Ramón del Valle-Inclán for endorsing the Mexican Revolution in the 1920s; this had improved Spain's image in the country. Now he denounced the late novelist as a "bad Spaniard" for his comments on Mexico. Valle-Inclán's references to the Spanish colony as exploitative *gachupines* had been damaging to national interests since resident Spaniards had always helped Mexicans defend their country against "foreign absorption." In commerce, for example, Spanish businessmen formed a barrier against Jewish, Syrian, and Lebanese merchants, "the real enemies of Mexico."[68] Revising almost everything that he had written about Spain in 1931–32, Vasconcelos accused the Loyalists of being from the start in league with the world's "evil" forces: Calles, Léon Blum, Jewish newspapers, international bankers, and the United States of America. Rather illogically he also accused them of being Communists; their misrule in Spain demonstrated the need for middle-class people in Mexico and elsewhere to protect themselves against Marxism's tendency to destroy them.

Vasconcelos claimed to have warned his Republican friends in 1931–32 against starting a religious conflict; he had been appalled by their anticlericalism. (As has been noted, the Mexican writer was still an anticlerical Mexican Revolutionary himself at that time and had praised Azaña's "moderation" in handling Spain's Church-state controversy.) Their most grievous offense, however, was to allow Russian agents to infiltrate the Spanish army during the months of the Popular Front regime. Franco's rebellion thus represented a struggle against Communism and for "civilized life." Only the future would tell if the rebels were fascists, monarchists, or republicans, but they were definitely "nationalist patriots." Franco wanted to make Spain a world power once again; after the leftists had been defeated, it would become such a power. Mexicans and other Spanish Americans could then shed their inferiority complex for they would be children of a Great Spain. Under Popular Front rule the peninsula could be no more than "a poor imitation of Callista Mexico."[69]

Although most conservative Mexican observers expressed pleasure when Spain's new Republic appeared, some dissenters predicted disaster. In retrospect these men seem to have possessed prophetic vision. Nemesio García Naranjo, a cabinet member under Huerta and one of Mexico's most widely published conservatives, argued that the 1931 election results, although clearly indicating repudiation of King Alfonso XIII, did not represent popular desire for the kind of Republic that had been established. Spaniards had accepted the Republic due to "patriotic frenzy and hope of redemption," but they would soon realize that mere political turnovers did not alter the nature of things: "Poor people do not become rich simply because they change from Crown to Republic; misery is not eradicated by covering it with a democratic mantle; and all this will soon become apparent to the Spaniards as they lose their most cherished illusions." There were already ominous signs. The government had made two serious mistakes: failure to deal forcefully with Catalan separatism and weakness concerning attacks on the Catholic clergy. More and more Spaniards would turn against the Republican administration "upon seeing Spain divided by regionalism and inflamed with religious conflict."[70]

Querido Moheno, another old Huertista veteran of many political battles, also offered a pessimistic appraisal of the Spanish situation. In June 1931 he maintained that since the new regime had not been institutionalized, no Republic really existed. President Alcalá-Zamora, he charged, was "an overseas Madero" whose "suicidal optimism" boded ill for Spain's political future. Moheno wondered how Alcalá-Zamora could continue to speak of the Spanish people's "romantic enthusiasm" for the Republic "after the burning of over one hundred churches, convents, and public monuments." There had indeed been enthusiasm in the Republic's first days, "but it was not exactly romantic." The only romanticism Moheno saw in Spain was in the political outlook of its president, whose obsolete ideas belonged to the nineteenth century. The immediate dangers to Spain—totalitarian impulses from left and right, the threat of dictatorships patterned after either Mussolini or Stalin—would have to be confronted by something more realistic than the Republic's present spirit of faith and confidence.[71]

El Universal's conservative editors also forecast a troubled future for Republican Spain. An April 1931 editorial characterized the monarchy's fall as resulting from a "process of social transformation" that had begun to be manifested in the 1920s. Primo de Rivera's dictatorship had tried to direct this process as part of what

El Universal termed the crown's "last heroic effort" to solve Spain's social and economic problems with traditional political methods. The country's new leaders would have to satisfy popular aspirations rapidly if they hoped to succeed; for "revolutionary" Spain in 1931 resembled the Mexico of 1911. It had many of the same problems to solve; the government's political task would be just as difficult as that faced by Madero; and there was no reason to believe that the Spaniards would work miracles. Mexico had plunged into anarchic violence. Spain seemed likely to do that, too. *El Universal* predicted that Alcalá-Zamora would prove powerless to calm the restless proletariat and that there would be a period of bloody struggle that might last for years "in keeping with Spanish custom."[72]

Reactions of the Spanish Colony

Members of Mexico's Spanish colony divided sharply on the Republic from its initial days. On the evening of April 14, 1931, for example, a Spaniard began to shout *vivas* for the defunct monarchy outside the office of *España Nueva,* a Republican newspaper in Mexico City. A group of men from inside rushed out and attacked him. When several other Spanish monarchists came to his defense, they were pummeled, too. Then some Mexican bystanders joined the fray to help the outnumbered supporters of the crown. Eventually police arrived to break up the fight and disperse the large crowd of onlookers who had gathered.[73] Such militancy by the generally demoralized Spanish royalists in Mexico, however, was unusual. It had become awkward for them to advocate preservation or restoration of Alfonso XIII's inept, discredited rule. Most Spanish conservatives, when they entered the debate over peninsular politics, backed such right-wing leaders as José María Gil Robles or Alejandro Lerroux. Braulio Suárez, co-editor of the Spanish businessman's newspaper, *El Diario Español,* endorsed the pro-Catholic stand of Gil Robles.[74] His colleague on the paper, Mario Fernández, wrote that the disappearance of the monarchy had been a beneficial event for Spain.[75]

In contrast to most Spaniards, Pedro Serrano, a conservative journalist, continued to be as partisanly loyal to Alfonso as he had been during the 1920s. Serrano, long a resident in Mexico, had been one of the king's most energetic apologists. During the previous decade, one of his books lavishly praised the character and record of Spain's reigning monarch.[76] Serrano in April 1931 began to reiterate his favorite theme even more urgently on the editorial pages of *Excelsior*, where his column on Spanish politics was regularly featured. He lamented the passing of the Primo de Rivera regime, which he brazenly claimed had "shed not one drop of blood." He deplored the fall of Spain's "democratic king" and berated the Republic for its anticlericalism and leftism. In the Iberian peninsula patriotism meant loyalty to crown and Church, two of the country's most glorious traditions according to Serrano.[77]

The opinions of hard-line royalists notwithstanding, many Spaniards in Mexico initially were sincerely committed to the Republic and even to some of its anticipated reforms. Among them, however, no consensus developed as to what directions these reforms should take. In addition to marching in demonstrations of joy with Mexican well-wishers, Spanish Republicans all over the country flooded newspapers with articles and letters.[78] Liberals such as G. B. Camargo y Angulo stressed the need for the recently inaugurated administration to bring about a genuine "social renovation" in Spain by eliminating the "intransigent ecclesiasticism" that kept the country gripped by "tenacious medievalism."[79] Catalans applauded what they called the long-overdue arrival of justice for their region as the Republic moved toward adoption of an autonomy statute for that province. Other Republicans belabored Catalonia for its disruptive separatism. Liberals denounced the "insolence" of anarchists and Communists, while for their part leftists demanded that "reactionaries" be purged from the government.[80]

Not all of the Spaniards resident in Mexico viewed the Republic with such partisan eyes. Fernando Mota, one of many Spanish contributors to the editorial page of *Excelsior*, displayed little bias in his analytical articles. Following the 1933 elections, which brought to power a conservative government, Mota offered an explanation of the Republic's political difficulties. Spaniards had adopted Republic "with feeling but not with conviction. . . . The transition from monarchy to republic was . . . neither the conquest of a goal, nor the triumph of an idea in the collective sense, but merely the most immediate remedy to ease the profound pain of a people who during the previous half century had seen Spain's glory and grandeur destroyed. . . ." Mota continued: Spaniards had romantically embraced the Republic with the "slightly ingenuous gaiety of a new love affair"; thus they were not prepared for the "radical spirit" of the 1931 Constitution and reformist laws that hit the country "like an avalanche" and disoriented national life. To capture the hearts of the Spanish people the Republic now needed responsible, patriotic leadership, something that the Azaña regime had lacked according to Mota. Alejandro Lerroux might provide this direction. Yet should the extreme right thwart him, Spain's left would become even more irresponsible, and the ensuing power struggle would probably end in either a military or a socialist dictatorship. At the heart of the problem lay the difficulty of reconciling innovation with tradition.[81] By late 1934, however, Mota had concluded that Lerroux was as bad an influence as Azaña. He called him a political liar who had so "defrauded" the Spanish people that they became disillusioned with the republican idea itself. Expressing sympathy for the rebels of "Red October," Mota said that they had been fighting for a new social order that would have established "a more equalitarian way of life than the present one, in which privileges and cast distinctions are still maintained." Their desperate measures had grown out of hunger, poverty, political chicanery, and the aristocratic mentality that had compromised the republicanism of Spain's middle and upper classes. Although the Republic had turned out to be so bitterly disappointing, the workers at least should not be blamed for its failure.[82]

Despite considerable animosity toward the 1936 Popular Front government in Spain, conservative Spaniards in Mexico tended to conceal the degree of their hostility toward that ill-fated regime prior to the military uprising. No doubt these less than sincere signs of goodwill were considered prudent by those Spaniards who believed that Mexico's uncertain political situation under Cárdenas threatened their economic interests. They might have to appeal for help to the Spanish embassy at any time. Thus when Popular Front Ambassador Félix Gordón Ordás arrived at Veracruz in May 1936, among those on hand to welcome him were Elías Pando and Ricardo de Alcázar, officers of the Casino Español, a businessmen's club in Mexico City. Ramón Blanco, secretary of the Spanish Chamber of Commerce in Veracruz, was also there. Ambassador Gordón later spoke by invitation at the Casino. Members listened to him politely, although some of them made unflattering comments about his "Bolshevist" remarks as they left the building.[83] *El Diario Español,* certainly no friend of the Popular Front, nonetheless extended a warm welcome to the new ambassador and minimized its criticism of the Republican administration until mid-July and the murder of monarchist deputy José Calvo Sotelo by some government policemen. At that point the paper turned furiously against the Republic.[84] Upper-class Spanish women followed a similar course in their treatment of Gordón's wife. Shortly before the rebellion, a number of them visited the embassy to invite her to serve as president of the Mexican branch of the Spanish Red Cross. An embassy tea was scheduled for July 22 to work out details, but the Civil War having begun by that date none of the women appeared at the building on Londres Street, for they now considered it to be "enemy territory."[85]

Mexico and the Republic, from 1933 to 1936

The warm friendship and mutual ideological admiration that had developed between Mexico's PNR and Azaña's liberal-left administration in Spain made Mexico an obvious target for Spanish conservatives as part of their domestic political strategy. Since much of the world had for some time regarded the Mexican government as a "Bolshevist tyranny," emphasis on Azaña's close ties to Mexico heightened popular sensitiveness to what was termed the Communist menace at home. During the 1933 election campaign, one Spanish rightist party widely distributed a poster showing a bloody Spain pierced by an arrow on which appeared the words Moscow and Mexico.[86] After Spanish conservatives came to power in late 1933, their supporters continued to attack Calles for his anticlerical and allegedly left-wing policies. This introduced an element of strain into relations between the Republic and Mexico that had not previously existed. During the period 1934–1935, Mexican diplomats in Spain noted with displeasure what they reported as a "campaign against Mexico" in the press and in statements by Spanish religious leaders. In December 1934 Madrid's *Informaciones* published an editorial, reprinted in various provincial papers, warning Spaniards to be on guard against Communism lest Spain become "another Mexico," where the "horrible consequences of Marxist rule" could be plainly seen.

Spain's Cardinal Gomá, moreover, was actively helping the Mexican hierarchy resist the PNR by means of public statements and support for a "protest pilgrimage" by members of Spain's Catholic Action to the Virgin of Guadalupe shrine in Mexico City. Mexican diplomatic officials tried to get their version of the "truth" about Mexico published in the Spanish press, but they were frustrated because most papers agreed with the conservatives.[87]

Spain's rightward move in 1933 brought to Mexico a new ambassador, Emiliano Iglesias, and a less amiable tone to Republican diplomacy. The wealthy Iglesias was a personal friend of Prime Minister Lerroux and had the reputation of being corrupt. Left-wing Spaniards despised him. During his stay in Mexico (late 1933 to early 1936), Iglesias vigorously defended Spain and the Spanish colony against attacks by Mexican radicals and supernationalists. He demanded that the PNR regime suppress such activity. Among his targets were Mexican films with anti-Spanish content; public school materials that denigrated Spain's historical role in Mexico; and the defamatory propaganda leaflets distributed by the Economic Reintegration Group in Veracruz.[88]

In December 1935 Iglesias delivered to the Mexican secretary of Foreign Relations a heated official protest about the content of school textbooks. By endorsing "blasphemies against Spain," Mexico's leaders were threatening to disrupt cordial relations between the two nations. Iglesias expressed the hope that reasons of truth and mutual respect would prompt the secretariat of Public Education to correct immediately its "unfortunate curricular errors." Such mistakes had "deplorable consequences" for Mexican-Spanish relations and for "the cultural progress that with laudable firmness the Mexican state is seeking." Iglesias charged that behind the problem were individuals who deliberately sought to prejudice generations of Mexican schoolchildren against Spaniards and Spain by filling their minds with lies. Everyone knew that Spain's influence had enabled the Mexican people to become one of the leading nations of the modern world.[89] Despite such frictions, Cárdenas and the PNR maintained a basically friendly attitude toward Iglesias. The Chamber of Deputies invited him to address them in the fall of 1935 and applauded his speech heartily.[90]

The Spanish right's electoral victory in November 1933 pleased *Excelsior*, which by then had turned against the leftist government of Azaña. Greatly disturbed by what it saw as Azaña's failure to control anarchists and Communists, the paper also accused the man himself of extremism; he had persecuted his conservative opponents. The Mexican paper interpreted Spain's election results as popular revulsion against politicians who had lost their sense of moderation. Spaniards had clearly shown that they wanted to be governed "by the right hand, man's most intelligent organ, after his head." *Excelsior* hoped that Spain's new administration would avoid right-wing excesses, but noted rather ruefully that Spanish politics had never been noted for moderation. Showing little optimism about democracy's chances in Spain, it predicted that the country's political crisis would be solved only when "the superior man appears—the caudillo who puts an end to dissensions and directs with energy and intelligence all social forces."[91]

Republican Spain's "Red October" of 1934 gave *Excelsior* another opportunity to castigate the villainy of Azaña and the Spanish left. The newspaper accused them of attempting to convert Spain into a "parody" of the Soviet Union, "with all the radicalisms, infamies, and exaggerations of Marxist Communism." Azaña's two years in power had been a "Bolshevist chaos of treason, disorder, and crime," and he had plotted with Catalan separatists to destroy Spanish unity. Fortunately the seditious movement had failed, and Lerroux's "conciliatory" administration was repairing damage done by the "bestial" rebels.[92]

Excelsior's plaudits notwithstanding, by the end of 1935 countless Spaniards had wearied of corrupt, reactionary Lerroux. Oppression united the left, which won general elections held in February 1936 and established a Popular Front coalition government. Yet the Spanish political situation gave no cause for expectations of stability. Hatreds had been too inflamed by the 1934 revolt and by Lerroux's dismal record as prime minister ("the two black years" his opponents called them). Violent activities by left- and right-wing extremists multiplied, leaving the country literally drenched in blood. Disloyal army officers openly plotted a coup. The Popular Front regime, which chose Azaña to preside over the unruly scene, found itself with dangerously few allies at home or abroad. Mexico, however, resumed its cordial relationship with a Republican Spain that had returned to "revolutionary" policies.[93]

Presenting his credentials to President Cárdenas in June 1936, Republican Ambassador Gordón repeated sentiments expressed five years earlier by Julio Álvarez del Vayo. More than ever, he said,

Mexico and Spain were linked together by common social philosophies and programs.

> Today, once again, we have parallel historical destinies. Both peoples are confronting the same problems in a similarly dramatic way, and in both of them the same pressure of the great masses, filled with a strong sense of social justice, is being felt. For this reason . . . Republican Spain understands thoroughly Mexico's monumental efforts to realize fully its historical destiny. It is logical, therefore, that the Spanish people and their government fervently desire . . . that Mexico will be able to translate into the most felicitous reality all of the idealism of its generous aspirations.[94]

Cárdenas's response to this echoed earlier Mexican leaders and also Gordón by stressing the firm ideological ties that once again bound Mexico closely to the Republican regime.

> Personally I share Your Excellency's ideas about the mutual historical destiny that unites Mexico and Spain, now that . . . the parallel extends to a common social task that should be immediately and effectively accomplished [in both countries]. . . . Please tell your government, Mr. Ambassador, that Mexico understands and appreciates its demonstrations of international cordiality, and that we will now and in the future work to achieve in both countries a unity of objectives and action that will serve our two peoples, who have joined together permanently to seek the same solution to our social problems.[95]

Despite their outward show of courtesy toward Ambassador Gordón, conservative Spaniards resident in Mexico and their Mexican ideological counterparts had to be upset by his immediate enthusiasm for Cardenism. It brought to mind Álvarez del Vayo's eulogies of Calles, an irritating memory. Ambassador Gordón had worked as a veterinarian prior to entering politics as a member of the Radical Socialist Party. He had been under-secretary of Development in 1931 and secretary of Industry and Commerce in 1933. The middle-aged envoy was short, plump, energetic, scrupulously honest, yet rather dull-witted. Mexican conservatives and pro-Franco Spaniards concentrated much of their fire on the ambassador's unsophisticated behavior, effectively exploiting his many mistakes and unfortunate statements.[96]

Some students of the Spanish Civil War express wonder at Gordón's being allowed to continue as ambassador in Mexico, given his ineptitude. A Spanish Republican source who wishes to remain anonymous provides the following information. President Cárdenas did indeed eventually ask the Loyalist government to replace Gordón. This was due to the president's irritation at the envoy's general lack of tact, but also to some misinformation about Gordón supplied to Cárdenas by one of his closest advisers. This man had tried to extort fifty thousand dollars from Gordón as the price of allowing certain military materials to be shipped from Mexico to Spain. When Gordón refused to pay the bribe, the man began to tell lies to Cárdenas about the ambassador. In Spain, President Azaña agreed to replace Gordón, and indeed named him ambassador to Cuba (because Gordón and Cuban dictator Fulgencio Batista were friends), but because of internecine strife within the Republican government, no acceptable replacement for Gordón in Mexico could be found. Indalecio Prieto had been nominated for the job, but Azaña wanted to keep Prieto in Spain. So Gordón acquired a second ambassadorial post in Cuba, and he spent some time during the civil war in Havana. A chargé d'affaires ran the embassy in Mexico City during his absence.

Gordón compounded his public relations problem during a talk at the Casino Español in June 1936. He urged members of the Spanish colony to support the Popular Front, then finished with a glowing tribute to the programs of the Mexican Revolution, which he recommended to his listeners as worthy of their sympathetic understanding.[97] The ambassador, however, did not find much sympathy for the PNR among wealthy Spaniards. The unpaid claims that many of them had filed against Mexico for losses suffered during the turbulent years since 1910 continued to be one major source of resentment in the Spanish colony and a diplomatic sore point between Mexico and Spain. Part of the problem lay in the Spaniards' intransigence; they refused to compromise on their claims despite the Mexican government's obviously precarious financial condition. Gordón negotiated a compromise formula with Cárdenas, but when he attempted to get Spanish claimants to accept the pact most of them rejected it.[98] Adding to the ambassador's woes was a dispute over the rights of Mexican bullfighters in the peninsula. The controversy, sensationally reported in the press, had aroused Mexican wrath against Spain all over the country. Spanish bullfighters were refusing to perform on programs with Mexicans because they could not obtain guarantees of jobs in Mexico. Unless the Mexican bullfighting business promised them the same number of fights as Mexican matadors received in Spain, they would forcibly exclude Mexicans from Spanish programs. Gordón tried to make it clear that his government was working on the problem, but due to repeated press charges of peninsular discrimination against Mexicans he accomplished little.[99] Thus on the eve of the civil war historic antagonisms and vexing new issues still troubled relations between Republican Spain and Mexico.

3

Mexican Government Aid to the Spanish Republic

Mexico and the Spanish War: An Overview

Mexico played a unique and rather lonely role in Spain's civil war. When the conflict started, President Lázaro Cárdenas without hesitation committed his country to support of the Spanish Loyalists. Although this assistance was extensive, certain domestic and international considerations tempered Mexico's ability to act unreservedly in the Republic's defense. The Cárdenas administration indeed took a strong ideological stance on the Spanish question, but it also protected Mexico's own best interests whenever these interests would have been jeopardized by certain forms of aid to the Republicans. Such constraints upon Mexican policy were especially evident in the international sphere, where foreign powers took a dim view of Cárdenas's military assistance to the Republic and pressured the Mexican president to keep this help to a minimum or to discontinue it altogether. At home, the Cárdenas position on Spain aroused considerable opposition among moderates and conservatives throughout the country. It is doubtful if even a majority of Mexicans favored their president's Spanish policy, and this factor also significantly limited the degree to which the Mexican government could become involved in the attempt to save the Republic. Cárdenas had to avoid certain pro-Loyalist actions that would have been too effectively exploited by his political opponents.

In Republican Spain itself, two closely related issues created a terrible dilemma for President Cárdenas, especially in diplomatic circles abroad. These issues, too, had the effect of limiting Mexico's response to the Republic's plight, and they tended to pull Cárdenas's policy in contradictory directions. The issues were the presence in Madrid's many foreign embassies of thousands of Spaniards who had successfully appealed for diplomatic asylum, and the widespread extremist Terror that was causing the deaths of innumerable noncombatants, some of them foreigners. When the Republican government proved unable to control the extremists, and indeed when this government appeared to be chiefly interested in negating the asylum principle so that it could punish many of the embassy refugees, Mexico came under intense pressure to join other countries in condemning the Loyalists. Both issues forced the Mexicans into a defensive posture for much of the war.

After consistently supplying generous military, economic, and diplomatic aid to the Republic during the war, Mexico rescued thousands of Republican refugees by helping them emigrate to the Americas, where they could reconstruct their shattered lives. Mexico itself took in about thirty thousand refugees between 1937 and 1945.[1] Only Mexico among the Latin American nations so consistently aided Republican Spain. Other Spanish American republics either remained neutral or openly sided with General Franco. For many of them Cárdenas's support of the Spanish Republic provided additional evidence that the PNR regime could not be trusted. Combined with its economic nationalism, Mexico's Spanish policy also increased the exasperation of Western powers, especially England and the United States. As Mexico's political isolation deepened, Loyalist Spain remained virtually its only friend.

Ideological sympathy for the Republic unquestionably was a major factor behind Cárdenas's diplomacy. The president and many of his associates saw the besieged Republican government as carrying out a revolution similar to the one that had been underway in Mexico for several decades. Spanish Loyalists championed such causes as agrarian reform, rights of industrial workers, and elevation of popular culture through secular, progressive education. Staunchly anticlerical, moreover, they planned to eliminate the Catholic Church's influence in society. Revolutionary Mexicans obviously found comfort in Spanish imitation of their own programs. In August 1936 Cárdenas explained in some diary notes his rationale for sending military aid to the Republic. He felt politically obligated to help put down the Franquista insurrection because Azaña headed a legal government that maintained friendly relations with Mexico. The Republicans also had his sympathy because they stood for the moral and economic emancipation of the Spanish people and because they were fighting to liberate the workers from "oppression" by Spain's "privileged castes."[2]

Cárdenas and such key advisers as diplomat Isidro Fabela had additional motives for supporting the Republic so resolutely. The Mexican president loved Spain, was morally offended by the reactionary attacks upon attempts to bring social justice to the country, and abhorrently feared fascism. Both he and Fabela, moreover, realized that Spain gave Mexico a chance to strengthen its own sagging international position. They wanted to persuade the Western powers that the Spanish war was another instance of outside aggression against weak countries that endangered world peace (fascism on the march). If this viewpoint could be convincingly established, then the powers might commit themselves to saving the Republic and at the same time agree to oppose in principle any imperialistic intervention by one country in another's affairs. The United States had already made nonintervention promises to the Latin American nations. Such a development would benefit Mexico, whose nationalistic economic policies rendered it still susceptible to foreign attacks. Despite Washington's assurances, the Mexicans continued to fear U.S. intervention. Unfortunately for Mexican foreign policy, the major powers never interpreted the Spanish conflict as Cárdenas did. Europe's most outspoken advocate of resistance to fascist aggression, Winston Churchill, favored Franco's rebellion.[3]

Long before the Spanish Civil War, Mexico had been campaigning in the League of Nations for collective resistance to imperialism. Mexican delegate Narciso Bassols urged assistance to Ethiopia, and Cárdenas issued a flurry of decrees in November 1935 to comply fully with the League's sanctions against Italy. After Ethiopia's fall, Bassols explained to the League why Mexico felt so strongly about the issue:

> It was not merely attachment to the abstract principles of international law that obliged us to act as we did. The Mexican people . . . throughout their history of independent life have more than once come to know the harsh significance of imperialism's conquering invasions. . . . For that reason, respect for the independence and territorial integrity of a country is an organic element of our national sensibility and a fundamental demand of all our people.[4]

As the Spanish war raged, moreover, Mexico consistently brought up Japan's invasion of China, linked it to Spain and resistance to imperialism, and urged the League to help the Chinese as well as the Loyalists.[5]

In contrast to partisan claims of overwhelming popular sympathy for Republican Spain in Mexico, available historical evidence suggests an opposite thesis: only a minority of Mexicans backed the Republic from 1936 to 1939; most people remained apathetic about the civil war or even sided with the Nationalists. The Spanish Republican Víctor Alba has written that most Mexicans adopted an indifferent attitude toward the war.[6] Other Spaniards confirm that relatively few Mexicans had any interest in the civil war or indeed in anything external to Mexico during the 1930s.[7] Even so pro-Loyalist a writer as Lois E. Smith perceived in the historical record strong popular opposition to Cárdenas's Spanish policy. Smith quoted Marcelino Domingo, a former cabinet minister for Azaña who spent the Civil War years in Mexico making innumerable pro-Republican speeches all over the country, as saying that most Mexicans opposed Spain's Popular Front government. Her revealing passage in *Mexico and the Spanish Republicans* merits reproduction here. According to Smith:

> . . . a large sector of Mexican public opinion looked on President Cárdenas's Spanish policy with extreme disfavor. It served as a focal point uniting the president's opponents. The pressures of the opposition from outside the government was tremendous; reportedly there was also pressure from within

> the government. . . . the long association between Spain and
> Mexico tended more to create hostility than to arouse
> friendship in Mexico for the Spanish Republic. . . . chiefly
> because the institutions which the Spaniards transplanted to
> Mexico were the very ones that furthered the anti-Republican
> cause.[8]

Despite the PNR's claim to speak for the nation, General
Franco's crusade against the Republic had many Mexican supporters. For years Mexicans had been bitterly divided over their own
Revolution. Hispanic conservatism and Catholicism still had a
powerful hold on much of the population, and this grip of
traditional forces was evident on all social classes. Mexico contained millions of rural people—impoverished peons and peasants
—many of whom were suspicious of change. For the middle and
upper classes, Republican Spain's alleged horrors confirmed fears
about their own likely fate if the PNR continued along its
antireligious and demagogic course. The Spanish Civil War gave
them numerous arguments to use against Cárdenas's Revolutionary
administration. Since 1931 they had been able to see striking
parallels between the social and political struggles of Spain and
those of their own country and they could draw many anti-
Revolutionary lessons from these similarities after July 1936.

From 1931 to 1939 Spanish events and the manner in which they
were perceived became integral aspects of Mexico's political life.
The experience came to have lasting importance for Mexicans as
political leaders after the civil war refused to recognize Franco's
regime, and a large colony of Loyalist exiles found a second home
in the country. Both of these circumstances, along with the debacle
and worldwide repudiation of fascism during World War II, helped
Mexico's role in the Spanish conflict achieve national myth status.
History seemed to be vindicating at last a policy that had received
little sympathy at the time Cárdenas put it into effect. The United
Nations, for example, ostracized Franco for six years after the war.

Yet Mexican traditionalists could still point to Spain as a place
where, at least in their view, Western civilization took a stand
against communist barbarism. The conservatives who had supported Franco—in however tacit a way—pointed to the West's
many confrontations with the Soviet Union and China after 1945
and also to their own government's steadily increasing conservatism

as justification for their views. As the decades passed and great changes swept across the world, however, the Spanish Civil War became less useful as a propaganda instrument for Mexican rightists. Decolonization of Asia and Africa, civil rights movements, students' and women's revolutions, and the impact of television and massive tourism eroded the cultural and social norms on which so much enthusiasm for Franco had been based. Even the papacy and the Latin American clergy moved to the left. Caught up in all this innovation, and increasingly a cultural as well as an economic satellite of the United States, Mexico ceased to be a place where conservative ideological axes could be ground with any profit on the stone of Franquism. It was just too hard to sell Hispanic traditionalism in the 1960s to a nation composed predominantly, in the cities at least, of young people in love with the Beatles. The Spanish dictator's regime, despite some resemblance to Mexico's authoritarian, elitist government, was simply too retrograde culturally, too clerical, and too repressive politically to be anything more than an embarrassing anachronism in the contemporary world. By the 1970s, shopworn right-wing talk about anti-Bolshevist lessons to be drawn from the peninsular conflict of the 1930s had long ceased to have popular appeal or validity.

Throughout the Civil War, Mexican Foreign Secretary Eduardo Hay displayed scant enthusiasm for the Republic. Although frequently invited to the Spanish embassy's social gatherings, he rarely attended. Cárdenas mistrusted Hay, perhaps viewing him as one of the army's many conservative generals, and tended to bypass him whenever possible on matters pertaining to Spain. On these occasions the president dealt directly with Under-Secretary Ramón Beteta. Hay for his part appears to have carried out faithfully if not enthusiastically all aspects of Cárdenas's Spanish policy.[9] Hay's cool propriety coupled with Cárdenas's rather careless supervision of Civil War matters kept Republican Ambassador Gordón constantly agitated. Since the Mexicans usually did whatever they could to help the Republic, Gordón would seem to have had few justifiable reasons for his many complaints.

Bad luck plagued the ambassador's entire mission in Mexico. Even the embassy's location at 7 Londres seemed to be an ill omen. The building had a second entrance on Roma Street, with Berlín Street just a half block away; next door stood a Catholic Church. As has been noted, Gordón arrived in Mexico to find most people

furious about peninsular discrimination against Mexican bullfighters. He was still trying to mollify public opinion on this issue
when the Civil War broke out. Because of a paralyzing electrical
workers strike in Mexico City, the ambassador could get no local
radio news from Spain and thus remained largely ignorant about
the nature and extent of the rebellion for some time. His first public
appearance during the Civil War touched off a riot at the National
Preparatory School. Several days later he proclaimed to a CTM
audience that if forced to choose between militarism and Communism the Republicans would opt for the latter, an oratorical
blunder that Mexican conservatives never tired of resurrecting.
Abandoned by his own inept government, Gordón had to turn to
the Mexicans for pamphlets, posters, and other propaganda
materials. The Azaña regime did not even send him regular news
dispatches about the war. For this information he turned (unwisely
as it developed) to shortwave transmissions from Radio Madrid.
The ambassador enlisted his aptly named daughter, Ofelia, for the
tedious job of listening to broadcasts and writing down their
content. Then he issued the "news" to the Mexican press in
bulletin form. The stories were largely fictional accounts of
Loyalist military triumphs and nonexistent Nationalist disasters.
Contradicted immediately by wire service stories coming directly
from Spain, the embassy bulletins soon had no credibility whatever.
His dispatches were not only discredited, they were the object of
derision. The Franquista *El Diario Español* started a daily column
called "The Embassy of the Bulletins" to ridicule them. Gordón
persisted with his news releases until October 1938 when pro-
Franco Mexicans discovered his secret source of contact with
Madrid and jammed incoming radio signals.

Defections by the Republic's foreign service personnel in Mexico
added to Gordón's problems. Spanish consular officials all over
Mexico resigned or were dismissed from July to September 1936 for
openly adhering to the Nationalist uprising. The first and second
secretaries at the embassy itself also quit, First Secretary Ramón M.
de Pujadas accepting appointment as the Nationalist's ambassador
to Mexico. *El Diario Español* gleefully published the defectors'
statements denouncing the Republic. Although Gordón and his
wife assiduously courted Spaniards resident in Mexico, only Catalans and Basques responded with friendship. The ambassador flew
to the United States in January 1937 on an arms-buying mission at

the very moment when Preident Roosevelt and the Congress prohibited any sales of American war materials to either side in the Spanish conflict. Although he always denied it, Gordón did at least manage to recruit and send off to fight in Spain numerous Mexican volunteers. They received false passports and travel money at the embassy. Some North American volunteers apparently also reached the peninsula via Mexico with the Spanish envoy's help.[10]

Factional strife, personal intrigue, incompetence, and disorganization manifested themselves frequently as Mexico implemented its Spanish policy. To some extent these problems and flaws in the foreign service stemmed inevitably from the nature of Mexico's Revolutionary regime. The PNR was a house divided in many ways: ideologically, personalistically, socially, even culturally. Such divisions, along with ever-present maneuvering between Cardenistas and Callistas, could be seen clearly at Foreign Relations. Powerful men in the government and specifically in the foreign service were not always intelligent, honest, or loyal. The Revolution had elevated to political preeminence many crude, unlikely figures. Attached to them were opportunistic relatives, friends, and hangers-on. Not surprisingly a situation of confusion and inefficiency developed. In regard to Spanish policy, the most harm was done (perhaps intentionally) by Ramón P. de Negri, ambassador to the Republic during the first half of 1937. His activities will be detailed later.

At all levels, though, things constantly went wrong with implementation of diplomacy during the Civil War. In the spring of 1937, for example, Mexico asked the League of Nations and countries throughout the world to help end the Spanish conflict by giving military aid to the Republic. Mexican envoys abroad were instructed to send back local press clippings so that the Ministry of Foreign Relations could judge reaction to Cárdenas's proposal. That summer the president asked Secretary Hay for detailed information about this foreign response to his note on Spain. He was apparently considering another public appeal despite his failure to generate much official sympathy previously. Finding few press clippings on file, Hay wrote to many ambassadors in June, repeating his earlier request. Most of them answered that they had sent the clippings in April as ordered, and on their communications the secretary could only note: "Mr. Herrera is searching for the file."[11]

Cárdenas himself contributed greatly to disorder in the Mexican foreign service. As noted previously, he often bypassed Secretary Hay and dealt directly with lesser officials at the ministry. In addition, the president made many crucial diplomatic decisions and appointments haphazardly, often on the spur of the moment following conversations with personal friends. In late 1937 Cárdenas sent David A. Siqueiros to ask Narciso Bassols if he would serve as ambassador in Spain. Angry about the president's granting of asylum to Leon Trotsky, Bassols refused to take the job but suggested that it be given to Adalberto Tejeda, then minister to France. Cárdenas appointed Tejeda.[12] Although presidential reliance on such controversial figures as Bassols and Siqueiros might seem an unusual method of selecting ambassadors, the incident typified Cárdenas's approach to his foreign service.

Along with being faction ridden, burdened with dozens of bunglers, permeated with ambitious intriguers, and possibly penetrated by several Russian and German agents, Foreign Relations also had to contend with a general ignorance of Spain in trying to implement Cárdenas's policy. Apparently neither the president nor anyone at Foreign Relations had ever seriously studied Spanish politics. In June 1937 Cárdenas wanted to answer a communication to him from the Basque "government" at Bilbao but wondered if a direct response would be diplomatically appropriate. Secretary Hay did not know, so he wired the Mexican embassy in Spain for information about the constitutional relationship between the Basque provinces and the Republic's central government. Not only did Mexico obviously lack an effective intelligence-gathering operation overseas, evidently none of the employees at Foreign Relations were even assigned to read Spanish newspapers.[13]

Late in July 1936 the Spanish insurgents formed a government at Burgos, the Junta of National Defense. General Miguel Cabanellas communicated this news by letter to countries around the world and invited diplomatic recognition. Mexico did not answer Cabanellas; Secretary Hay merely scribbled "to the archives" on his letter. Cabanellas named the disloyal embassy first secretary, Ramón de Pujadas, as the Junta's official representative in Mexico. Gordón promptly fired him but was unable to prevent him from walking off with reams of embassy stationery. De Pujadas typed *Junta de Defensa Nacional* under the printed *Embajada de España en México* and began to write notes to the Mexican government on this stationery. Secretary Hay also sent these communications to the archives without answer. Not easily discouraged, de Pujadas continued to transmit messages to the Cárdenas administration. In August he protested against the announced formation of a volunteer Mexican Legion to fight in Spain (it never was organized) and against Mexico's arms shipments to the Republic. He also published an article in *Las Últimas Noticias* that labeled the Republican government "an instrument of destruction and barbarism that causes indignation and shame" and that referred to the military rising as "a sweeping movement against the outrages, crimes, assassinations, riots, burnings, and thefts committed by hordes that wanted to destroy Spain." Cárdenas threatened in August to expel de Pujadas but, perhaps fearing Madrid's fall to the Nationalists, delayed his deportation until the end of December.[14]

Cárdenas always saw the Spanish Civil War as related to the broader questions of colonialism, imperialistic wars, and the proletariat's worldwide struggle for what he termed "justice and freedom." He also feared that the United States, England, and France would passively watch fascism swallow up much of the world, Mexico and the rest of Latin America being likely victims of such a catastrophe. In 1937 he observed that if only the United States had acted to stop Germany and Italy, the Spanish War would have quickly ended with a Loyalist victory. A year having passed, however, the Franco rebels might win, and in league with Germany and Italy directly menace the Americas. He even thought it possible that all three countries might join with Japan in waging war against the United States itself. Cárdenas sent a message to President Roosevelt to this effect, but the United States did not change its neutrality policy in regard to Spain.[15]

By 1938 Cárdenas had virtually despaired of any "antifascist" action by the United States, and he increasingly began to emphasize "worldwide worker solidarity" as the only likely method of stopping "crimes" committed by imperialistic powers. Boycott actions taken by the United States following his oil nationalizations in 1937 especially irritated the Mexican president, for these American reprisals would force him to sell Mexican oil to Germany exactly at a time that country was helping Franco destroy the Spanish Republic. More than ever Cárdenas believed that fascism and "imperialistic capitalism" threatened Mexico and the rest of the Hispanic world and that the "political and economic democracy" that had started to emerge in Spain and Latin America stood in grave danger of extinction. Unless "working masses" in these places banded together for resistance, they would be "re-enslaved" by their class enemies. Cárdenas nevertheless continued to raise the Spanish question with President Roosevelt. In April 1938 he had his ambassador in Washington again ask Roosevelt to lift the arms embargo, but the American president replied that such a move would "uselessly agitate public opinion."[16]

In dealing with most foreign countries, Cárdenas usually downplayed Mexico's political and ideological sympathies with the Republican government. Mexican diplomatic notes on the Civil War implied that the PNR had formed no political alliance with the Popular Front regime, and they denied that Mexicans were communists helping other communists. Even in routine thank-you messages sent to people who had congratulated Mexico for helping the Loyalists, Foreign Relations included a statement that "Mexico only has acted in the Spanish conflict in accordance with law and justice."[17] Some Mexican diplomats, however, indiscreetly linked their country's support of the Republic to common leftist sentiments. In August 1936, during a discussion among members of the diplomatic corps in Madrid, Embassy First Secretary Francisco Navarro opposed a proposal of Chilean Ambassador Aurelio Núñez Morgado that all foreign envoys leave the Spanish capital because its government could not guarantee their safety. Navarro said that the Mexicans would remain despite the obvious dangers for they "had suffered a struggle similar to the one that has developed in Spain. . . . [and] out of this struggle . . . arose our left-wing government that in heart and spirit is with the Madrid regime."[18] Navarro's candor exposes the crux of the matter. Cárdenas obviously would not have rushed aid to the Spanish Republic if it had still been headed by conservative Alejandro Lerroux, and if it was facing a Soviet-assisted leftist rebellion. With equal certainty the Mexican president would not have instructed his representative in the League of Nations to press for international assistance to Lerroux's legal government on the same grounds that Isidro Fabela used on behalf of Azaña in 1937.

Well aware of Mexico's precarious international position, Cárdenas and Foreign Relations tried to keep Mexican actions on behalf of the Republic as circumspect as possible. They had only partial success. Worried about confrontations with Germany and Italy, the president rarely authorized a Mexican ship to carry supplies to Spain during the war. The Republicans usually had to furnish their own transport for goods they bought from their friend.[19] Certain wartime schemes, moreover, advanced by Spanish Loyalists or by other foreigners, were quickly rejected as being likely to damage Mexico's own interests. Obvious limits existed beyond which Cárdenas would not go in helping his ally. When an official delegate from the Propaganda Department of the Catalan autonomous government in December 1936 solicited Mexican "cover" for an "antifascist publicity campaign throughout Central and South America," Foreign Relations turned him down. Under-Secretary Ramón Beteta explained the refusal to Minister Tejeda, who had forwarded the request from Paris. The problem lay in the "vexation demonstrated by numerous right-wing Iberoamerican regimes in regard to Mexican policy." Beteta continued:

> This vexation could be easily converted into serious diplomatic tension as a result of activity of the type proposed. . . . The regimes to which I allude . . . move in the orbit of fascism or national socialism and would consider Mexico's assistance to such a propaganda mission as a clear violation of the nonintervention principle solemnly consecrated during the Inter-American Conference at Buenos Aires. . . .[20]

During the summer of 1937 the Cárdenas administration vetoed several other proposals that would have compromised Mexico. The Spanish embassy in Mexico City, without informing Foreign Relations, sent fifty copies of *No pasarán*, the Spanish-language edition of a book by Upton Sinclair, to the Mexican embassy in Guatemala City and asked the Mexican envoy there to distribute them. Guatemala had recognized Franco's government at Burgos, so the Republic had no diplomatic representation in the country. When the Mexican chargé at the embassy wired Hay for instructions, the secretary told him not to pass out the books.[21] Another project involved an offer by several men from the United States who contacted Ambassador Alfonso Reyes in Argentina. They proposed to sell several planes to the Republic. After purchase by the Spaniards, the aircraft would be flown to Spain from Mexico by

pilots trained in Mexico. Foreign Relations passed on the offer to
National Defense where Secretary Manuel Avila Camacho rejected
it as being too risky and probably illegal. He told Hay: "To
maintain friendly relations with the Spanish Republic our government is under no obligation to get involved in dubious actions that
violate international law. . . ."22

In conformity with Mexico's official line on Spain, both Cárdenas
and Foreign Relations tried to keep Mexican diplomatic personnel
away from pro-Republican activities obviously sponsored by local
extremists or subversives. Conservatives, the Catholic clergy, and
the press in hostile foreign countries already had enough inflammatory material to use against what they termed Bolshevist Mexico;
there was no need to add to their stockpile. Yet Foreign Relations
inconsistently policed its South American operations; some diplomats there stepped far beyond the bounds of discretion by publicly
joining with local communists in pro-Loyalist activities. These
cases will be examined later in the chapter.

Secretary Hay and the embassy in Washington kept a tight leash
on Mexican consuls in the United States. They had to clear public
appearances at pro-Republican functions with one of the two
higher authorities. When the Spanish Antifascist Committee of
New York in November 1936 invited Mexican consul Rafael de la
Colina to attend a fiesta in honor of Mexico (for its help to the
Republic), de la Colina sent a full report to the embassy in
Washington before answering the invitation. The Committee, he
said, was dominated by Spanish and Spanish American communists,
and several well-known American authors had already refused to
attend, "probably due to their antipathy toward Communism."
The consul added that his attendance at the program might give
rise to "new attacks against our government by New York City's
Catholic and reactionary press." The embassy told de la Colina to
decline the invitation since there might be speeches at the fiesta
that would embarrass Mexico. At approximately the same time the
embassy ordered the Mexican consul at St. Louis to refuse an
invitation he had received from the American League Against War
and Fascism to speak at its fund-raising rally for the Republic. The
consul sent two friends to observe the rally, and they reported that
many American communists were involved in the program, which
had been picketed by anticommunist demonstrators.23

Mexico Helps Arm the Republic

Early in August 1936 Cárdenas responded to a Republican plea for arms. Without waiting to negotiate a sale price with the Spaniards, he had the Mexican army move twenty thousand 7MM Mauser rifles and twenty million cartridges to Veracruz, from where they went to Spain on the Republican ship *Magallanes*. Not until October did Ambassador Gordón sign a Mexican government contract covering the arms sale. The Spaniards agreed to pay Mexico 3.5 million pesos ($962,000) for this initial shipment. Since the Republic anticipated more arms purchases, it sent to Gordón, through banks in Paris and New York, six million dollars to cover them. At the Republic's request, Cárdenas also authorized Minister Tejeda in Paris to buy for the Spaniards arms and aircraft sufficient to equip two regiments. Later the Mexican president permitted Tejeda to acquire unlimited supplies of European arms for Republican Spain. Cárdenas also tried in August to obtain arms for Spain in England, but the British government refused to authorize any such sales. Although Mexico's diplomatic representative in England promised that the material his country wanted (thousands of rifles and machine guns, millions of bullets) was destined solely for its own army, the British refused "to risk the possibility that these arms would be reshipped to Spain."[24]

Cárdenas at first tried to keep secret the Mexican arms sale to Republican Spain because he knew that his action would create an international uproar. Newspapers all over the world, however, reported the story even before the shipment reached Veracruz. Mexico thus began its long commitment to the Spanish Republicans in a burst of highly unfavorable publicity. From his vantage point at the legation in Lisbon, Minister Daniel Cosío Villegas observed that in Europe and Latin America hostile countries were scoring propaganda victories at Mexico's expense. A newspaper cartoon sent from Portugal by Cosío showed a hydrophobic-looking Spanish "Red" murdering several noncombatants with a gun marked "from Mexico." In Chile, where radio stations joined newspapers in calling for a break in diplomatic relations with the Cárdenas regime, the Mexican ambasssador considered the situation serious enough to ask President Arturo Alesandri to announce that his government intended to maintain friendly relations with Mexico. After about three weeks of silence on the matter, Cárdenas confirmed what the press had reported by detailing his action to Congress during an annual report to the nation at the beginning of September.[25]

Conservative publications throughout the Americas and in Europe continued to attack Mexico on the arms issue for the war's duration. Mario Ribas, a socially prominent pro-Franco Spaniard who lived in Honduras, did typical journalistic damage. He wrote in Tegucigalpa's *Renacimiento* that Mexican shipments did not really have Spain as their destination. All war materials, he charged, secretly went to Brazil and other Latin American countries for use in local communist uprisings. (Brazil had recently experienced such a revolt.) According to Ribas: "General Franco's armies need not fear these Mexican arms; it is rather the American governments who should keep their eyes open in this matter." As will be seen, Mexico was highly vulnerable to such propaganda, especially in Central America where the Revolutionary regime inspired fear as well as hatred.[26] In November 1937, for example, the Jorge Ubico government in Guatemala accused Mexico of complicity in a Spanish Republican-Comintern plot to smuggle arms into the country. The Guatemalans named Emilio Zapico, Spain's Consul General in Mexico, as the "Soviet agent" who was involved in the conspiracy. Allegedly the weapons would be used by communist revolutionaries to "liberate" Central America. Mexico politely denied the charges as unfounded, but even to have such accusations made constituted a diplomatic setback in that region.[27]

Cárdenas initially intended to supplement Mexican arms sales to the Republic by purchasing for them in the United States airplanes, airplane engines, and other war materials. Ostensibly Mexico would be acquiring the military hardware for itself. Late in 1936 Mexico bought ten planes in the United States after assuring the State Department that they were destined for the Mexican air force. A Mexican corporation purchased six other planes from American Airlines, presumably for use in the mining industry. But in January 1937 all sixteen planes were in Veracruz awaiting shipment to Spain on the Loyalist ship *Motomar.* Upon discovering this the American press, led by Hearst's papers, played up the story. American warplanes, the Washington *Herald* objected, were being sent to help "the Spanish Communist forces." President Roosevelt was determined to avoid domestic political trouble on the issue and asked Cárdenas not to forward planes or any other American-made arms to Spain. The Mexican leader cancelled the plane shipment, then announced that Mexico's policy henceforth would be to send no foreign-made weaponry to Spain unless it had permission to do so from the government of the country concerned.[28]

For the most part Cárdenas kept his promise to Roosevelt not to transship to Spain any war materials that Mexico acquired in the United States. He did this despite urgent pleas from Spanish Republicans and against the advice of some key members of his administration. During much of the war he also insisted that any European arms purchases from Spain by Mexico be approved by authorities in the country involved. "Under no circumstances are we to deceive friendly governments," he once told his ambassador in Spain. With the Republic facing imminent destruction in 1938, however, Cárdenas relented. When Narciso Bassols wired Foreign Relations from the legation in Paris requesting permission to supply Mexican cover for a Loyalist acquisition of ten airplanes in Holland, Cárdenas after some delay finally told Secretary Hay to authorize the secret transaction.[29]

On several occasions North American war materials did go to Spain from Mexico, apparently without President Cárdenas's knowledge. Perhaps hoping that Roosevelt would eventually change his mind, Cárdenas allowed fifty planes and a large number of airplane engines—all made in the U.S.—to accumulate in Veracruz. Throughout 1937, however, he refused to let them be shipped. Exasperated with the delays, Ambassador Gordón went to Defense Secretary Avila Camacho for help in December of that year, when the president was temporarily away from Mexico City. A strong supporter of Republican Spain, the secretary agreed to participate in a sham conspiracy: Gordón would be depicted as having spirited away the planes and engines without government knowledge. With the help of Avila Camacho and of generals Molinar and Mange in Veracruz, the large shipment left for Spain on the Republican vessel *Ibai* on December 26. When *Excelsior* was about to publish a "rumor" that the planes and engines were to be loaded on the *Ibai*, a telephone call from Avila Camacho to the paper's managing editor killed the story. Cárdenas later forgave Gordón with the observation that he would have done the same thing had he been in the ambassador's position. Avila Camacho helped the Republic additionally by devising a way to keep Mexican arms flowing to Spain. He persuaded Cárdenas to buy from United States companies new weapons for Mexico's armed forces, at the same time selling to the Loyalists equal quantities of old Mexican arms. Military assistance to the Republic thus contributed to standardization and modernization of the country's weaponry, a development that even conservative Mexican generals who might prefer Franco to the Loyalists would have to appreciate.[30]

From September 1936 to September 1937 Mexico sold to the Republic armaments worth about eight million pesos ($2.2 million). Most of these weapons, which included artillery pieces, anti-aircraft guns, mortars, and gas masks, as well as more rifles and ammunition, left Mexico on the Republican ships *Motomar, Ibai,* and *Mar Cantábrico,* the latter captured by the Nationalist navy in 1937. The Mexicans also loaded food, medical supplies, fuel, and military clothing that the Republic had bought on these ships, and occasionally Mexican volunteers sailed off to Spain on them.[31]

Lack of secrecy was a major factor in the capture of the *Mar Cantábrico,* for the Nationalists knew when and where to expect it.[32] The vessel left Veracruz loaded with arms on February 19, 1937. On March 8 Franquista ships captured it off the Spanish coast. Letters subsequently stolen from some Franco agents in New York and published in U.S. newspapers revealed that information about the *Mar Cantábrico's* contents, exact destination, and sailing time was sent to the New York spies by Federico Varela, a Spanish businessman resident in Veracruz. The published copy of a letter from one of the agents to Varela exposed the latter's role. He told Varela: "I appreciate your cablegram, which I at once passed on to the person who is to warn our government in Spain so that they will be watching the arrival of this ship at those shores." Once informed (by the press of another country) about Varela's espionage activity, the Mexicans took steps to deport him.[33]

Mexican diplomatic officials in Paris purchased (outside of France) substantial quantities of European-made arms for the Republic throughout the Civil War. Foreign Relations warned Minister Tejeda in Paris to avoid antagonizing the French government, so Tejeda either operated in secrecy or informed the French that he was buying the weapons for Mexico's army. In August 1936 the Mexicans in Paris contracted to buy fifty thousand bombs and two hundred thousand hand grenades from a company in Brussels. The sales agreement allowed Mexico to cede contract rights to a third party, and this it did, naming as third party Antonio Fernández Bolaños, an agent of Republican Spain. In October Tejeda reported additional purchases of military equipment for the Republic from companies in Switzerland and Poland, reporting to Foreign Relations that payment had been made "in a way that will not compromise our government." Tejeda continued to seek sources of weaponry for Spain as long as he remained in Paris. When he left at the end of 1937 to become ambassador to the Republic, his successor carried on with the project.[34]

On the Diplomatic Front

Mexico stood by Loyalist Spain in the international diplomatic arena, but in the early months of the war some members of the diplomatic corps expressed reservations about the extent of violence in the Republican zone. When the League of Nations took up the Spanish question in late September 1936 and responded with the Nonintervention Committee rather than with assistance to Azaña's regime, Mexican delegate Bassols objected at his first opportunity. Speaking to the League's Assembly on October 2, 1936, he called nonintervention a tragic step backward in international relations. Paralyzed by deficiencies in its charter, the League could not protect member states from aggression and thus could not preserve world peace. He went on to allege that unless charter revisions were made immediately, the League would be destroyed by its enemies. Mexico would continue to aid the Republic; its policy rested on "solid juridical bases" and stemmed from a sympathetic understanding of the Republican government's dilemma, for Mexicans themselves had suffered frequently from "the scourge of antisocial military uprisings."[35]

Early in 1937 Isidro Fabela replaced Bassols at the League. Fabela was a distinguished old liberal from the Revolution's early days and an experienced diplomat. His name invariably comes up in connection with Cárdenas's decision to champion the Loyalist cause, for he and Bassols are regarded as important influences on the president at that critical moment.[36] Prior to Fabela's departure for Geneva, Cárdenas personally gave him instructions. Mexico must defend not only Republican Spain but "any country that suffers foreign aggression from whatever power." It would insist that Spain, having been attacked by Germany and Italy, could properly request and rightfully expect protection from the League's member states under provisions of Article Ten of the organization's charter. Azaña's government being legitimate, Mexico would recognize no other Spanish regime. Fabela must remain intransigent on these points and also on the question of Ethiopia, which Mexico would continue to regard as being illegally occupied by a foreign power.[37]

Cárdenas sent additional instructions in February to his new representative at Geneva. He wanted Fabela to make clear that Mexico considered the League's nonintervention policy to be a form of indirect aid to Franquista rebels and to the foreign powers helping them. Fabela should state emphatically that Mexico's assistance to the Republic, including arms shipments, was the "logical result" of a correct interpretation of nonintervention, namely that aggression was to be discouraged by resistance. He must also emphasize Mexico's "scrupulous observance of the principles of international morality" on which the League justified its existence; and he must explain that Mexico transshipped arms to Spain only when the government of the country from whence they came gave its approval.[38] Upon his arrival, Fabela made these and other points verbally and in writing, and he repeated Mexico's position on Spain at every opportunity.

On September 20 and 28, 1937, Fabela made major speeches to the League on the Spanish question. He had had to wait months for Spain to come up on the official agenda. Along with Japanese aggression against China, he said, foreign attacks on Spain constituted an especially dangerous crisis, since they involved violations of both international law and the League's charter and assaults on human rights that "presage the downfall of our civilization." Fabela chided League members for refusing to accept jurisdiction over the Spanish war and called the Nonintervention Committee an instrument for obscuring reality with fictions. Mexico believed that if the League had applied vigorously those sanctions that foreign intervention in Spain deserved, the Nationalist rebellion would have collapsed quickly and the League have scored a resounding triumph. Supporters of nonintervention claimed that the League had avoided war in Europe, but Fabela asked: "Is it not more accurate to say that war is being prolonged in Spain and merely postponed in the rest of Europe?" Since Spain was clearly under heavy German and Italian attack, with the object of imposing on the country through terror an external political ideology, the League had an obligation to dissolve the Nonintervention Committee immediately and take steps to halt the aggression. Mexico would continue to aid Spain's legitimate government, doing this in accord with the general principles of the Rights of Man and as a signatory of the 1928 Panamerican Convention on the Duties and Rights of States in Cases of Civil Wars, a treaty that "authorizes giving material aid to legally constituted governments and prohibits such aid to rebels."[39]

Throughout the Civil War Cárdenas insisted that Mexico take no action that in any way even implied Mexican recognition of a Nationalist government at Burgos, and Secretary Hay strictly imposed this policy on diplomatic personnel. This kept Mexico from taking certain humanitarian actions that might have been beneficial to Republicans and also precluded their joining other countries in seeking a negotiated settlement of the conflict. In 1936 the Mexicans rejected such a proposal by Uruguay, and they vetoed a similar Cuban suggestion in 1937. Inflexibility also meant that Mexico had to abandon any of its citizens unlucky enough to have been arrested by the Nationalists. The Mexican embassy in London tried to get British help in such cases, but the British Foreign Office replied that England had no diplomatic relations with Franco's regime either.[40]

Mexico's ambassador at Madrid in July 1936 was General Manuel Pérez Treviño, a follower of Carranza and Obregón in the Revolution. Along with Calles, he had been one of the PNR's founders. Pérez had held cabinet posts in several administrations and had unsuccessfully tried for the official party's presidential nomination in 1933. In his mid-forties, the ambassador had a spreading paunch, fleshy jowls, a rapidly receding hairline, nervous eyes, and very little political luck. He and some other Callistas considered to be major rivals of Cárdenas—Tejeda for example —had been assigned to diplomatic posts in Europe, primarily to get them out of the country. Pérez went to Spain in 1935, the year of Cárdenas's break with Calles.[41]

Pérez's first crucial decision when the Civil War started involved requests for political asylum by over eight hundred people, most of them conservative Spaniards. When the ambassador chose to harbor them in the embassy and other buildings protected by Mexican diplomatic immunity, leftists at home called him a fascist.[42] Pérez's action also displeased President Cárdenas, for it created several complex problems, not the least of which was Spanish Republican anger with its ally for shielding people marked for execution. The United Press news service correctly reported in October that Cárdenas would replace Pérez with Ramón P. de Negri, Mexico's ambassador to Chile.[43]

Cárdenas had an even better reason than the asylum policy for removing Pérez from Spain. He knew that his envoy saw the Spanish war in terms that contradicted Mexico's official interpretation of the conflict as being between a constitutional, democratic government and seditious militarists in league with international fascism. In October the ambassador had told Foreign Relations:

> The formation of popular militias occurred so quickly and on such a large scale that their Committees immediately assumed almost all government functions. This created a situation that, far from involving the struggle of the legitimate government against the rebellious army, should be seen as an extremely violent clash between two uprisings—one militarist and of completely conservative tendencies and the other popular, Red, of the masses, undoubtedly aimed at the revolutionary transformation of Spain.[44]

Ambassador Pérez and other Mexican officials in Spain had been profoundly shocked by the magnitude of indiscriminate Republican terror. Pérez explained this to Foreign Relations after learning that the president was angry with him. He informed Secretary Hay:

> Despite my recognized revolutionary and left-wing sympathies . . . I have given asylum to many people obviously in immediate danger of death. I want to make clear that these persons . . . are not, for the most part, political refugees in the strict sense; their anxieties did not result from specific accusations or prosecutions on the part of the constituted authorities; rather they feared becoming victims of the numerous *chekas* operating anarchically in Madrid and other locations.[45]

While he awaited de Negri's arrival, Pérez continued to stress to Foreign Relations the lack of guarantees and anarchy prevailing in revolutionary Madrid to justify his asylum policy. He even signed a joint diplomatic protest to the Loyalist government about its inability to control the extremist death squads that were still carrying out numerous murders and massacres months after the July rebellion.[46] The protest, signed also by the ambassador of Chile and the chargés of England, France, and Argentina, was delivered confidentially to the Republican minister of state on October 8. The diplomats reminded the Spanish government that its pledge to prevent such excesses remained unfulfilled, and they expressed dismay at the continuing incarceration, physical abuse, and execution of people of both sexes in "irregular jails." Such things, they said, "manifestly conflict with universally accepted principles of legality and humanity." In transmitting a copy of the note to Foreign Relations, Pérez pointed out how angry the continuing Terror made the diplomatic corps in Madrid. He also registered his own repugnance at the "great number of bodies" discovered every morning in the streets of the Spanish capital.[47]

Although accused of sympathy for the Nationalist rebellion and for fascism, Pérez acted consistently in granting political asylum under provisions of the 1928 Panamerican Convention. When Franquista troops appeared on the verge of capturing Madrid in November, the ambassador gave refuge in the embassy to numerous leftists and some Republican officials. His action created a bizarre situation at the embassy where two hostile, armed camps of refugees were each obtaining protection against their enemies outside. Despite Mexican fears of an outbreak of shooting inside the building, none occurred.[48] On December 10 Pérez again reminded Foreign Relations about the Terror in Madrid. "A completely anarchic situation prevails here and each day it becomes more acute," he said. Even the Loyalist *alcalde* of Madrid could not safely leave the city for Valencia, new home of the Azaña government. Despite the efforts of several cabinet ministers to help the man, he remained sheltered at the Mexican embassy, for militiamen patrolling the streets refused to let him make the trip.[49]

Embassy First Secretary Francisco Navarro shared Pérez's feelings about the Terror. In August 1936 he told Secretary Hay that the Chilean ambassador in Madrid had been "basically correct" when he charged that there was "no government" in Spain's capital. Leftist militias ignored government orders to stop the killings. Seven Colombians had just been murdered despite their being under diplomatic protection and having "guarantees of safety" from the Republican administration. Militiamen disobeying official orders had executed 225 prisoners from Jaén, and "every night individuals frequently having no connection whatever with the military rising are dragged from their homes and shot by the militias." Revolutionary trade unions held real power, he maintained, and their armed members exercised far more authority than Azaña and his cabinet.[50] Two months later Navarro again emphasized terror as the salient characteristic of a Spanish Republic that he described as being on the brink of "sovietization." By rebelling against the Popular Front administration, Spain's army had precipitated the very political development that it had claimed to be forestalling: a radical workers revolution. The Republic's elected government had "abdicated" all responsibility in favor of extremist unions and political parties. Under present circumstances, should the Popular Front win the war, "the Spanish Republic will become the world's second soviet state. . . ." Navarro added that "left-wing bourgeois" members of the Loyalist regime continued in office only at the militias' pleasure and that they had no power to stop arbitrary persecutions of noncombatants. Armed groups of communists, with no more authority than the orders of three or four chieftains, regularly carried out searches, arrests, and executions throughout Republican territory. Anarchist police squads behaved even more irresponsibly, for they "killed their enemies on the basis of a single vote by one of their members."[51]

Loyalist terror in the summer of 1936 shocked another Mexican diplomat, the consul general in Barcelona, José Rubén Romero. Writing to Under-Secretary Beteta at the Ministry of Foreign Relations, Romero described conditions that filled him with much anxiety.

> The militiamen, armed and deployed throughout the city, give rise to constant unrest, since many of them act irresponsibly, and outrages, public assassinations, vengeances, and persecutions are repeated much too frequently. We witness here in 1936 scenes reminiscent of the French Revolution, the only difference being that Madame Guillotine has been replaced by the modern Mauser. Every day people accused of being fascists, industrialists, landlords, etc. are taken from their homes and shot. One urgently hopes for the emergence of a popular caudillo with the necessary evergy and intelli-

gence to dominate the situation and stop the lawless movement that is consuming so many lives and gravely endanger-
ing the military campaign at the fronts.[52]

Romero added that the Catalans presented another serious problem
for the Republican war effort. They seemed determined to separate
their province from Spain "in order to establish a soviet-type state,
with abolition of private property and bureaucratic regulation of
all of the individual's activities."[53]

As had been the case with arms sales to the Republic, the refugee
and Terror issues became diplomatic nightmares for Mexico. Other
countries asked the Mexicans to intercede with the Loyalist
government to obtain an easing of Madrid's tense situation, to get
safe conduct out of Spain for thousands of refugees in numerous
embassies, and to prevent their own nationals or Spaniards related
to their nationals from being killed by militiamen. Some countries
also pressured Mexico to join them in demanding that Republicans
strictly observe their right to grant political asylum. When Mexico
refused to cooperate fully with the hard line taken by Argentina
and Chile, who wanted all Latin American countries to break
relations with the Republic if there were any violations of asylum,
several governments and much of the world press accused Mexico
of preparing to yield to demands by Popular Front officials that
many of the refugees be turned over to them for punishment.[54]

In October 1936, Minister Cosío sent an anxious message to
Foreign Relations from Lisbon:

> I greatly fear that the unconfirmed news reported by Havas,
> AP, and UP concerning Mexico's position on Spanish matters
> is causing irreparable harm to the prestige and interests of our
> country. Havas reports that in regard to the political refugees
> it assumes Mexico's willingness to hand them over to the
> Madrid government if required to do so; this has caused
> indignation here equal to that aroused by our sale of arms [to
> the Republic] and our willingness to let its ships fly the
> Mexican flag.[55]

A month later he reported that relations between Mexico and
Portugal, never very warm, had become "singularly delicate" due
to the continuing refugee controversy and that the Portuguese
press, moreover, was being most unfavorable toward Mexico's
position.

> Whereas the newspapers depict [Argentine Foreign Secretary] Saavedra Lamas as feverishly trying to arrange the evacuation of the refugees from Spain, and present the Chilean government as daily insisting on complete respect for the right of asylum, in contrast they describe the Madrid government as denying this right. . . . And in this arbitrary assignment of roles they represent Mexico as being so friendly to Madrid that it lacks even a trace of the other countries' gallantry and will do nothing to save the lives of innocent people.[56]

Given the frightful situation in Madrid and elsewhere in Spain, Mexico's justifications for its refusal to join other governments in demanding that the Popular Front end the Terror were lame enough to cause many people to wonder whether or not Cárdenas really cared about this issue. As thousands of Spaniards were slaughtered, embassies and diplomatic missions invaded, and foreign nationals shot down in cold blood, Mexicans officially voiced unwillingness to "exert excessive pressure on a legitimate government with which friendly relations are maintained." Mexican politicians also complained that the pressure being applied by such countries as Argentina and Chile threatened to inflict moral injury upon Azaña's administration. Such statements enabled unfriendly critics to accuse the Mexicans of being willing to hand over the political refugees in their embassy if they thought that they could get away with it.[57] At home conservative newspapers exploited the Loyalist Terror and Cárdenas's position on asylum, which remained ambiguous to the public due to a series of contradictory statements made by various members of the administration. *Las Últimas Noticias* in January 1937 even suggested that Cárdenas might abandon Mexico's asylum policy in Madrid. The paper urged him not to "throw to the lions" people sheltered at the embassy.[58]

Among the refugees were soldiers, airmen, civil guards, policemen, and conservative politicians. Falangists, noblemen, newspapermen, and relatives of rebel leaders had also been saved by Ambassador Pérez. Some Mexicans had come to the embassy for protection, too. Conservative writer Rodolfo Reyes was there with his two sons, both of whom had been active as rightists in Spanish politics. Pedro de Alba, a pro-PNR educator, had also sought safety in the embassy, apparently worried that militiamen might shoot him before he could explain that he was on their side. Former Spanish ambassador to Mexico, Emiliano Iglesias, and his wife had entered the embassy on July 26. The couple remained there until the spring of 1937 when the Mexicans smuggled them (disguised and carrying Mexican passports) out of Spain by getting them secretly aboard a British warship.[59]

Ramón P. de Negri replaced Pérez early in 1937. Opportunism and good political connections had provided the new Mexican envoy with high government posts in the 1920s: chargé d'affaires in Washington; secretary of Agriculture under Obregón; ambassador to Germany and secretary of Industry, Commerce, and Labor under Calles. By the 1930s he had settled comfortably into the foreign service. Cárdenas made him ambassador to Chile, then assigned him to Spain at the end of 1936. At the time of this appointment de Negri was a flabby, bespectacled, gray-haired man of middle age. Deceptively innocuous in appearance, he resembled more an insurance salesman than a diplomat. He had an attractive Argentine wife (her second marriage) and a decidedly unattractive stepson, Carlos, a chronic drunk given to violent rampages. De Negri was an enigma (to say the least), and he proved to be such a total diplomatic failure in both Chile and Spain that some people suspected him of having been recruited as an agent either by the Germans or the Russians or by both of these powers. Others thought that his many failings stemmed from the evil influence of Carlos, who dominated his stepfather.[60] Superficially de Negri was at least a fellow-traveler if not a crypto-communist. His reports to Foreign Relations from Spain followed the Soviet and Spanish Communist party lines, and he formed close ties with the communists in Spain. When he came back from Spain (in disgrace), he continued to work on behalf of the Republican war effort. Yet in 1939–40 he defected from the PRM to join General Juan Andreu Almazán's rightist campaign for the presidency, a movement that attracted some profascist support despite Almazán's declarations of sympathy for the Western democracies.[61]

De Negri's irresponsibility in Chile in 1936 had almost precipitated a break in diplomatic relations between Mexico and that country. Confronted with a conservative government hostile to leftism at home and abroad, the ambassador chose to be aggressive in his office and champion the Spanish Republic and encourage the Chilean masses to make a Mexican-style revolution of their own.

Secretary Hay warned de Negri that his tactics only increased Mexico's isolation in South America and ordered him to be more prudent; yet de Negri persisted in his reckless behavior. Mexican radicals operating out of the embassy in Santiago harangued audiences with predictions that Mexico's "proletarian revolution" would spread throughout the hemisphere. Chilean newspapers excoriated Cárdenas and called on President Alesandri to sever ties with Mexico, and eventually Chile expelled from the country a third secretary of the Mexican embassy. Upon de Negri's reassignment to Spain, the Chilean crisis passed; according to the diplomat left in charge of the embassy, however, Mexico's interests had suffered greatly in that country as a consequence of de Negri's "subversive acts."[62] Cárdenas could not have been familiar with de Negri's character and record when he named him ambassador to Spain. Foreign Secretary Hay certainly could have enlightened the president about the bungling envoy, but perhaps he wished to avoid an argument with his chief, or perhaps he was not even consulted about the appointment. Given his lack of enthusiasm for the Republic, Hay may have just smiled grimly and concluded that de Negri was his best choice for the job.

De Negri got off to a typically disastrous start in Spain. It took him sixty-seven days (not counting allotted travel time) to arrive at his new post. En route he stopped in Paris and began to defame the character of former ambassador Pérez. When he finally reached Spain, he also embarrassed Cárdenas by suggesting to the press that he would turn over political refugees at the Mexican embassy in Madrid to the vengeful Loyalists. Upon arrival in Valencia, Republican capital for much of the war, de Negri immediately began to quarrel with his staff, virtually all of whom he had selected himself. When he asked Foreign Relations to allow him to fire Second Secretary Efraín Brito Rosado, Hay refused permission, reminding the ambassador that he himself had chosen Brito and that to fire him so soon "would give the impression that we choose our personnel carelessly." De Negri then scandalized Republicans by failing to observe any diplomatic protocol when presenting his credentials to the Azaña government. He arrived at the ceremony attired in nondescript street clothes and accompanied by two "aides," both of whom wore Mexican cowboy hats and carried large pistols on their hips.[63]

De Negri badly wanted to turn the refugees over to the Loyalists.

Even before he reached Spain, he sent inflammatory reports to Cárdenas about their alleged behavior in an effort to persuade the president to let him clear them out of the embassy. From Paris he had Minister Tejeda forward to Cárdenas a message accusing the refugees of numerous outrages: conspiring against the Republic; celebrating religious acts; and expressing disdain for the Mexican government. He promised the president that when he arrived in Spain, "I will energetically move to put an end to the embarrassing and abusive refugee situation." Cárdenas responded with a cable ordering de Negri to refrain from expelling the refugees and to treat them with all the consideration that their position as guests of the Mexican government merited.[64] If at this time de Negri was secretly a German agent only feigning leftist sympathies (as some authorities have suggested), his ability to have the refugees massacred would certainly have pleased the Germans. Such deaths would have been a devastating propaganda setback for both Mexico and the Republic. Having failed to move Cárdenas, de Negri was left with the unwanted job of negotiating safe conduct out of Spain for the refugees. When he eventually achieved this in the spring of 1937, he also had to escort them from Madrid to Valencia, from where they sailed for France. On March 13, after some dangerous moments at the pier when crowds of workers and militiamen insisted on executing several of the departing rightists, de Negri managed to get all but four of them aboard a ship bound for Marseilles. Four refugees had to stay in the country under Mexican diplomatic protection because the Loyalists accused them of possessing military secrets.[65]

De Negri remained in Spain a mere six months, from late January to late July 1937, yet his stay in the peninsula must have seemed an eternity to the Republican government and to responsible Mexican officials at Foreign Relations. Terrified by Nationalist air raids against Valencia, the ambassador domiciled himself in a village far removed from the city. Even during working hours his appearances at the embassy were rare. Business did not get transacted; communications from Mexico City went unanswered. Reviewing his performance in July, Foreign Relations told Cárdenas that de Negri had not sent back one useful report on the Spanish situation. In addition he had ignored instructions to protect *all* Mexicans in Spain, regardless of their politics, and Secretary Hay thought that he did not even know how many of his

countrymen remained in the peninsula. Hay further charged de
Negri with complete neglect of his duties in regard to the
president's March 1937 note on the civil war and with mishandling
negotiations over several hundred Republican war orphans sent to
Mexico as refugees. The orphan question will be discussed elsewhere in the book.

Despite his official truancy, de Negri did keep busy in Spain.
Investigations by other foreign service officers indicated that he had
more than once extorted money from wealthy Spaniards as the
price for smuggling them out of the country under Mexican
protection. He also sold diplomatic passports indiscriminately to
Spaniards and commissioned numerous confidential agents (to
whom he also gave Mexican documentation) for special assign-
ments, none of which had been authorized by Foreign Relations.
When the ambassador finally reached agreement with Republicans
about the eight hundred people sheltered in the Mexican embassy,
he overcharged the refugees for travel expenses to Valencia and
pocketed the extra money. Constant turmoil surrounded de Negri,
his stepson Carlos, and the embassy staff in Valencia. Carlos
repeatedly got into serious trouble with Spanish police. His
drunken carousals among adventurers and low-life types often
ended in violence. Yet when police arrested him for shooting up a
bar or a street, his stepfather obtained his release. After one
nocturnal binge, Carlos allegedly returned drunk to the embassy
and shot to death several staff members. The murders were
effectively concealed. De Negri himself behaved erratically and
shared his stepson's criminal tendencies. On one occasion he
requested from Foreign Relations permission to name as honorary
consul in Valencia a man wanted for murder in Mexico. Embassy
staffers also contributed to the chaos. First Secretary Jesús Sansón
Flores, a friend of Cárdenas, began abusing his wife when she
objected to his many love affairs. During one of their heated
domestic battles at the embassy, Sansón struck her on the head
several times with the butt of his revolver. (Evidently everyone at
the embassy went about armed, no doubt as a precaution against a
quarrel with Carlos rather than from fear of a Nationalist attack.)
Sansón finally sent his wife back to Mexico "in order to have
complete freedom for his orgies," as one diplomat put it in a report
to Foreign Relations.[66]

The interlude between the departure of de Negri, recalled by

Cárdenas in July 1937, and the arrival of Adalberto Tejeda from France at year's end was ably filled by General Leobardo Ruiz, Mexican Consul General in Barcelona. An astute, no-nonsense soldier-politician in his forties, Ruiz worked well with the Republicans, did not meddle in Spanish politics or cause scandal, and kept a suspicious eye on Communist and Russian activities. When Tejeda took over the embassy, Ruiz returned to his consular office in Barcelona.[67]

Colonel Tejeda looked both mean and cunning; he was big, bald, and in his mid-fifties. If ever a man had boss stamped all over his face, that man was Tejeda. A terror to Catholics in Veracruz where he had been governor, Tejeda nonetheless could be warm and compassionate. At the Mexican embassy in Barcelona (the Republican government having moved there from Valencia in the fall of 1937) Tejeda maintained an orphanage-school for two hundred children. He personally adopted one of these waifs and raised her in Mexico as his own daughter.

By the time of his appointment, Tejeda had already accomplished his major services to the Spanish republic in Paris. His tenure as Mexico's minister to France was spent in arranging Mexican cover for arms shipments to Spain. Although his diplomatic work in Spain was largely ceremonial—visiting factories, hospitals, peasant communes, and schools—Spaniards developed strong affection for him. Despite his friendship with the Communists, he apparently avoided any involvement in the Republic's internal politics. Consequently he came out of Spain with his reputation intact, although some Spaniards found him rather crude and stupid. Tejeda, along with Isidro Fabela and Narciso Bassols, played an important role in rescuing thousands of Republican refugees in France by keeping the issue before President Cárdenas in 1939. Spanish exiles in Mexico never forgot this. Years after the war had ended they still came to Tejeda's house in Coyoacán to thank him personally for helping them escape from certain death at the hands of Franco or as a result of French indifference.[68]

Mexican Diplomacy in Spanish America

Cárdenas tried to find support for the Spanish Republic in Latin America, but political dominance by conservatives in Spain's former empire doomed his efforts to failure. As has been noted, with few exceptions regimes throughout the hemisphere viewed Revolutionary Mexico with as much animosity as they did Popular Front Spain. Right-wing politicians, the press, middle- and upper-class people, and the Catholic Church tended to lump Mexico together with the USSR and the Republic as major components of a worldwide communist conspiracy. In addition the pro-Republican activities of Mexican diplomats in Latin America drew some of them deep into local left-wing circles, and these associations only confirmed existing suspicions about Mexico's revolutionary intentions in the Americas. In 1937 most Latin American members of the League of Nations voted to expel the Spanish Republic from the League Council, an action that Mexican newspaper columnist Salvador Novo ironically noted "clearly shows us how much sympathy we enjoy among our dear sister republics to the south."[69]

Several South American countries followed Chile's lead in 1936 in trying to organize "an American front against Communism," a movement that included Mexico as one of its targets.[70] The Mexican embassy in Santiago reported that members of the Alessandri administration regarded Mexico's influence as a greater revolutionary threat than Soviet Communism, since Chilean leftists realized that social and economic conditions in their country made imitation of the Russian Revolution unlikely.[71] Mexican diplomats saw among Chileans little evidence of popular support for the Loyalists or even of a spirit of neutrality or fair play. Press and clergy in Chile propagandized relentlessly for Franco, and church services held on behalf of a Nationalist victory invariably attracted Santiago's most important people. When newsreels about the Spanish war were shown in Chilean movie houses, "the audience hisses whenever Popular Front loyalists or members of the government appear on the screen and noisily applauds any scenes featuring the reactionary rebels." In rural areas the largely illiterate laborers obtained their news about Spain during masses celebrated on large estates, when local priests praised Franco and denounced the "diabolical" ideas of the Republicans.[72]

Mexico was under heavy fire elsewhere in South America as well. In Paraguay a National Committee of Paraguayan Rightists repeatedly accused the Mexican legation in Asunción of distributing Communist propaganda and of supplying funds to local Marxists, charges publicized by newspapers in Argentina.[73] Members of the Paraguayan government were so pro-Franco that the

Mexican chargé only brought up the Spanish question with them when directly ordered to do so by Foreign Relations and even then he assured them beforehand that everything would be "off the record and strictly informal."[74]

The Argentine political situation as reported by Ambassador Alfonso Reyes afforded the Mexicans small hope of gaining their foreign policy objectives. Reyes said that "a thousand fascist influences and pressures within and without the government" were working against the Spanish Republic in Argentina. The Argentine ambassador in Madrid made no secret of his hostility to the Popular Front regime. President Agustín P. Justo's Acting Foreign Secretary, Ramón S. Castillo, tormented the Republican ambassador in Buenos Aires through such deliberate obstructionist tactics as the seizure of two Republican freighters to prevent them from reaching Mexico where they would have loaded arms for Spain. Reyes predicted that the ship incidents would be remembered as "one of the most shameful chapters in the history of South American diplomacy."[75]

Mexican diplomats in Peru also found themselves in a totally unpromising situation. Local leftists had been suppressed by a conservative military dictatorship, the press universally lauded Franco, and some newspapers were serving as outlets for Italian attacks on both the Spanish Republic and Mexico as Communist states. Peruvian fascists openly campaigned against Mexico. The Benavides government favored the Nationalists and had received a diplomatic representative from the Burgos regime—Luis Avilés y Tíscar. Avilés had been Spain's minister in Lima when the war started. He defected to the rebel side and the Peruvians allowed him to retain control over the Spanish Legation building. From this base he solicited contributions for Franco from Peru's Spanish colony. According to the Mexican envoys, as early as August 1936 the Peruvian government had sounded out both Argentina and Chile as to the feasibility of their joint recognition of the Nationalist government.[76]

Inept Mexican diplomats made things even more difficult for Cárdenas in hostile South America by committing tactical errors. Ambassador de Negri's blunders in Chile have been noted.[77] Equally damaging to Mexico's position in Chile were public statements made in Madrid in early 1937 by Narciso Bassols. At the time Bassols held no government position, yet he was invariably identified with the Mexican regime because he had served it so prominently in the recent past. Bassols described Chile to a Republican audience as being owned by one hundred families and he called it "a fascist country that sells its products cheaply to other fascist countries." When Chile's government lodged an angry protest with Mexico, Foreign Secretary Hay pointed out that Bassols was merely a private citizen, but this did little to mollify the incensed Chileans. Bassols exacerbated tense diplomatic relations by publicly referring to Argentine Foreign Minister Saavedra Lamas as a fascist in 1937.[78]

In Peru, Ambassador Moisés Sáenz and First Secretary Bernardo Reyes appeared unable to do anything right. Both of them transmitted sensitive documents pertinent to Mexico's Spanish policy back to Foreign Relations without observing mandated security measures. They also communicated directly with the Spanish Republican government, whose interests Mexico represented in Peru, instead of routing their messages through Mexico City as required by protocol. To the great chagrin of Secretary Hay, Reyes had also distributed Loyalist recruiting propaganda throughout Peru without informing Foreign Relations of his actions, and he had inadvertently revealed the key to Mexico's diplomatic cipher in his unauthorized direct correspondence with the Spaniards.[79]

Indiscretion that hurt Mexico politically in South America was not limited to blundering diplomats. The PNR itself, through its newspaper *El Nacional*, occasionally published extremely derogatory material about pro-Franco regimes in the hemisphere. These attacks were invariably reprinted by the press of the country concerned, and they dimmed even further any prospects for the success of Cárdenas's Spanish policy. Typical of the imbroglio between Mexico and South American countries was an incident in Argentina. Mexico was already unpopular in Argentina where local politicians balefully watched Ambassador Reyes try to assist his beleaguered Spanish Republican colleague Enrique Diez-Canedo. Then in October 1936 a Buenos Aires newspaper prominently displayed a PNR blast at the Justo administration. *El Nacional* had personally attacked Acting Foreign Secretary Castillo "and his friends at the Jockey Club" and had lamented that "the winds of fascism have now arrived on the banks of La Plata, where in former times San Martín, Rivadavia, and Sarmiento battled for liberty."[80]

Perhaps the PNR's example, along with his own emotional

sympathy for the Republic, caused Ambassador Reyes himself to lose normal diplomatic prudence. He had little use for the Republic's communists and anarchists, but he was easily drawn into public associations with the very political extremists regarded as most dangerous by Argentina's conservative leaders. He spoke at pro-Loyalist rallies organized by Argentine communists. At a celebration of the Republic's sixth anniversary, press photographers captured him sitting amidst a group of leftists giving clenched-fist salutes. The ambassador's problems were compounded by occurrences that reflected unfavorably on him and the embassy. Resident Spaniards who sympathized with the Republic, a suspect group in government circles, streamed to the Mexican embassy to thank Reyes for Cárdenas's Civil War policy. Finally, some of Reyes's subordinates went to the Centro Republicano Español to help raise money for the war effort.[81]

In La Paz, Alfonso Rosenzweig Díaz behaved as indiscreetly as Reyes. During the spring of 1937 he joined the Spanish Republican chargé Manuel Martínez Feduchy in a scheme to rally local support for Mexico's position on Spain. Minister Rosenzweig told Foreign Relations that he hoped to show the Bolivian government that its sympathy for Franco ignored public opinion. His notions about Bolivian attitudes were decidedly limited and derived chiefly from communist-dominated organizations such as the Bolivian Popular Front and the Spanish Democratic Group. Rosenzweig also associated openly with the Marxist Circle of Intellectuals and Artists. At a Circle program honoring Mexico, the minister blamed Spain's conservatives for the civil war, which he characterized as a struggle between rebel "egoism" and Loyalist "ideals of human fraternity." Circle members saw it as "the great and heroic tragedy of the Spanish workers." Rosenzweig concluded his speech by assuring those present that Mexicans admired their efforts to shape Bolivia's future in accordance with "the new social ideologies" that Mexico itself had adopted.[82]

Mexico's diplomatic position in Central America was perhaps even worse than in the southern continent, for military rulers of the small states in this area, as well as sharing Franco's social and political outlook, viewed their allegedly communist northern neighbor with visible apprehension. Both Guatemala and Nicaragua early in the war recognized the Nationalist government and courted its favor. Guatemalan dictator Jorge Ubico sent an ambassador to the rebel regime in 1937 who assured Franquistas that his country stood as "a bulwark against Bolshevism" in Spanish America and that "Guatemala was following with sympathy and interest the Nationalist uprising's development." When a Franco spokesman later responded to this by praising Guatemala as Spanish America's first line of defense against "Bolshevist Mexico," major Guatemalan newspapers gave his remarks special emphasis.[83] Official attitudes toward Mexico in Costa Rica, Honduras, and El Salvador were just as unfriendly.

Cuba and Colombia offered some hope of success for Mexican Civil War diplomacy in Spanish America, yet even they disappointed Cárdenas. Cuban strongman Fulgencio Batista adopted a friendly attitude toward Mexico and seemingly toward Republican Spain, in part because he was cultivating a progressive image at home. When he made a state visit to Mexico in 1938, the PRM welcomed him as a hero. A joint session of the Mexican Congress cheered wildly when he promised that "Cuba will never recognize Franco." Yet Cuba offered little beyond promises as support for the Republic. Batista, moreover, did recognize Franco (rather soon after the war ended), and the Cuban government responded less than enthusiastically to Mexico's postwar pleas for acceptance of large numbers of Loyalist refugees.[84] In Colombia, Mexico could always count on expressions of solidarity with the Republic by liberal politicians, labor organizations, and even major newspapers; Colombians, however, never fulfilled their many promises to join Mexico eventually in helping its Spanish friends. To some extent the behavior of Colombian liberals when approached by Mexicans on the Spanish issue resembled that of French premier Léon Blum, who told the Republic's ambassador to France that he could not help a regime he loved. Blum urged the ambassador to "tell the Spanish workers that you have seen me weep for them."[85]

The Mexican Note of March 1937

On March 29, 1937, Mexico formally submitted a note on the Spanish war to the League of Nations, and Mexican envoys abroad presented the same statement to governments to which they were accredited. Cárdenas again denounced the League's nonintervention policy as depriving a freely elected government of the help from friendly nations to which it was entitled under international law. Failure of League members to cooperate with Republican authorities was "cruelly prolonging a fratricidal struggle." Given the involvement of foreign powers, Cárdenas continued, the League's inaction also threatened world peace. No legitimate government "representing the national will" should be at the mercy of a "faction" aided by outside elements. Mexico urged League members to assist the Republic and thus bring to an end the "lamentable Spanish situation." The League, however, continued to rely on the Nonintervention Committee, a body that the Republic itself had accepted much to Isidro Fabela's dismay. Responses to Cárdenas's appeal, when governments even bothered to give them, showed that Mexico remained thoroughly isolated in its Spanish policy.[86]

Sweden did not even want to acknowledge the Mexican note since it was a member of the Nonintervention Committee. This attitude fellow Committee members England and France shared. England and France, moreover, shunned discussions about Spain with the Mexicans at all times.[87] The Belgian Foreign Secretary, Paul-Henri Spaak, professed disenchantment with nonintervention because it "favored the fascists," yet he indicated to the Mexican ambassador that Belgium would continue to follow League policy on Spain because it could not afford to alienate England and France.[88] Belgian socialists spoke on behalf of Mexico's position only to be answered by conservative newspapers, one of which described Mexican aid to the Republic as part of a Russian plot to export communism and characterized the Spanish war as having been provoked by the Popular Front's "ragamuffin dictatorship," which had committed "innumerable exactions and atrocities."[89] In Warsaw, Under-Secretary of Foreign Relations Count Schoenbeck told the Mexican chargé that Poland regarded assistance to the Republic as "intervention in Spain's internal affairs" and thus improper. Provoked by what he called the speciousness of this argument, the Mexican diplomat asked Schoenbeck what his reaction would be if the Polish government were in danger of being overthrown by a communist uprising and Germany refused to sell it arms. The Under-Secretary grudgingly replied that Poland would feel that it had a right to purchase such arms, but he refused to discuss the Spanish question further.[90]

Latin American answers to the Mexican proposal, Colombia's excepted, were all negative. Most regimes politely advanced their neutrality on Spain as the reason for rejecting Mexico's suggestion; some governments, however, used the occasion to taunt Cárdenas. Interviewed by the Mexican ambassador, both the president and foreign secretary of Colombia "approved" the plan and offered to collaborate with Mexico "in favor of Spain's legitimate government." But Mexican diplomats in Bogotá were still waiting for the promised assistance five months later. None ever came.[91] The Cuban government initially misinterpreted Mexico's statement as a call for Latin American mediation of the Civil War, both Spanish parties to be treated as equals. When Mexico explained that it sought help for the Republic not arbitration, the Cubans replied that they would not play what they termed a partisan role in the conflict.[92]

Anastasio Somoza's rightist administration in Nicaragua merely informed Mexico that it would adhere to its "nonintervention policy." Somoza had already recognized Franco. But Guatemala's military ruler goaded the Mexicans by having his foreign secretary point out to them that "democratic" Guatemala would have nothing to do with intervention designed to set up a "communist" regime in Spain.[93] In El Salvador the Mexican minister saw no chance of even presenting the Cárdenas note to that country's pro-Franco government. Suspicious Salvadorean authorities were openly violating his diplomatic mail, so he refrained from antagonizing them further by raising the Spanish question.[94] Costa Rican animosity toward both Mexico and the Republic was so great that Salvador Martínez de Alva in San José did not even request an answer to Cárdenas's note when he presented it. Foreign Secretary Manuel F. Jiménez Ortiz owned a conservative newspaper that regularly denounced Mexico and the Spanish Republic as foci of Marxism. The administration's treasury secretary had already complained informally to Martínez that aid to the Valencia government would represent a step toward the imposition of communism in Central America. Throughout Costa Rica, suspicion of Mexico was so great that "even persons of relative culture" saw communist tendencies in Mexico's actions, "however insignificant or innocent they might be." Undoubtedly the Costa Rican government did stand well to the right in 1937 (a journalist received ten days in jail for writing an anti-Mussolini article that year), but Mexican activities in San José were hardly innocent. Martínez himself systematically planted pro-Mexican material in a friendly communist newspaper.[95] Venezuela's rulers chose to continue their nonintervention policy toward Spain. In addition they allegedly supervised the press to prevent newspapers from making favorable allusions to the Republic.[96]

The Benavides military regime in Peru politely rejected the note. Lima's conservative press impolitely ridiculed the basic assumption on which Mexican policy was based. According to *La Crónica:*

> Mexico believes that the "legitimate government of Spain is that headed by Mr. Azaña. The Iberian reality, however, namely . . . the political action of the militias, the expanding force of anarchosyndicalism . . . demonstrates that the government in those zones not yet captured by the Nationalists, far from being in the hands of authorities named by Azaña, is directed by the armed militias and union representatives, without whose stamp of approval not even the safe conducts issued by [Minister of State] Álvarez del Vayo have any validity. The Mexican thesis totally ignores this reality.[97]

Bolivia's government formulated a provocative answer to Cárdenas. Foreign Secretary Enrique Finot expressed satisfaction with League policy on Spain, then critiqued the Mexican note. In his opinion, Mexico was asking the world to adopt a reactionary international policy that would shut the door on popular revolutions or movements of national renovation. That at least would be the effect of accepting a definition of all political rebels as "aggressors." Bolivia could not accept this position "since the Mexican thesis emphasizes the obligation to help legitimate governments, and Colonel Toro's administration is the product of a coup carried out by the army against a civilian government. . . ." A disgusted Mexican minister in La Paz told Foreign Relations that most members of the Toro regime sympathized with Franco.[98]

Cárdenas probably realized that his statement would convert few governments to his point of view. But he did expect the note to stimulate press commentary and thus make clear to newspaper readers what he considered to be the obvious justice of the Spanish Republican cause. In this expectation he was disappointed, for most newspapers reacted with hostility or derision. In Latin America much of the independent liberal press had been intimidated or suppressed. Thus in some places where Cárdenas had hoped to arouse pro-Republic sentiment among the masses and progressive middle sectors, Mexico's appeal received no publicity whatever. Socialist newspapers in the hemisphere generally supported the Mexican position, but these publications had limited impact on political opinion and their backing probably did Mexico more harm than good.[99]

Other Mexican Diplomatic Aid to the Republic

Mexico, besides making assistance to Loyalist Spain a central feature of its foreign policy, extended personal diplomatic protection to Republicans and to their sympathizers throughout the war. Mexican diplomats also interceded as third parties to settle disputes or problems arising between the Republic and other nations. In some Latin American countries Mexico agreed to represent the interests of Loyalist Spain when their governments suspended or broke relations with the Azaña regime. In Paris, Minister Tejeda gave Republican politician Juan-Simeón Vidarte a Mexican passport so that he could make his many wartime journeys safely. Vidarte thus became Juan Valdés of Veracruz, a fictional person who could even travel through countries sympathetic to Franco.[100] Minister Cosío in Lisbon helped six Spanish peasants who had survived the bloody fall of Badajoz to escape from Portugal, where they would have been turned over to the Nationalists if caught, by giving them money and Mexican passports.[101] Foreign Relations itself provided similar shields, apparently without Secretary Hay's knowledge. In 1937, for example, Teresa Proenza traveled from Mexico to Spain with a Mexican diplomatic passport. She was a Cuban who belonged to the Mexican Communist Party and her mission was to work with the Women's Committee of the Spanish Communist Party.[102]

Mexico's third party intercessions with governments aggrieved by Loyalist actions usually involved pleas to the Republicans not to execute alleged subversive foreign nationals, not to seize political refugees sheltered in foreign embassies, and not to violate the immunity of diplomats from countries hostile to the Popular Front. When these things happened Mexico tried to appease the offended parties by getting the Republicans to apologize and to promise that the incidents would not be repeated. In January 1937, Consul General Romero came to the aid of his Nicaraguan counterpart in

Barcelona. Loyalist police had arrested the man for allegedly issuing Nicaraguan passports to Franquista Spaniards. They had also invaded the consulate. Romero obtained the Nicaraguan's release (the Catalans then deported him) as well as a promise from the provincial authorities to respect consular offices. Later in the year Mexico responded to a request by the Peruvian government for help in protecting twelve Spanish youths sheltered at Peru's legation building in Valencia. The Peruvian regime feared an imminent assault on its legation because of the presence of pro-Franco refugees, but Mexican chargé Ruiz appealed to the Spaniards, who immediately offered guarantees that no attack would be made.[103]

The hapless Republicans certainly needed Mexico's aid. They had virtually no friends abroad, and most of their foreign service personnel overseas defected to Franco. There were so many resignations or dismissals of consuls for disloyalty in Uruguay that eventually resident Spaniards there came to be without diplomatic representation of their interests.[104] From Peru, Mexican chargé Bernardo Reyes reported that the entire Spanish embassy staff and all consuls had gone over to the Nationalists. The honorary consul at Arequipa was "the only one remaining faithful to the Republican government."[105] Embassy staffers in Argentina resigned en masse in September 1937 when they heard that Francisco Largo Caballero had formed a new Republican cabinet that included two Communists.[106] Manuel del Moral, the Spanish minister in Colombia, resigned and departed for Switzerland to join his family, who had fled from the Terror unleashed in Madrid. He made the reason for his decision clear to the Colombian press before going:

> I am leaving before anybody receives the impression that I sympathize with the assassinations that are occurring under a government that is rapidly disintegrating, nullified by Communists, anarchists, and sindicalists. . . . The crusade begun by the Junta of National Defense at Burgos, on behalf of the independence of authentic, traditional Spain, will soon end in a great victory for civilization and for the Hispanic spirit over barbarism.[107]

He added that he had faithfully served the Azaña government even though he did not agree with its political philosophy, yet a mob in Madrid had nonetheless burned down his house. In a country such as Colombia, where public opinion initially opposed the military uprising, del Moral's defection had to be a major blow to the Republic.[108]

Uruguay suspended diplomatic relations with the Popular Front government after militiamen in Madrid murdered the Uruguayan vice-consul's three sisters in the late summer of 1936. Mexico proposed to represent the Republic's interests there in February 1937. The Uruguayan administration delayed its decision until May, when it agreed to the arrangement. By that time, though, the Spanish legation building had been stripped of its archives and other contents by the former staff, all of whom (the minister excepted) had defected to Franco. Mexico also assumed Loyalist interests in Peru where, despite a situation similar to that in Uruguay, Mexican officials managed to save the Spanish legation's archives. In April 1938 Mexico began to look after the Republic's interests in Costa Rica.[109]

Mexico tried to protect Republican interests in Germany, Italy, and Portugal, but this was virtually impossible. The best that the Mexicans could do was occasionally to help out beleaguered Spanish diplomats. Chargé F. A. de Icaza in Berlin used Mexico's diplomatic pouch to forward to their destination some secret papers left with him by Loyalist chargé José Rovira Armengol. Rovira had fled to France after being beaten and robbed of other government documents by Nazi police. De Icaza also interceded with the Germans on behalf of several pro-Republican Spaniards stranded in the Third Reich and marked for internment in a concentration camp.[110] Cosío faced an equally inhibiting situation at Lisbon. He told Foreign Relations that there were no Spanish Republican interests in Portugal to represent. Only a few resident Spaniards favored the Popular Front, he reported, and they should simply be evacuated as soon as possible. The Mexican minister did manage to help Republican Ambassador Claudio Sánchez Albornoz by giving him some expense money when the Portuguese government froze his bank account just prior to recognizing Franco. But Cosío could do little more since the authorities had him under constant surveillance. Both his driver and maid were government spies; the legation building had been burglarized, presumably by the political police; and Portuguese newspapers referred to him as a dangerous communist.[111]

When feasible, Mexican diplomats and consular officials acted as couriers for the Republicans if their own communications channels had become blocked. The Mexicans were even willing to perform tasks for their Loyalist colleagues that the Spaniards with a little effort and imagination could have easily accomplished themselves. In May 1937, for example, the Mexican consul in Chicago procured for his counterpart in that city an English translation of Cárdenas's March 29 appeal to the League of Nations to end the Civil War by aiding the Republic.[112] Mexican envoys also passed on to the Popular Front some useful information. From Luis Padilla Nervo at Montevideo came a report about five disloyal vice-consuls in Uruguay. The Spaniards still did not realize as late as the summer of 1937 that these men had defected to Franco and were engaging in pro-Nationalist activities.[113]

Republican Gratitude to Mexico

Spanish Republicans regularly demonstrated their profound gratitude to Mexico for its help during the Civil War. President Cárdenas and Mexicans generally were idolized in Loyalist zones, where Spaniards enthusiastically celebrated the virtues of their allies time after time. Not even ostracism and insult by the powerful Spanish Communist party, which took its cue from the Kremlin and turned on Mexico in mid-war over the Trotsky issue, could prevent displays of affection. To this day Cárdenas is unquestionably the foreign figure most revered by old Republicans when they remember the Civil War. Embassy First Secretary Navarro accurately described Spanish sentiments in October 1936.

> In all sectors of public opinion, in the press, at high government levels, in every phase of national life where manifestation of sentiment is possible, great thanks are clearly and sincerely expressed toward Mexico and its president. . . . The current of sympathy is unanimous, and everyone talks about Mexico. . . .[114]

Mexicans who came to Spain were effusively welcomed, lionized, even pampered by rank and file Republicans. Typical of the cordial greeting was the reception given three young Mexican volunteers headed for Barcelona in 1937. Along the way they met some Spanish soldiers who shouted *vivas* for President Cárdenas and asked them for news from Mexico. The trio then boarded a

train and their fellow passengers offered them armfuls of food when
they learned that the youths were Mexicans. "We owe you much,"
said one of the Spaniards, "it is just that you receive something
from us in return."[115] Popular wartime ballads often referred to
Mexico's pro-Republican stand. In Barcelona, Mexican consul
Alejandro Gómez Maganda heard the following verses in one of
them:

> Do not be afraid Spain
> Even though they hurl Italians against you!
> Justice is on your side
> As are all the Mexicans.[116]

Throughout the war, organizations at all levels of Loyalist
society sent greetings and messages of thanks to Mexican diplomatic personnel in Spain (for transmittal back to Mexico) and staged
formal acts of homage to their ally as lavish as conditions would
permit. Prior to breaking with the Mexicans over Trotsky's asylum,
Spanish communists joined with other Republicans in these tributes. From collectivized factories came "fraternal Communist
salutes" to the "noble Mexican people" and their government.
From its Spanish headquarters and from local committees of
International Red Aid, a Comintern-sponsored group, came statements by "antifascist comrades" lauding Mexicans for "supporting
our democratic cause and for rendering unconditional assistance to
their brother workers." Speaking for Red Aid of Spain, Estebán
Vega thanked the Mexican people for "undergoing so many
sacrifices in order to make possible our victory over fascist
aggression."[117]

In December 1936, Spanish teachers serving in the Félix Barzana
Battalion at the Madrid front passed on to the Mexican consul at
Barcelona a fraternal salute to their counterparts in Mexico. Two
months later proletarian militiamen in control of Almendricos,
Murcia, renamed one of the town's streets "México" to show their
appreciation for disinterested help rendered. During ceremonies
that marked the occasion, speakers praised Mexico's government
and its antifascist citizens. Barcelona's city council at this time
asked President Cárdenas (through the Mexican consulate and
Foreign Relations) if he would permit them to rename a city street
in his honor. Cárdenas suggested that instead the Catalans choose
some figure from Mexican history for the street name, and

prompted by Consul Romero they selected Benito Juárez.[118] At the beginning of March 1937 the municipal council of Cieza, Murcia, renamed one of its squares the Plaza de Méjico out of gratitude for Mexican aid.[119] Messages of greetings and thanks continued to pour in to the Mexican embassy at Valencia and to the consulate at Barcelona throughout 1937. Included among those who expressed such sentiments were local executive committees of the Socialist party, federations of municipal workers, labor unions, and the staff and students at a Carabinero Academy in Orihuela.[120]

The Republican government itself made many formal demonstrations of gratitude to the Mexicans. In September 1937 it sponsored an Exposition of Mexican Art in Madrid as a way of celebrating the anniversary of Mexico's independence, a gesture that pleased Mexicans in Spain and at home.[121] Two months later Republican authorities in Madrid paid homage to the Mexican Revolution during an emotional program at the Teatro Zarzuela. The event began noisily when Loyalist General José Miaja embraced Mexican Chargé Leobardo Ruiz and touched off "delirious, spontaneous enthusiasm and a long ovation . . . with repeated *vivas* for Mexico and General Cárdenas."[122] The Popular Front also created Los Amigos de México, an organization affiliated with the regime's Propaganda Department. Local chapters of the Amigos throughout Republican territory staged periodic rallies to honor Mexico as "the antifascist country *par excellence*" and offered thanks to the Mexicans (sometimes in verse) for contributing to their war effort.[123] Pro-Republican Spaniards resident in the Americas also showed their appreciation of Mexico's stand on the Civil War. Individuals and groups wrote letters of thanks to President Cárdenas and to Mexico's foreign service personnel, and they visited Mexican embassies and consulates to express personally their feelings. Spanish organizations from New York to southern Argentina sponsored many programs of homage to Mexico during the war years.[124]

After the war Cárdenas continued to receive much personal adulation from the Republicans; until his death in 1970, the former president was the object of countless tributes. Lombardo, Tejeda, and other Mexicans who played major roles in the Spanish drama were also honored and formally decorated by Republican officials exiled in Mexico. After Cárdenas, however, most Republicans reserved their warmest sentiments for Isidro Fabela and Alfonso

Reyes. Fabela had been instrumental in persuading Cárdenas to help the Republic in 1936; he had argued its case eloquently before the League of Nations; he had insisted on the evacuation of the refugees from France to Mexico in 1939; and he had adopted two Spanish orphans. Among the Republicans, therefore, the diplomat enjoyed virtually universal respect. Exiles of all factions saw him as standing above any particular political sect or creed. For many of them, he personified the humanitarianism in their mission to reform Spain. Among other official awards, Fabela received the Order of Grand Chancellor of the Spanish Republic. In 1962 a Spanish woman, Estrella Morales, wrote a poem eulogizing his role in the Civil War.[125] Republican intellectuals indicated clearly their generous feelings toward Alfonso Reyes in 1947 when, from Franquista Spain, philosopher José Ortega y Gasset attacked his former Mexican friend. Ortega's remarks appeared in a Mexico City newspaper and promptly several Republicans banded together to produce a series of articles called "The Truth about Ortega y Gasset," which they published in *El Nacional*. After defending Reyes, José Gaos went on to hang the albatross of Franquism around Ortega's neck. "Can it be," he asked rhetorically, "that Ortega shares the fury and, where this does not apply, the resentment of the Franco government? In anti-Franco Spain . . . Ortega has lost his intellectual and above all his moral authority almost completely."[126] Despite the passage of four decades since the Civil War, Spaniards in Mexico retain a strong sense of grateful loyalty to the Mexicans. In the 1970s they still demonstrate, consistently and in diverse ways, their appreciation for help rendered during the years of their tragic ordeal.

4

Mexicans in Spain and on the Home Front, 1936-39

Mexicans in Spain

Much misinformation has been published about the Mexican volunteers who went to Spain. In *Mexico and the Spanish Republicans,* Lois Smith asserted that 150 Mexicans fought in Spain, that they "formed part of the International Brigades," and that "several" of them were killed; all these statements are inaccurate. Spanish Republican politician Juan-Simeón Vidarte got closer to the truth when he wrote that approximately 300 Mexicans went to Spain, but he also incorrectly assigned them to membership in the International Brigades. He even invented a fictitious Lázaro Cárdenas Battalion allegedly composed of Mexican and other Latin American soldiers. *El Universal* made a similar error in 1938 by printing a United Press story from Barcelona that mentioned "the battalion of Mexicans" being concentrated in that city for repatriation. Actually these men were the surviving 59 out of roughly 330 Mexicans who had enlisted.[1] Far from being members of the same battalion, most of them had never even seen each other in Spain, so widely scattered were the army units to which they had been assigned. Several other Mexican volunteers escaped death but did not come home with this group. They were prisoners of war, repatriated after Franco's victory.[2] A final misconception derives from remarks by Republican Ambassador Gordón, who wrote in his memoirs that neither the Spanish embassy nor any Spanish consulates ever solicited or accepted Mexican enlistments. The embassy, however, both recruited Mexicans and paid their way to Spain. Capt. Félix Guerrero obtained leave from the Mexican army to serve with the Spaniards; he signed up at the Spanish embassy in Mexico City where he was given money to pay for his passage.[3]

Two major factors prevented the Mexican government from actively encouraging or helping combatants go to Spain: Mexico's weak international position and the unpopularity of Cárdenas's pro-Loyalist policy with so many Mexicans. The PNR gave very little financial assistance to volunteers. Usually such men were recruited by Spanish Republicans at the embassy or by the CTM, which also supplied funds to cover travel expenses. Communists who joined up had their fares paid by the Party. Some men sailed to Spain from Veracruz on the Republican freighters *Magallanes, Motomar,* and *Mar Cantábrico.* On August 21, 1937 three Mexicans and several Spaniards were on the *Motomar* when it left Veracruz loaded with arms and food for Spain. Other recruits traveled by train to New York where they boarded luxury liners bound for Europe. A few Mexicans appear to have sailed off to the Spanish war on the *Queen Mary.*[4]

At the request of Foreign Relations, Spanish Defense Minister Indalecio Prieto in August 1937 supplied a list of Mexicans known to be serving as officers in the Loyalist army. (Some others were commissioned later.) They ranged in rank from captain to colonel, and none of them had signed their contracts with the Spanish government prior to 1937.[5] In alphabetical order the eleven officers were:

Name and Rank	Contract Date (1937)	Location or Unit
Capt. Isaías Acosta	February 4	Medellín
Col. Carlos Álvarez Alegría	March 20	Ejército del Centro
Lt. Col. Rafael B. Aguilar	June 20	Ejército del Centro
Capt. Julio Cancino	June 20	46th Brigade
Capt. Félix Guerrero	February 4	Medellín

Maj. Antonio Gómez Cuellar	March 20	Ejército del Centro
Col. Juan B. Gómez Ortiz	March 20	Ejército del Sur
Maj. Ruperto García Arana	May 3	46th Brigade
Capt. Héctor Hernández	June 20	46th Brigade
Col. Santiago J. Philemore	June 20	Ejército del Centro
Lt. Col. David A. Siqueiros	March 20	Frente del Tajo

Some of these men were professional soldiers (Captain Guerrero); others were political activists with no professional training or combat experience (Siqueiros). Siqueiros, a communist, owed his largely bogus military rank to his position as a political commissar for the Republic. He bought his uniform in New York City, where he had been living and doing paintings prior to departing for Spain. It was a United States Army uniform. A picture of Siqueiros wearing this outfit in Spain can be seen in the painter's book *Me llamaban el coronelazo.*

Only about twenty percent of the Mexican volunteers survived the Spanish carnage to return to Mexico and resume their careers. Siqueiros's subsequent history is well known. Capt. Félix Guerrero had been an artillery officer in Mexico's army when the Spanish war started. He had graduated from the Colegio Militar in 1932. In January 1937 he obtained a certificate of separation from active duty to join the Loyalist army. He fought on various fronts (Estremadura, Tajo, Guadalajara, Granada), and his Spanish commanding officer praised him for heroism under fire. After the war Captain Guerrero rejoined the Mexican army, eventually rising to the rank of general.[6] Other Mexicans who fought for the Republic (and not listed by Prieto) included David Serrano, Barnabé Barrios, and men named Pujol, Gabucio, and Domenzáin. Pujol served in the Madrid Tank Corps, and Gabucio was "the greatest artilleryman during the defense of Madrid," according to Loyalist General Kleber as quoted by Siqueiros. Another Mexican volunteer, Néstor Sánchez, joined a Polish battalion in the International Brigades; he thus became one of the few Latin Americans to fight with those units rather than with the Popular Army. Mexican Communist David Serrano survived the war and became president of the PCM's political committee after returning to Mexico. Barrios was a drifter who attached himself to Siqueiros's *Taller Experimental* in New York and followed his boss to Spain. Some Mexicans remember him as a peasant type who the Spaniards called Pancho Villa. After the war Barrios got a job with Mexican Customs at the U.S. border. That he got back to Mexico at all appears to have been due to Siqueiros's influence. Barrios took his military duties lightly and would have been shot for desertion had not the painter intervened with the Popular Front authorities to save him. After being expelled from the Republican army, Barrios spent his time loafing in Valencia's bars.

The mixture of motives that drew Mexicans to Spain—ranging from ideological fervor to adventurism—is well illustrated by the Mexican pilot Luis Monter Cerrillo. He lived in Spain during the Civil War, but it is hard to say just how much fighting he did. Lt. Monter seems to have gone to Spain mainly to get away from his wife and four children, since he left them destitute and with no promise of return. He became a companion of Carlos de Negri, and together they periodically terrorized Valencia's residents. When Foreign Relations inquired about Monter on behalf of his distraught wife, Ambassador de Negri falsely reported his status as "killed in action" to prevent him from being sent back home.[7]

Republican military leaders found many of the Mexican and other Latin American volunteers especially useful as they tried to create a functional army out of an undisciplined, badly fragmented collection of political extremist groups. For this reason they assigned most Latin Americans to Popular Army units rather than to units of the International Brigades and commissioned many of them officers. One here recalls George Orwell's remark in *Homage to Catalonia* that Spaniards tended to assume that any foreigner knew more about military matters than they did. Siqueiros, who claimed to have commanded the 82nd Mixed Brigade and later the 46th Brigade, offered some insight into the situation that made Mexican soldiers so valuable to the Republic.

> Because I was a Mexican officer, I was given command of a unit composed of anarchists from the old Iron Column and the Rosal Column. . . . Other Mexican officers and myself were given command of such units . . . , because the love that the anarchists had for Mexico, in contrast to their hatred of the Soviet Union, facilitated our organizational work.[8]

Presumably Siqueiros discreetly avoided publicizing his own Stalinism while in the presence of his anti-Soviet troops—if indeed he ever actually held a command in Spain. After the Civil War Octavio Paz, who had seen Siqueiros in Spain, challenged his war stories; Mexico's famous muralist uncharacteristically let the matter drop without a reply.[9]

Probably most Mexican soldiers in Spain had been recruited by the PCM. Communist writer Miguel A. Velasco said that many PCM militants went to Spain to help the Republic in various ways, including enlistment in its armed forces, but he provided no specific numbers or names. Velasco and other sources, however, have precisely described one ill-starred group of Young Communists who sailed for Spain on the *Mar Cantábrico* in 1937. Nationalists took them prisoner and shot them after capturing the ship off Spain's coast. Executed in El Ferrol were Ricardo Solórzano and Manuel Zavala (students at the University of Guadalajara), José Carlos Gallo, and Alejandro Franco. PCM member Rosendo Gómez Lorenzo apparently recruited most of the communists who went to Spain.[10]

The youngest Mexicans to enlist were four teenage ex-cadets from Mexico's prestigious Colegio Militar. In the summer of 1937 they and five other cadets reportedly deserted from the Colegio to take ship for Spain. They had been recruited by regular army Capt. Ricardo Balderas Carrillo and several anonymous persons (from the Spanish embassy *Excelsior* charged). All were caught and returned under military arrest; authorities at the Colegio then discharged them dishonorably from the Mexican army. Capt. Balderas went to prison for his part in the affair. Five of the youths dropped their plans to fight for the Republic, but the remaining four went to Spain. Commissioned lieutenants in the Popular Army, they served in different units: Roberto Vega González (20th Corps); Roberto Mercado Tinoco (23rd Corps); José Conti Varcé (9th Corps); and Humberto Villela Vélez (unit unknown). Conti died in combat. Vega was captured by the Nationalists and remained a prisoner of war for several years after the Franquista triumph but eventually made it back to Mexico.[11] In a subsequent book about his experiences, he outlined the cadets' motivations. All of them were "morally outraged" at the prospect of a "free people" about to be subjected to "fascist tyranny." They had not expected anyone at the Colegio Militar to object to their leaving for Spain.

> All of us assumed that our action would not be seen in a bad light by the Mexican government, which itself was standing at the side of a friendly country that was fighting for the same principles that had been the cause of so much bloodshed in our Republic; especially when one could see so clearly that the Mexican government was openly and disinterestedly helping the Spanish Republic.[12]

In 1937, however, another cadet deserter told the press that their main inducements to leave had been promises of money, rank of instructor in the Popular Army, and an officer's commission in that army after the war. He said nothing about moral outrage.[13]

Mexican civilians also played an active role in the peninsula during the Spanish conflict. The most prominent noncombatants belonged to the League of Revolutionary Writers and Artists (LEAR). They specialized in propaganda assistance to the Republicans. These activities were secretly financed by the Mexican Treasury, which in 1937 subsidized LEAR's delegation to an international writers conference in Spain. (The Mexican government also paid the expenses of Cuba's largely communist delegation to this meeting.) Some LEAR notables who went to Spain were José Revueltas, Octavio Paz, Carlos Pellicer, Blanca Trejo, and Susana Gamboa. Ideological tiffs were frequent. Trejo later charged that Susana Gamboa worked as a Soviet agent under the direction of Narciso Bassols. LEAR was headed by José Mancisidor, a fat, middle-aged teacher who belonged to the PCM. His so-called sectarian servility before Russian and Spanish Communists alienated some of the organization's less doctrinaire fellow-travelers, who could not reconcile Stalinist cruelties and intrigues with their conception of Spain's battle for freedom and democracy.[14]

LEAR members during their time in Spain sponsored programs honoring the Republic and were feted in return by Spaniards, made speeches, and wrote newspaper articles. On their return they brought back to Mexico pro-Loyalist books and movies. Returning from the writers conference, LEAR delegates carried with them for showings in Mexico two copies each of the films *Madrid, sufrido y heróico, Invasión,* and *Guerra en el campo.*[15] Octavio Paz, although he is no longer a Marxist, years later emotionally recalled his trip to Republican Spain. He learned the meaning of the word *fraternity* there, he has said. While walking toward Valencia one night with two Spanish friends, Paz and his companions were caught in an air raid.

> We went through [a village] singing the *Internationale* to keep up our own courage and also to encourage the inhabitants, and then we took shelter in a vegetable garden. The peasants

came to look at us and were interested to hear that I was a Mexican. Mexico was sending help to the Republicans, and some of those peasants were anarchists. They went back to their houses in the middle of the bombardment to look for food, and brought us a little bread, a melon, cheese and wine. Eating with those peasants during a bombardment . . . that's something that I can't forget.[16]

Writer Blanca Trejo, in contrast to Paz, found her Spanish experiences mainly disillusioning because of the petty infighting of political factions that resulted in a total disregard for the principles of liberty all espoused. She traveled to Spain in the guise of a consular official assigned to Barcelona. Trejo, after observing Mancisidor and Spanish Communist leaders, developed a strong dislike for them. She complained that Mancisidor once spoke at a LEAR-sponsored Homage to Mexico in Valencia where neither the Mexican flag nor President Cárdenas's picture was displayed. Standing under the Soviet flag and Stalin's picture, Mancisidor lauded the USSR rather than Mexico, ostensibly the object of LEAR's tribute. Trejo characterized Margarita Nelkin, a Republican Cortes delegate and leading feminist, as a fraud who lived luxuriously while claiming to be a champion of Spain's hungry proletariat. Dolores Ibarruri, the famed *La Pasionaria*, behaved so doctrinairely that she refused to sign an autograph requested by Mexican women because the Communist Party line called for ostracizing the country that had given asylum to Trotsky. (Siqueiros mentions in his memoirs that at a Spanish Communist party congress he heard a speech paying tribute to countries helping the Republic, and the orator did not even mention Mexico.) Other Spanish Communist leaders, according to Trejo, made fortunes speculating on food sales "while the people slowly starved." In February 1938 the Mexican embassy sent Trejo back to Mexico as a gesture to appease the Spanish Communists. Although she wanted to stay and help the Republic, her criticisms were no longer tolerated by Mancisidor and other PCM members. They convinced the Spaniards that she was a Trotskyist who had been selling Mexican passports to alleged fascists so that they could get out of Spain.[17]

The Home Front: Conservatives Justify
Their Support of Franco

When the Spanish Civil War was in progress, Mexicans acknowledged that the conflict divided them. Even PNR zealots admitted that Cárdenas's support for the Republic enjoyed only limited approval. Alejandro Gómez Maganda, a left-wing federal deputy from Guerrero and Mexican Consul General in Barcelona during part of the war, described the "Revolution in power" as backing the Popular Front; but "traitorously" siding with Franco were many other Mexicans, among them capitalists and businessmen, "creole fascists," conservative survivors from the Porfirio Díaz era, and "workers with bourgeois ideas."[18] Gómez might have added several other obvious Franquista elements in the Mexican population: Roman Catholics and their clergy, those students opposed to what they termed the PNR's socialistic programs, many government employees, and political moderates.

Mexico's Roman Catholic hierarchy, despite sympathy for Franco's so-called religious crusade, spent little time writing or preaching about the peninsular conflict. They had serious problems of their own, including getting exiled bishops back into the country and preventing Catholics from being murdered by mobs or by the police. Their principal antagonists, moreover, remained President Cárdenas and the PNR, not communism or Spain's Popular Front. Noisy advocacy of the Nationalist cause certainly would have been counterproductive and might have been interpreted by Cárdenas as breaking the truce negotiated by ecclesiastics and the PNR in 1929. At that time the Church had pledged to shun politics in return for the right to exist. During the Civil War, Pius XI and the Vatican made far more official references to Spain than did Mexico's bishops, and that was evidently the way the pope wanted it. Less than two weeks after issuing a papal encyclical on communism in 1937, the Vatican published another one, *On the Religious Situation in Mexico*, in which the pope specifically instructed clergy and laity in Mexico to avoid any political activism that might produce renewed government persecution.[19]

Pius XI drew parallels between Mexico and Spain on several occasions during the Civil War. His most pointed remarks came in his encyclical *On Atheistic Communism* dated March 19, 1937. Inspired by what he called "a communist danger that daily grows more serious under the impulse of able agitators," the pope raised the spectre of a "conspiracy of silence" among non-Catholic newspaper owners and editors; they helped communism spread by "virtually ignoring the horrors committed in Russia, Mexico, and also in much of Spain." Rarely did these newspapers even mention "a worldwide organization so vast as Russian Communism." The sad consequences of Marxism could be seen in Russia and in Mexico, where bishops and priests had been jailed, assassinated, or exiled during a campaign to "destroy civilization and the Christian religion." Now in Spain, he argued, "the communist lash" fell furiously on the Catholic religion in an effort to eliminate it. Thousands of clergy had been killed, uncounted numbers of Catholics slaughtered "for the mere circumstance of their being good Christians." Such barbarous hatred, said the pope, should make all men tremble "for what happens in Spain today might well be repeated tomorrow in other civilized nations."[20]

The Mexican Church supported Franco, but not as aggressively as Piux XI. In 1936 the hierarchy's Executive Committee instructed bishops to tell all priests to join their parishioners in offering up "fervent and persistent prayers for the peace and true liberty of the Spanish nation, from which we have received our civilization and our faith, and which is now undergoing one of the most sorrowful crises of its history." Mexican bishops also sent to Spain's clergy a message of sympathy that made clear their desire for a Nationalist victory in 1937.[21] Beyond this modest moral and spiritual support, however, Mexico's Church chose not to go. This left the polemical burden of advocating Spain's military rebellion to individual Catholics and conservatives. Their activities showed none of the Church's calculated reserve.

Rubén Salazar Mallén, a young law professor and journalist, enthusiastically stumped for Franco and for Spanish fascism throughout the war. One of his first articles on Spain appeared at the end of July 1936 and made him a hated figure in pro-Republican circles. Salazar wrote that even if the Nationalist revolt failed it would have served as a noble protest against communism. Spain's Western culture had made the army uprising inevitable, for culture and communism were antithetical terms, the latter only thriving in the East "where men are used to slavery and patiently endure [its] slow suffocation." Spain's rebels were telling the world that their country still had a Western culture. The Civil War, in his view, did not represent a conflict between monarchism and republicanism since Franco's movement had "fascist roots" and promised to supercede those political forms. It would "synthesize" fascism and democracy to produce a "pure" political order superior to anything that had preceded it. "Spain," he concluded, "preserves its historical prestige by means of the present rebellion."[22]

Unfortunately for Salazar's immediate comfort and safety, he attended a program at the National Preparatory School on the same day that *El Universal* printed his article. The meeting, organized by the National School of Economics Alumni Society, featured Republican Ambassador Gordón as one of the speakers. When Gordón began his talk, Salazar found himself a target of abuse and threats: students in the audience, divided between pro-Loyalists and Franquistas, grew disorderly and then rioted. A newspaper reporter described the opening scene:

> Frequently there were shouts demanding that Professor Salazar Mallén, whom the shouters accused of being a fascist, and several other persons, leave the hall. They all, however, stayed in their seats, even Lic. Salazar Mallén, although his face had grown intensely pale.[23]

When Salazar started to leave the room during one of many pauses in the ambassador's speech (necessitated by fist fights and release of tear gas), "there was a moment when he seemed likely to fall victim to violent acts," but a group of conservative students came to his aid and escorted him from the building.[24] Salazar took a more reflective position on Spain late in the war, though he remained extremely partisan about communism and Popular Fronts wherever they appeared. He believed the conflict signified the end of traditional Spain. Every shot fired, whether by the rebels or by the Loyalists, represented a bullet flying at the heart of Spain itself, and out of the "spiritual ashes" of the struggle, whichever side won, a tyranny would emerge to rule over an exhausted people. Spain had the sad destiny of repeating Revolutionary Mexico's mournful experience.[25]

Catholic militant Fernando Robles interpreted the Nationalist uprising in Spain as a move toward corporatism and authentic *hispanidad* that should be imitated in Latin America. Robles still openly sympathized with Mexican Cristeros, whose cause he had championed in the 1920s. In 1937 he paid homage to the Franquistas and to the memory of Ramiro de Maeztu, a Spanish Catholic author who had long argued that corporatism and Hispanism were essential bases for Spanish and Spanish American societies. After a period of what he termed material and spiritual poverty, during which Spaniards had lost faith in themselves, forgotten their historic destiny to defend Western civilization, and embraced the false doctrine of materialism, they had rediscovered their native spiritualism. In response to the Republican attack on Christianity, Spain had become the principal battlefield between incompatible philosophies of life. As heirs to the Christian ideals of their Spanish ancestors, Latin Americans had a vital interest in the conflict.

> We are involved in that battle where our faith and our ideals are tested. The people of America, children of the hidalgos who yesterday brought them life in the vessel of Christian humanism, cannot remain indifferent to the struggle. By the will of Queen Isabella . . . we are spiritually Hispanic, and for that reason the Spanish war is our war, and Spain's destiny will be our destiny.[26]

More representative of genuine Christian humanism during the Spanish Civil War was *Ábside,* which described itself as a journal of Mexican culture and was edited by a scholarly young priest, Gabriel Méndez Plancarte. *Ábside* contained few openly political articles on Mexico or Spain and it rarely even mentioned the peninsular conflict. Yet by opposing communism and defending Catholicism the journal implicitly rejected both Revolutionary Mexico and Loyalist Spain. Right-wing *Ábside* spurned both fascism and corporatism as incompatible with a truly humanistic Catholic society. Méndez did print some pro-fascist articles and many of his regular contributors were intransigent reactionaries; but *Ábside's* general tone remained consistently antitotalitarian. It even contained commentary by such Republican sympathizers as journalist Pedro Gringoire and Enrique González Martínez, a former Mexican minister in Spain.[27]

Articles published in 1937 by Manuel de la Cueva and Carlos Gómez Lomelí typified *Ábside's* refusal to accept the totalitarian state. De la Cueva attacked communism, fascism, and corporatism in an essay advocating return to the principles of "medieval, Christian humanism" as a remedy for the modern world's social and political strife.[28] Gómez characterized as unacceptable for Catholics any type of totalitarian politics. His essay took its departure from the central thesis of Jacques Maritain's *Integral Humanism.* Gómez repeated many of the French writer's arguments. Christian principles and values constituted the best guarantees of the "personal liberty threatened by contradictions of the materialistic world." Communism and fascism were "rebellious errors" against Christian teachings and provided no answer to the modern world's perennial crisis; that answer could only come from a new Christianity based on integral humanism. Truly Christian political movements had to be concerned with "a just idea of liberty" and they had to oppose totalitarianism's "dictatorial violence of left and right." The "democratic liberal idea" had failed, for it could not overcome internal contradictions of the materialistic world, which was now "decomposing." Only a new, revolutionary Christian political party had any chance of success. Conflict between Communism and fascism made civil war inevitable, and due to prevailing hatreds this meant "a war of extermination." Upset by some Catholic approval of fascist military movements in Austria, Portugal, and above all Spain, Gómez warned the Faithful to shun such false solutions to social problems.[29]

The conservative journal *Lectura* stood much farther to the right than *Ábside.* It had a clearly pro-totalitarian bias and Spain occupied a central position in its ideological promotions. Edited by Catholic nationalist Jesús Guisa y Azevedo, *Lectura* mixed together clericalism and fascism. In addition to printing articles by Mexican rightists, it featured considerable foreign material: excerpts from the propaganda classic *Blood Drenched Altars;* translations of speeches and articles by General Franco and Portuguese dictator Antonio Oliveira Salazar; and the writings of Frenchmen associated with Action Française, a political movement with fascistic inclinations.[30] For Guisa y Azevedo, a Catholic totalitarian state that would unite the Mexican people by eliminating "democracy and class warfare" could best defend Mexico against the United States, which was trying to destroy the country's Hispano-Catholic culture as a prelude to actual takeover.[31] Such a state would also be a bulwark against communism, an infectious disease that had originated in the Soviet Union and was being spread all over the world by "the children of Israel." Revolutionary Mexico had voluntarily allowed entry to the disease for reasons that were not clear: perhaps due to a superstitious belief that this would cause it to "treat us with a certain leniency," or possibly from mere "suicidal desperation" among political leaders, or possibly from their hope that "something new and better will arise from our ruin, as is the case now in [Republican] Spain."[32]

After September 1, 1939, Mexican conservatives had an increasingly difficult public relations problem. History inexorably linked the Spanish Nationalists to totalitarian regimes in Germany and Italy that had become objects of hatred throughout the West. General Franco overtly consorted with his Civil War allies, and his authoritarian state ostentatiously displayed the heavily symbolic trappings of fascism. The situation grew darker for Mexican Franquistas in 1942: President Avila Camacho declared war upon the Axis powers. Yet pro-Franco Mexicans braved the unfavorable climate of opinion and continued to use Spain as a political issue in attacking the Revolution. Many of them were Catholic ideologues who had long since repudiated totalitarianism as contrary to Christian doctrine. Satisfied in their own minds at least that Spain remained free from fascism or Axis domination, they insisted on the indigenous, traditional character of the Nationalist movement. Franco represented Catholic hispanidad, not fascism, and hispanidad had a natural compatibility with Mexican culture. To be true to their own nature, and to defend the country patriotically against North American inroads (a greater "threat" than German foreign policy), Mexicans had to be Hispanic; and to be genuinely Hispanic, they had to be Catholic.

As it had done during the Civil War, *Ábside* provided a forum for Catholic, Hispanist justifications of Franco that sought to separate the man and his movement from fascism.[33] Conservative writer Alfonso Junco rather perfunctorily rejected totalitarianism (nonexistent in Spain he insisted) while at the same time eulogizing José Antonio Primo de Rivera. Falangism was an inspiring, "truly democratic" solution to the Hispanic world's modern crisis. Junco, an accountant originally from Monterrey, had won a prominent place among right-wing polemicists in Mexico City with his tireless pro-Catholic journalism. In 1940 Junco published *El difícil paraíso,* a series of essays on Spain that he had written the year before. Claiming that he represented "the voice of Mexico," the author lamented that the PRM remained "absurdly belligerent" toward Franco and that it had brought into the country thousands of Spanish Republicans, "refugees who arrive at Veracruz clenching their fists under the 'international' yoke of Negrín and Lombardo. . . ."[34]

Junco denied charges that Franco's government was totalitarian. The general headed a "Catholic" regime that had "instituted a bold program of social justice," had rejected "idolatry of the State," and had repudiated "those aspects of fascism and Nazism that were unacceptable." In formulating his policies, Franco had followed the Spanish hierarchy's "antifascist" leadership. (One wonders what aspects of Nazism Junco considered "acceptable" and how he missed seeing the famous photograph of Spain's bishops giving fascist salutes during the Civil War.) According to Junco under Franco Christian humanism prevailed in Spain. Spanish America had much to gain from close association with Nationalist Spain. Spanish tutelage could help in "exaltation of the values of our truest essence," which Hispanic Americans could use profitably in opposing "a fraudulent and incoherent Pan-Americanism that is nothing more than the sarcastic brotherhood of sheep with the wolf!" With its war over, "resurgent Spain" experienced the "difficult paradise" that José Antonio Primo de Rivera and the Falange had desired.[35]

Actions and Opinions in the Spanish Colony

Mexico's Spanish colony remained as divided over the Civil War as it had been split by the major issues troubling the Republic. Due to these bitter antagonisms, all of Mexico City's Spanish clubs agreed in August 1936 to suspend their customary festive events until the conflict had ended. Openly pro-Franco Spaniards clearly outnumbered supporters of the Popular Front. Even Ambassador Gordón admitted that within the colony only workers and "a select intellectual and bourgeois minority" had Loyalist sympathies. Mexican writer Blanca Trejo unhappily observed that "almost all the resident Spaniards" in Mexico City got drunk celebrating Málaga's fall to the Nationalists in 1937. From Puebla, the newspaper *La Opinión* reported that most Spaniards there threw parties upon hearing of Franquista victories and that only ten of the city's 3,000 Spaniards attended a pro-Republican rally in late

1936.[36] The many resident Spaniards who showed little interest in the Civil War were probably for the insurgents; Mexicans certainly regarded them as such. Former ambassador de Negri complained in 1937 about "the passivity and apathy of almost all the Spaniards in Mexico" concerning the Republic's plight.[37] Journalist Salvador Novo drew the same picture of indifference:

> The most dedicated Republicans here without doubt are Mexicans, and while our Colonel Siqueiros fights in the *madre patria*, throughout Mexico [the Spaniards] . . . calmly listen to the latest news on their radios, imperturbably go on managing their clothing shops, grocery stores, and bakeries, attend the soccer matches on Sundays, and even have the extravagance to fill up the bullfight ring on the day of the Covadonga bullfights.[38]

Franquista Spaniards who wanted to be heard had no trouble publicizing their views. Newspapers and magazines were open to them, and they made full use of their opportunities. When the Cárdenas regime prohibited the showing of pro-Nationalist films, Spanish theater owners boldly hired orators to make political speeches to crowds of Mexican movie-goers. Some Spaniards even wrote to the president to reproach him for aiding the Republic and to urge him to recognize the military government at Burgos without delay. One of these writers reminded Cárdenas that his speeches addressed to the Mexican army usually emphasized the soldier's duty to defend his nation's institutions and that this was exactly what the Spanish soldiers following Franco had undertaken to do.[39] Although Cárdenas deported those Spaniards caught raising money for the rebels, or in suspicious contact with them, or engaged in espionage, he made no move to suppress less threatening types of political action. Even known Falangists operated under few restraints until after the war. Thus in August 1936 a group of pro-Franco Spaniards publically petitioned both the French government and the French legation in Mexico City to give no aid to the Popular Front. Falangist agent Augusto Ibáñez Serrano worked overtly among his compatriots and had an office at the Portuguese legation. On one occasion several Falangists wore their uniforms to a religious ceremony honoring Nationalist soldiers killed in battle.[40]

Such things infuriated Mexican leftists and Ambassador Gordón.

From the embassy and from the Chamber of Deputies emerged long lists of names: Spaniards to be deported immediately for engaging in Franquista activity. (Mexican bureaucrats filed the lists.) To make their case stronger, Gordón and his allies from the CTM and the Revolutionary Bloc of deputies tried to link the Spaniards with what they termed fascist plots to overthrow the government. To save himself and the Revolution, Cárdenas should expel from the country those pro-Franco Spaniards guilty of "fascist crimes." Among these alleged offenses were: manipulations designed to cause Mexico's economy to collapse; propaganda intended to divide people ideologically; suggestions to Franco that he use German and Italian help in a reconquest of the Americas for Spain; and plans to "poison" the Mexican populace by adulterating milk and fine wines. Columnist Salvador Novo had a good laugh at the notion that the majority of his countrymen regularly drank "fine wines."[41]

Republicans in the Spanish colony worked hard for their cause, but at times the same ideological discord that divided peninsular leftists reduced the effectiveness of their efforts. A Mexican branch of Spain's Popular Front became active as soon as the Civil War started. Its members organized special demonstrations of support for the Loyalist regime and took part in the many pro-Republican rallies sponsored by the PNR, CTM, and PCM.[42] Within the colony, Catalans were especially prominent propagandists and fund-raisers for the war effort and for humanitarian projects intended to relieve the suffering of Republican civilians and refugees. When the Orfeó Catalá openly lent itself to a wide variety of political actions, many Catalan businessmen and professionals contributed their energy, money, and prestige to these endeavors. Catalans, however, tended to be preoccupied with the grievances of their separatist province, and much of what they said and wrote about the Civil War must have bewildered the Mexicans, most of whom regarded political regionalism as an evil that had caused much of their own nation's historic unrest.[43]

Serious public relations problems developed for Spanish Republicans in Mexico when some of them aired publicly their partisan resentments and bitterly blamed certain groups for the Popular Front's failure in 1936. R. García Treviño, a radical writing in the magazine *Rumbo* in September of that year, attributed the disaster to the Republic's "petty-bourgeois, democratic reformists." Had it not been for the bungling of these Republican politicians, the Civil War could have been avoided. They had paved the way for fascism by preventing the workers from seizing dictatorial power. Ambassador Gordón had said proudly in July 1936 that the socialists had been successful in "attracting the working masses to the legal struggle." Unfortunately, García noted with sarcasm, "the fruits of this success are the thousands of corpses of revolutionaries that now lie rotting in the fields of Spain."[44]

Spaniards sent over from the peninsula supplemented the activities of Loyalists in the Spanish colony. Militiamen toured the country, usually under the auspices of the CTM, and told rallies of Mexican workers that the Spanish proletariat was fighting for its very existence and desperately needed their contributions of money. Energetic Marcelino Domingo, a socialist deputy known and liked by the Mexicans, spent most of the war in Mexico City. He seemed to turn up at every pro-Republic function, ready with a fiery if not especially accurate speech. Once he charged that Spain's armed conflict had been started by Spanish newspapers, right-wingers who had infiltrated the trade unions and caused a series of strikes, and a large number of German nationals who had been secretly operating in every part of the country. At the Chamber of Deputies, Domingo drew cheers and evoked from the galleries shouts of "Arms for Spain!" in a demonstration that may not have been totally spontaneous. Some of the visiting Spaniards found it necessary to downplay combative rhetoric and issue quiet, reassuring disclaimers about the radicalism of the Popular Front. During a short stay in Mexico City in early 1938, Republican emissary Juan-Simeón Vidarte told a group of sympathetic but worried fellow Masons that Loyalist Spain was not as antibourgeois as they had heard.[45]

The Home Front: Support for the Republic

Much of Mexico's assistance to Loyalist Spain was humanitarian rather than political; yet such activity often lent itself to political exploitation. During the spring of 1937 some Mexican women who had formed a Committee to Aid the Children of the Spanish People, joined by Ambassador Gordón, pressured President Cárdenas to accept into Mexico several hundred war orphans. Cárdenas agreed to do this in hopes of "setting a humanitarian precedent," but he and the PNR also saw prospects for some good publicity in the project. Ambassador de Negri and Republican representatives fixed terms and conditions in Valencia. Most of the 464 orphans came from that city. De Negri astounded Foreign Relations and Cárdenas by not even consulting them before agreeing to Spanish proposals. The Mexican government thus found itself obligated to provide for transportation of an unknown number of children to Mexico, to support these youngsters indefinitely, and to provide for their education. De Negri's action ultimately resulted in creation of the Spain-Mexico School at Morelia, a government institution that was intended to provide a left-wing environment in which the proletarian orphans could grow up. Mexican conservatives immediately attacked the school as an abomination (contributing to the communist delinquency of minors), and in subsequent months strife among the factionalized Spaniards on the faculty created a scandal that critics of the PNR quickly exploited. When these attacks appeared elsewhere in Latin America in newspaper reprints, Mexico obviously lost some of the public relations ground that it had initially gained by "providing a home for war orphans."[46]

The Cárdenas administration gave the children a big welcome when they arrived at Veracruz in June 1937. Ernesto Hidalgo, Chief Clerk at Foreign Relations, made the main speech. In addition to reassuring the young people about their future in Mexico, he reaffirmed Mexican solidarity with Republican Spain. The youngsters would find themselves growing up in a political democracy characterized by "a revolutionary conscience and a firm social orientation." A simple, honest man who sought social justice through economic reforms headed the government. No Mexican faced persecution for political reasons; all people expressed their opinions freely. Spanish events had "touched Mexican hearts" because they reminded Mexicans of their own Revolution's early years: both Madero in 1913 and Alcalá-Zamora in 1936 had been so "beatifically naive" in their republicanism that they had failed to see enemy plots against them. Mexican assistance to the Republic was only natural: "Victim of identical treasons, torn apart by the same base appetites . . . [Mexico] offers to Spain the fruit of its experience, as logically all other democratic countries should also provide help."[47]

Dissemination of such pro-Loyalist publicity had become a PNR concern in all parts of the country at the start of the civil war.

Various government agencies regularly promoted and financed ideological programs about Spain. In September 1937, for example, Ambassador Gordón gave several speeches in Morelia under the auspices of Michoacán's state government and state university. Two months later he appeared at a Mexico City rally sponsored by the Public Education Secretariat where he and a series of left-wing speakers paid tribute to the Spanish American volunteers killed in Spain. The Mexican government's Official Propaganda Department broadcast this address to the nation.[48] Cárdenas also did what he could to offset private communications media bias in favor of Franco. Programs on the government's *Radio Nacional* featured pro-Republican commentary by Mexicans and speeches by Ambassador Gordón. Communications Secretary Francisco J. Múgica prohibited privately owned networks and radio stations from broadcasting Franquista propaganda or even news of Nationalist victories. *El Nacional* printed much material favorable to the Republic and during the last half of 1936 alone it ran eight articles on the Civil War by Gordón. Other PNR publications made contributions, too. *Revolución,* a monthly journal put out by leftists in the Chamber of Deputies, contained articles written by peninsular Loyalists praising Spanish workers and the masses for their "resistance to fascism."[49]

Supplementing Secretary Múgica's ban on pro-Franco radio broadcasts, the PNR prohibited movie theaters or private organizations from showing films that backed the Nationalists. Cárdenas even bowed to demands by Ambassador Gordón and personally ordered destroyed the two Mexican copies of Paramount Pictures 1935 film *The Devil is a Woman* on grounds that it "insulted Spain." Anyone who has seen this nonpolitical picture, which depicts "a courtesan making a fool of a pompous old Spanish general," will immediately be struck by the nonsensicality of Gordón's charge. Yet the Republican ambassador refers to this incident in his memoirs as if it were one of his major diplomatic triumphs in Mexico, a circumstance that casts some doubt on his professional if not mental competence. Cárdenas's censorship of movies and radio programs, when he made no similar moves against the pro-Franco press, suggests that unfriendly newspaper comment in predominantly illiterate Mexico did not overly worry him.[50]

Whether out of genuine conviction, political ambition, or simple prudence, most Mexican army officers gave Cárdenas their cooperation in regard to his Spanish policy. Indeed, some of the Republic's most enthusiastic and helpful adherents came from the military. Many of these officers had risen to prominence by commanding troops in the Revolution; some had been famous radicals in earlier decades. Among those providing especially valuable assistance to the Republic were generals Manuel Avila Camacho (secretary of National Defense); Francisco J. Múgica (successively secretary of National Economy and secretary of Communications); Leobardo Ruiz (chargé d'affaires and consul in Spain); and Col. Adalberto Tejeda (diplomat in France and later in Republican Spain).

Despite their friendship toward the Republic, however, Mexican professional soliders tended to be disturbed by its internal politics. Col. Reynaldo A. Híjar, military attaché at the embassy in Barcelona in 1938, recorded his criticisms in a report sent to the Foreign Relations and National Defense secretariats. He complained that "establishing control of the armed forces has been extremely difficult for the authorities" and that even after a "titanic struggle" there still remained excessive political meddling with the Popular Army by left-wing parties and labor groups. "The military authorities are gradually trying to free the army from partisan influence so that it will become truly the army of the people," he noted. Late in 1938 the Republican army "was not exactly a marvel," but it had the advantage of fighting for a just cause.[51]

For many officers the Spanish conflict provided a clear lesson for Mexico: organized labor must never become a rival armed force, nor should its political influence be permitted to grow too strong. Broad military support for Cárdenas's Spanish policy thus coincided with deep foreboding in the minds of many officers about leftist influences on Cárdenas. They worried about the potential for "another Spain" erupting in Mexico. They voiced their fears publicly, and they made concerted efforts to forestall any such development. On various domestic issues, then, Cárdenas faced significant opposition within the army.[57] In June 1938 a group of officers aggressively denounced Lombardo, but their statement contained a message for Cárdenas, too.

> Lombardo Toledano cannot hide now that he seeks the
> dissolution of the revolutionary army, and one proof of this is

the formation of the so-called workers militia in order to install a proletarian dictatorship in Mexico. The army is tired of the anti-army calumny by labor leaders like Lombardo who are seeking to fool the workers into starting a fight like that in Spain.[53]

They promised that in due time military men would deal with Mexico's "perverse" labor leaders, who only "exploited" the working class.

A few generals broke with Cárdenas, left the army, and launched right-wing political movements or parties of their own. Of these defectors the most prominent were Saturnino Cedillo, a regional boss of San Luis Potosí state and sometime secretary of Agriculture in the Cárdenas cabinet; Manuel Pérez Treviño, the harassed ambassador to Spain in 1935–36; and Juan Andreu Almazán, a cabinet member in the early 1930s and the major opposition candidate in the 1940 presidential election. All three men made much of Cárdenas's allegedly communistic regime.[54] Cárdenas offset this conservatism, evident among many general officers from the outset of his presidency, by courting majors and captains, and by attempting to provide a progressive political orientation for all members of the military. Assisted by Defense Secretary Avila Camacho, he enjoyed a measure of success in this endeavor. Many junior officers contributed articles to the *Revista del Ejército (Army Journal)* applauding the administration's social and economic reforms, taking anticapitalist positions, and lavishly proclaiming their solidarity with workers and peasants. Several of them wrote pro-Loyalist articles, but the *Revista* made few references to Spain's Civil War.[55]

The Mexican congress reflected presidential patronage within the PNR rather than popular will; consequently it gave Cárdenas no trouble in regard to Spain. Such foreign policy moves as the arms sale received rubber-stamp approval, and the most active congressional group, the left-wing Revolutionary Bloc, periodically staged emotional tributes to Republican Spain in the Chamber of Deputies. The congress also sent messages to United States lawmakers, urging them to rescind their embargo on arms to Spain. Such differences over Spanish policy as existed between the president and PNR legislators generally involved congressional appeals for more extreme measures by Cárdenas to aid the Spaniards. CTM leader Lombardo had friends in the national legislature, and they frequently helped along his demagogic schemes by demanding repressive action against pro-Franco resident Spaniards and Mexican conservatives, invariably depicted as "fascist conspirators against the Revolution." The president refused to be intimidated by these maneuvers, so Mexican rightists remained free to support the Nationalists in most ways. Any fund-raising activities on behalf of Franco that came to light, however, were suppressed.[56]

Ambassador Gordón once described Mexico's pro-Republic activists as being made up of "workers and peasants, intellectuals of the left, members of the PNR . . . Masons, the Veterans of the Revolution organization, public functionaries supporting President Cárdenas's policies, and . . . teachers."[57] Communists, some secondary school and university students, and various women's organizations also worked for the Republic. Pro-Loyalist students usually belonged to socialist youth groups, but some of them simply identified with the PNR and had no Marxist commitments.

A representative campus event took place in May 1937 at the State Institute of Sciences in Durango. Lawyer Miguel Mendoza Schwerdtfeger spoke by invitation to an assembly of students, the faculty, and rector about Spain. Mendoza told his audience that the Republic and its revolution "arose from the long and patient preparatory labor . . . of venerable university professors and enthusiastic young students. . . ." They had persuaded the Spanish people to liberate themselves from their "traditions and worn-out institutions." Heroic Republicans now fought to establish a "more just social state" in which thought would no longer be shackled by the prejudices of the past and in which "the magnates" would no longer dominate labor. Mendoza went on to warn that Mexico would soon have to imitate the Spanish Loyalists by demanding that technological advances be matched by corresponding progress in social justice. Only through such courageous action could they confound those who, like the Nationalists in Spain, sought to "destroy their country."[58]

The lawyer's thesis, however, would not have convinced most Mexican college students, for they stood well to the right of socialism and the PNR. As previously noted, the socialist education issue had produced massive alienation at all school levels, and the university population remained an elite minority drawn principally from upper and middle social strata. Neither they nor their parents had much interest in proletarian causes in Spain or in Mexico, and they certainly had a more accurate perception of what was at stake in the peninsula than did Mr. Mendoza. Fear of the proletariat, in fact, gave them a good reason for disliking the Cárdenas regime, which despite much ambiguity seemed to endorse collectivism.

Organized peasants and rural laborers under PNR or leftist control did indeed, as Gordón claimed, show sympathy for the Republic. Some of them marched in pro-Loyalist rallies, others gave money to be sent to Spanish militiamen. In the fall of 1937 villagers from Ytztacapa and Tetlapa, Hidalgo, collected a modest sum that they sent to Spain through the Regional Confederation of Workers and Peasants (FROC). Accompanying the money was a letter offering a "fraternal salute" to the Republic's "noble combatants."[59] For Porfirio del Castillo (also from Hidalgo) this action by the villagers demonstrated the natural affinity between Mexicans and the type of Spaniard who battled Franco. Hidalgo's simple peasants, he said

> . . . truly represent the Mexican people who [like the Spanish Republicans] deeply love their liberties and know how to defend them courageously. . . . Our rural folk and the masses generally only know the Spaniards from superficial contact and through commercial transactions with Spanish businessmen resident here, most of whom continue to be filled with prejudices and to treat Indians disdainfully. Our masses, however, possess a wonderful institution . . . [and] know how to distinguish . . . between those archaic Spaniards who still live in the past from the Spanish Republicans who are fighting for their integrity and autonomy as a sovereign state. Thus, across space and through time, in a supreme communion of ideals, Mexico and Spain identify with each other, and the two peoples draw together as brothers. Tyrants can neither force them from the course on which they have mutually embarked nor prevent them from justly realizing their common destinies.[60]

Del Castillo was here voicing an oft-repeated theme in propaganda on behalf of the Republic: however poor and uneducated, Mexicans perceived that they shared the same ideals and destiny as progressive Spaniards, whom they distinguished from traditional gachupines. Yet few Mexican peasants in the 1930s could have had anything beyond a dim conception of Spain, and most of them had probably never even heard of the Spanish Republic. The rural majority lacked PNR or leftist direction and had been largely bypassed by agrarian reforms. Not surprisingly these people remained susceptible to traditionalist appeals from the clergy or Catholic laymen, and the number of them that ever felt any solidarity with their Spanish brothers had to be relatively small.

Lombardo's CTM proved to be without question Mexico's most effective pro-Loyalist pressure group and source of funds. Its activities in this regard enjoyed Cárdenas's full approval and cooperation, although at times Lombardo's irresponsibility and pro-Soviet stance exasperated the president. On these occasions he either ignored Lombardo or stopped him from whatever he was doing or saying. During the first week of the Spanish conflict, Mexico City and other urban centers were paralyzed by a nationwide strike of electrical workers. Once that had been settled the CTM began its assistance to the Republic. Gigantic labor rallies took place all over the country to publicize the Loyalist cause; money began to be raised for transmittal to Spain; workers in the armaments industry volunteered free labor so that weapons and munitions could be sent to the Republicans as cheaply and as rapidly as possible; and a large volume of propaganda started circulating through the labor press, books and pamphlets, radio programs, films and special benefit programs.

CTM rallies usually drew large, enthusiastic crowds of workers and left-wing militants wherever in Mexico they took place. The events tended to be colorful, noisy, and full of emotion. An excursion to Guadalajara in March 1937, sponsored by CTM members of Mexico City's graphic arts and commercial engravers union, and featuring Ambassador Gordón and Marcelino Domingo, received a big welcome at the railroad station. On hand were workers, students from Industrial School Number 4, a Red Cross youth brigade, and Jalisco's state band, which played the *Internationale*. Red flags abounded at the Teatro Degollado as assembled workers raised clenched fists and again sang the socialist anthem. Francisco Rodríguez Gómez of the PNR addressed the rally as did the two visiting Spaniards.[61] A CTM program at the Teatro Hidalgo in Mexico City several months later left a lasting impression on youthful Roberto Vega González, on his way to Spain (with CTM money) to fight for the Republic. Present in the theater were

. . . an enormous multitude of workers from all branches of industry. Posters, flags, and signs bearing the names of unions could be seen everywhere. . . . The first speaker . . . talked about the Spanish war and asked the congregated workers to show their solidarity by contributing money to sustain the struggle of their class brothers. . . . Applause and shouts of "Viva España republicana" followed the speech.[62]

CTM appeals to its affiliated unions for assistance to the Republic usually evoked generous responses. Beginning in the summer of 1936, union members periodically contributed one day's pay to be sent to Spain by the Republican embassy in Mexico City. In August and September of 1936, electrical and streetcar workers in the capital began their donations as did schoolteachers throughout the country.[63] Money, food, clothing, and other supplies continued to be collected for the Republic by CTM unions until the war ended. A letter sent to Ambassador Gordón in January 1937 by two officers of a small union in Monterrey illustrates rank and file cooperation. In compliance with a CTM request, each worker had given a day's wages to help finance the Republic's war effort. The letter informed Gordón that a check for 309.47 pesos had been sent to him through the Banco de México. Poorly typed and marked by unconventional syntax and spelling, the letter indicated that the money was for

. . . the comrade worker militiamen of Spain. . . . who are sacrificing so heroically their lives in defense of the liberty and sovereignty of their country and for the government over which Don Manuel Azaña so honorably presides, under attack by the hordes of Hitler and Mussolini who wish to muzzle the liberties of the proletariat, drowning them in blood, but they will not accomplish this, those Dictators.[64]

CTM assistance to the Loyalists was not limited to periodic rallies and fund-raising drives. Mexican workers engaged in diverse activities to show their solidarity with the Republic and to publicize its cause. The Workers Federation of Jalisco in August 1937 staged an eight-hour general strike in Guadalajara, which included turning off all electricity, to remind residents of Mexico's second largest city about Spain. At the end of January 1938 the electricians union in Mexico City sent written protests to the

German and Italian legations condemning air raids against Barcelona. A month later CTM members joined militants from the Unified Socialist Youth of Mexico to picket businesses in the capital owned by Spaniards, Germans, Italians, and Japanese. They told prospective customers not to buy at the stores because any money they spent would be used to wage war against the people of Spain, China, and Ethiopia. The labor organization also sent pro-Loyalist materials to the United States. In January 1938 CTM money enabled the Spanish Republican exhibit "Fourteen Months of War" to be taken to Los Angeles.

Solidarity with the Republic through cultural events was a prominent part of the support rallied for the Loyalists. Universidad Obrera (Workers University) naturally became a forum for supporters of the Popular Front and a major disseminator of publicity about the war. Guest lecturers from such organizations as the Confederation of Miners Unions of Asturias spoke there on "The Real Significance of the Spanish Revolt"; and pro-Republican films sponsored by the school were shown continuously from 4 to 11 P.M. at the Hidalgo Theater during the first fifteen days of each month. In December 1937 the CTM campaigned to provide Christmas gifts for the hundreds of Loyalist orphans living at Morelia. The campaign closed with a program at the Bellas Artes Theater in Mexico City on December 19. In addition to speeches by Ambassador Gordón, several well-known leftists, and Francisco Macías of the film workers union, the CTM event featured an appearance by three pro-Republic activists from Hollywood: actresses Gale Sondergaard and Josephine Bright and director Herbert Biberman. Despite this added touch of glamour, most of those attending came from unions or left-wing political organizations.[65]

The CTM took two actions relative to Spain late in 1938 that indicated just how desperate the Republic's situation had become. The CTM National Committee decided to have the recently founded Latin American Workers Confederation (CTAL), which Lombardo dominated, ask all Latin American governments to restrict trade with fascist countries. The object was to hinder aggression against such democratic countries as Spain by withholding materials needed to wage war. To help the Spanish Republic further, the CTM and CTAL would request a Latin American boycott of all goods and products emanating from Nationalist territory. The Committee also desginated December 20 as Spanish

Republic Day. All CTM affiliates would sponsor meetings to call attention to Spain and to counter the propaganda of those they regarded as local fascists. During December, moreover, union members would be asked again to make donations for Spain: tobacco, food, condensed milk, and clothing. Although most of these things were to be obtained through unpaid labor, the Committee urged CTM families to give some of their own clothing as well, especially coats and sweaters.[66]

CTM publications such as *El Popular* and the journal *Futuro* provided a steady flow of Marxist interpretations of Spain's Civil War and its relevance to Mexico. In 1937 Narciso Bassols wrote two articles for *Futuro* explaining why Mexicans had an obligation to help defend the Republic. The peninsular conflict was "a modern struggle of workers against their natural enemies." He went on to argue that Spanish capitalists, aided by numerous foreign fascists—Hitler, Mussolini, Pope Pius XI, Roosevelt, Eden, and Blum—sought to destroy the Popular Front government. Yet even if this happened, the Spanish working class would emerge from the war much strengthened; no longer were workers weakened by nineteenth-century confusions and contradictions, which hitherto were powerful forces in the country's life. Since fascism directly menaced Latin America, Mexicans who aided the Spanish people also defended their own interests. Given Mexico's precarious position in the hemisphere, where "fascism had already won many victories," and with its progressive government under attack "by groups linked to international fascism," the country had to maintain solidarity with the Republicans. Bassols urged Mexican workers not to forget that a Popular Front victory would mean conquest of political power by Spain's proletariat: "The significance of the Spanish conflict, that which gives it worldwide importance, is precisely this. . . . conquest of power for the Spanish workers. Anything less than this objective would not be worth the effort."[67]

An *El Popular* editorial in July 1938 restated the idea that the Spanish war had direct relevance for the fate and future of Mexican workers and the democracy that worker rule represented.

> In the Spanish latifundium, in the clergy, in [foreign] capitalism, in the traitorous military rabble, Mexican workers are seeing a repetition of the Mexican Revolution's experience.

> . . . The Mexican people are witnessing in the Spanish war
> their civil war of 1910–1917. Fortunately, during our Revolu-
> tion, foreign intervention was minimal. . . . Mexican workers
> are deeply concerned about the fate of the Spanish workers.
> . . . Triumph of the Spanish Revolution will signify a new
> manner of struggle and progress for the Ibero-American
> nations; a step closer for all toward realization of a better
> society. Its defeat, however, will be our defeat, through a
> strengthening of fascism and its threat to the democratic
> countries.[68]

Despite this ongoing propaganda effort, and unfailing rank and
file CTM enthusiasm for the Republicans, Lombardo's personal
sincerity on the matter remains highly suspect. Ambassador Gordón
learned that Lombardo had given up on Spain as a lost cause as
early as 1937. He reportedly had begun to urge Cárdenas and other
PNR leaders to shift Mexico's support from the Spanish Republic to
China in the "worldwide proletarian struggle against fascism."[69]

Like the CTM, Mexico's Communist party became a persistent
advocate of the Loyalists and raised money for shipments of food,
clothing, and medicine to Spain. From its ranks, moreover, came
many of the Mexican volunteers who fought for the Republic.
Communists operated through the party itself and less openly
through front organizations that they created. PCM members were
especially active in Spain where the Popular Front government
gave them more political latitude than they enjoyed at home. In
Mexico, as in Spain, much party activity was channeled through
the League of Revolutionary Writers and Artists. A LEAR educational program at Bellas Artes Theater in February 1938 consisted
of lectures by individuals recently returned from Spain. All of the
principal speakers had Marxist backgrounds or PCM affiliation.
LEAR's José Mancisidor also helped run the Friends of Spain
Society, a source of pro-Loyalist publicity that closely followed the
communist line on the Civil War. Communists also controlled the
Spain-related projects of the Mexican Popular Front, a coalition of
labor groups and political parties. In addition to having one official
representative on the organization's governing board, the PCM
could count on the CTM's vote as well: party member Miguel A.
Velasco served on behalf of the labor confederation. Mexican Communists even got a measure of control over the Republican children

at Morelia. Party member Roberto Reyes Pérez directed their school.[70]

Events in Puebla in November 1936 indicate how communist and fellow-traveling organizations thoroughly dominated pro-Loyalist campaigns in that state. Since the late nineteenth century, economic conditions in this region had been especially conducive to labor activism and radical politics. Puebla's branch of the PCM co-sponsored a program on November 8 that commemorated the nineteenth anniversary of the Russian Revolution and paid tribute to the Spanish Republicans, then engaged in the dramatic defense of Madrid. Other sponsors included the Regional Federation of Workers and Peasants, local railroad workers, socialist students from the state Colegio, Revolutionary Youth of the State of Puebla, and United Front for Women's Rights. During the emotional rally, orators exhorted those present to send money to the Spanish workers who were "fighting for labor's cause." PCM and LEAR member María Luisa Vera read her poem "España Roja" (Red Spain) and reportedly was applauded deliriously. Among numerous PCM members and other leftists who spoke was the communist Gonzalo Beltrán, representing the Union of Editors and Employees of the Press of Puebla. Some of the socialist students analyzed revolutionary movements in recent world history and ranked "the late revolution of Asturias and the present Spanish conflict" alongside the great Russian and Mexican upheavals. Left-wing Spaniards and CTM officials addressed the crowd. According to a local paper sympathetic to the rally, children dressed as "red militiamen" and numerous radical posters "gave to the scene a decidedly Communist appearance."[71]

Two weeks later many of the same people and organizations joined with PNR officials and supporters in the state to celebrate the twenty-sixth anniversary of the Mexican Revolution. During a big parade many of the marchers raised clenched fists and sang the *Internationale*. Some Spanish militiamen from Aragón who were touring Mexico to raise funds for the war effort joined the festivities as guests of honor. Rafael Orea, Secretary General of the Regional Federation of Workers and Peasants, spoke at Puebla's city hall after the parade. He told his audience that in addition to glorifying their own Revolution they had come together that day "to sympathize publicly with the Spanish workers, who are fighting against the imposition of fascism in Spain by the hosts of Franco."

He also warned that "Mexican fascists are preparing a movement designed to deprive the proletariat of the few victories that it has won here." The Spanish Popular Front of Mexico organized the last pro-Republican rally of the month on November 28, 1936. It featured speeches by the visiting Aragonese militiamen. Left-wing journalist Moisés Mendoza and Communist Gonzalo Beltrán also addressed the assembled workers. [72]

Despite the scope of its actions relevant to Spain's Civil War, PCM commitment to the Republican cause seems open to doubt. One wonders how much interest the Party would have taken in the plight of Spanish Loyalists had not the Soviet Union decided to support them. There can be no question about the PCM line coinciding exactly with that of the Russians on major international issues or about the Party's complete subservience to Soviet dictates on even internal Mexican matters. As has been noted, it was only on direct orders from the USSR that the PCM grudgingly agreed to support President Cárdenas. In 1939, after almost three years of protesting "foreign aggression against the Spanish people," the PCM called the Finns "instruments of imperialism" and lauded the Soviet invasion of their country. Following the Spanish Republican defeat, moreover, José Mancisidor cheerfully made himself president of the newly created Friends of the USSR Society. [73] Mancisidor and the Communists did work hard on behalf of the Loyalists who fled to France after the Franquista victory; but many of these refugees, of course, were also Communists.

Whether or not they belonged to LEAR, Mexican writers and artists contributed in many ways to the wartime propaganda effort. A number of them attended the International Writers Conference for the Defense of Culture in Valencia in 1937. [74] None of the writers, however, produced a major work of art with Spain as its theme. Celebrated literary figures who wrote pro-Republican material or lent their names to the cause included poets Octavio Paz and Carlos Pellicer and essayist Andrés Iduarte. Writers Alfonso Reyes and José Rubén Romero actually implemented Cárdenas's Spanish policy from their diplomatic posts in Buenos Aires and Barcelona respectively. Fainter literary lights on the Loyalist side were Blanca L. Trejo, a prize-winning author of children's stories who briefly did public relations work for the Popular Front in Spain prior to running afoul of Mexican Communists in the peninsula, and dramatist Eutiquio Aragonés whose three-act tragedy about the Civil War opened in Mexico City in October 1936. In 1938 the Popular Graphics Workshop in Mexico City published *La España de Franco,* a collection of fifteen pro-Republican lithographs by Raúl Angiano, Luis Arenal, Xavier Guerrero, and Leopoldo Méndez. The book's prologue characterized the four artists as "workers in the plastic arts" whose democratic and revolutionary sentiments had led them to show their support for the "heroic Spanish people" and to express their determination to help defeat the "fascist assassins of popular liberties." Muralist David A. Siqueiros returned from Spain to paint "Portrait of the Bourgeoisie," a work that students of his art regard as originating in his Civil War experience.[75]

Some of the Spanish Republic's support in Mexico came from obscure, provincial activists who joined together in tiny left-wing clubs with grandiose names. In November 1936, the Unión Hispano-Americano-Oceánica of Santiago Tuxtla, Veracruz, sent a letter to the Buenos Aires Peace Conference. Typed on an obviously worn-out machine, the letter urged Conference delegates to help the Spanish Republic. In other communications this group referred to the Civil War as the "defense of our Mother Spain by rationalist, leftist Republicans against traitors" and emphasized that "the struggle of Spanish loyalists is the same struggle as that of Mexican loyalists." Provincial Mexicans also got involved in a week of homage to Loyalist Spain in August 1937. There were workers rallies in Jalisco state and the Federation of Veterans of the Revolution put on a program at the Teatro Degollado in Guadalajara. Teachers unions in Oaxaca organized various pro-Republican activities in the state's public schools. Similar events took place throughout the country, attracted thousands of participants, and generally were managed by either the PNR, the CTM, or the Mexican Communist party.[76] All these expressions of support, however small the gathering or quixotic the plea, are an indication of the emotional involvement of Mexican leftists with the Republic's plight.

Mexico's Press Reports and Evaluates the Spanish Conflict

Mexican supporters of the Republic have always claimed that the nation's press not only favored Franco, but that it also showed clear sympathy for fascism. This version of Civil War press coverage alleges that Mexican newspaper owners and editors, in collusion with fascist agents, conspired to keep people so badly informed about Spain that public opinion never had a chance to be shaped on the basis of reason and truth. These charges are made against both the Mexico City and the provincial press.[77] Complaints made in November 1936 by Puebla's pro-Cárdenas paper *La Opinión* are typical.

> Using the Spanish conflict as an excuse, the country's press, with few exceptions, has become a tenacious and terrible propagandist for Fascism; it shamelessly applauds Franco's rising in virtually the same manner that it welcomed the crimes of Victoriano Huerta; Madero was a lunatic whose ideas were ruining the country; Azaña is another crazy man whose rule has brought disaster to the glorious fatherland of Cabanellas and Mola. To the Mexican press, the wrecking of Toledo's Alcázar constituted a crime against humanity, but the destruction of Madrid is worthy of figuring homerically in any epic poem.[78]

As the war raged, left-wing organizations accused *Excelsior, El Universal,* and other newspapers of being sustained financially by Spanish fascists. Editors and reporters were called traitors to Mexico.[79] CTM leader Lombardo frequently raised the treason issue, the following statement being representative of his rhetoric.

> The Spanish war was used by Mexican daily papers, particularly *Excelsior* and its afternoon edition called *Las Últimas Noticias,* not only as an issue with which to defend fascism over there, but also to defend fascism here, in such a way as to encourage fascists living in Mexico to persevere until they succeeded in achieving in our country [the fascist victory] already won in other parts of the world.[80]

Shortly after the war's end, North American authors Nathaniel and Sylvia Weyl (whose work later appeared in Spanish in Mexico) charged that *Excelsior* and *Novedades* were journalistic instruments of the Axis. They also maintained that *Excelsior* and *El Universal* used German wire services exclusively for their news copy.[81]

Examination of Mexican newspapers from 1936 to 1939, however, reveals that these accusations go too far. Most Mexican papers certainly were pro-Franco, and they did tend to slant the news somewhat, especially in their headlines, but only a few extremely partisan papers showed enthusiasm for fascism. The general character of news coverage itself was accurate and fair. Charges of irresponsibility, excessive bias, and collusion with fascists on the part of almost all newspapers simply do not stand up to impartial analysis. They overlook the existence of papers that supported the Republic, the general rejection of totalitarianism by Mexico's conservative press, and the many efforts it made to present both sides of the conflict to the Mexican people. Far from relying on German wire services, *Excelsior* and *El Universal* obtained most of their international news copy, Spanish war stories included, from Associated Press and United Press. Both papers, moreover, used the French Havas-Anta wire service as often as its German counterpart, Transocean. Although relying heavily on the wire services for their copy, some Mexican papers, including the PNR's *El Nacional*, sent correspondents to Spain to cover the conflict, which was without question the single most important ongoing news story from 1936 to 1939.[82]

Loyalist Ambassador Gordón, who reproached the entire Mexican press for being unfair to the Republic and biased in favor of General Franco, nevertheless admitted that all Mexico City dailies and some regional papers regularly published his embassy "news bulletins" about the war. Since these handouts almost immediately were discovered to be propagandistic and largely inaccurate, their continued publication by Mexican papers would seem to indicate at least some spirit of fair play. Franquista Mexicans such as Alfonso Junco objected when the press kept on printing the ambassador's lies. *El Universal* regularly featured editorial columns on Spain by Lombardo, stoically ignoring his oft-repeated characterizations of the paper as fascist. It also printed the entire texts of his major speeches on Spain. The opinions of Marxist ideologue Narciso Bassols appeared in the pages of *El Universal* at this time, too.[83]

El Universal during the 1930s was run by Miguel Lanz Duret and José Gómez Ugarte. Lanz Duret, the paper's president and manager, also taught constitutional law at the National School of Jurisprudence and had once headed the Mexican Bar Association. Editor Gómez Ugarte was a journalist originally from Jalisco who, in the 1920s, had published three books of poetry. Under their direction *El Universal* took a strong capitalist, Hispanist, Christian editorial line. Although basically conservative, the editors maintained high standards and generously provided space for left-wing views. The paper featured a wide range of opinion on major issues of the day: Mexican politics, Communism, Fascism, and the Spanish Civil War. *El Universal* often slanted headlines against labor unions and political radicals, and sometimes conservative editorial comments appeared in the news stories themselves, but the paper generally reported news in a straightforward manner. *El Universal* editorials consistently attacked the "irresponsibility" of organized labor, arguing that the state should intervene in labor-management conflicts to curb the unions and thus protect "the public good." At the same time, however, criticism of Mexican capitalism did appear in the paper. In February 1938, federal deputy Salvador Ochoa Rentería contributed an article calling for nationalization of the electric industry. Fernando de la Fuente, a Supreme Court justice from 1929 to 1934, had a regular column in the paper in which he stressed Christian values, warned against the Communist menace, and related the spread of Communism in Mexico to Jewish and United States influence. Yet the Marxist opinions of Lombardo appeared on the same page. In their own editorials, *El Universal's* staff rejected both fascism and Communism and expressed preference for democracy as a political system. Although highly critical of the Cárdenas administration, *El Universal* nonetheless printed much Cardenista publicity, for example, tributes to his humanitarianism by loyal supporters of the Revolutionary Party.[84]

Contributors to *El Universal*, whether Mexican or Spanish, frequently referred in glowing terms to "our Spain." They commonly emphasized the Spanish origins of Mexico and paid tribute to Hernán Cortés, "founder" of the country. For the most part, their Spain was the conservative, traditional one, rather than the radical or revolutionary Spain of the left. The Hispanist writer most frequently and prominently featured in the paper both before and during the civil war was Carlos Pereyra, an old Huertista who had been living in Spain for years. Pereyra relentlessly attacked what he regarded as the Bolshevist Popular Front government and became one of General Franco's most enthusiastic supporters. Curiously, prior to the military rebellion, Pereyra did not number Communism among his grievances against the Popular Front; he correctly observed shortly before the war began that the Soviets did not want a Communist revolution in Spain.[85]

Despite a traditionalist bias, *El Universal's* editors handled Spanish Civil War news and comment without excessive distortion or prejudice. Regular columns by the moderate Enrique Marine offset the tirades of Pereyra. If the paper remained generally unsympathetic to the Republic, it still published propaganda handouts from the Spanish embassy. One of Ambassador Gordón's news bulletins early in 1938 described "fascist horrors" perpetrated in Teruel. *El Universal* did not tamper with the text, nor did it offer any editorial rebuttal. Another news release from the embassy ten days later described the "horrendous murders" committed by "fascist" airmen in bombardments of Barcelona and Valencia. It, too, was printed without change or comment. The large volume of Spanish war news printed by *El Universal* corresponded in content to that published by the press of France, England, Canada, and the United States. Most of the stories, in fact, originated with United Press and Havas-Anta; some of them came from the *New York Times*.[86] Extensive news coverage was not matched by a comparable amount of editorial comment by the paper's editors themselves, who left this journalistic task to columnists, political writers, and politicians. The staff wrote few editorials on Spain. Such reticence was sometimes revealing, as in the case of the bombings of Barcelona and Valencia in late January and early February 1938. Readers learned from news stories in the paper that public opinion throughout the world, even much conservative opinion, condemned the air raids; but *El Universal* made no criticism of Franco nor did it express any regret about what was happening to civilians in these cities.[87] Since the paper did reprove the Republicans editorially for far milder transgressions than the bombing of helpless noncombatants, it seems fair to conclude that its owners and editors were determined that they themselves would do no damage to the Nationalist cause in Spain. Editorial restraint by *El Universal* extended even to the reviews of books on Spain that it published, most of which merely summarized content and avoided partisan judgments or polemics.[88]

El Universal did strike at the Republic occasionally when the issues involved had immediate relevance for the Mexican political situation. Thus at the start of 1938, with the Loyalist economy in shambles, the paper published a lengthy editorial on the "collectivist failure" in Catalonia. The idea of collectivism, "so dear to extremists," had been shown to be erroneous by the dismal results produced in the Soviet Union and Catalonia. Citing Luis Companys, president of Catalonia's autonomous government, as an expert source, *El Universal* quoted his comments about the disastrous results of collectivization. Companys had recently gone to Belgium to meet with exiled Catalan capitalists in an effort to get them to return home and thus contribute to the revival of Catalonia's industry. According to the editorial, Catalan workers themselves showed discontent with the collective system because they earned less than before the revolution and were required to spend much of their free time at "useless meetings." In the Catalan countryside the situation was even worse than in the cities, an inevitable development because "the land, belonging to nobody (and the land belongs to nobody when it belongs to everybody), nobody works it." Companys had made the same observation, complaining that due to collectivization "nobody is interested in working the [land]" and charging that extreme leftists "were on the verge of annihilating the economic and social life of our region." In *El Universal's* view, the Catalan experience again demonstrated the truth that "a body cannot govern itself without a head," and that in any economy empresarios performed indispensable functions; indeed, they constituted the principal workers in all industry. The editorial ended by claiming that many people throughout the world now saw the sophistry of collectivism and realized that "order and common sense" had to prevail over "the empty rhetoric of myopic ideologies and opportunistic agitators."[89] No Mexican reader could fail to miss the implied criticism of President Cárdenas's economic and social policies in all this.

Excelsior stood to the right of *El Universal* on many issues, including Spain. During the Civil War, veteran journalist Rodrigo de Llano ran the paper. A prodigy in his youth, de Llano had been editor-in-chief of Mexico City's *El Imparcial* in 1910 at the astonishing age of twenty. Openly hostile to Azaña's Popular Front government from the start, *Excelsior* nevertheless reported most Spanish news straightforwardly. Republican Ambassador Gordón, one of the paper's major targets after July 1936, had been treated with courteous respect upon his arrival in Mexico in May of that year. *Excelsior* reported extensively and fairly pro-Loyalist activities throughout the country, and issues of the paper often contained lengthy excerpts of speeches by Mexican and Spanish politicians. When Ambassador Gordón visited Tallares Gráficos de la Nación in October 1936, *Excelsior* printed long passages of his remarks to the assembled employees.[90]

Excelsior's editorials opposed what they called "the Azañist faction" and the "republican-communist-sindicalist regime of Red Spain." Its staff often slanted the news against the Republic and occasionally concocted sensational stories of a semifictional character in an effort to embarrass Loyalists and their Mexican sympathizers. Most columnists featured on the editorial pages came from the right. Pedro Gringoire was one of the few liberal contributors, yet his column appeared quite frequently. Far from being pro-fascist, as mythologists have so often charged, *Excelsior* editorially rejected fascism as a solution to Mexico's many problems.[91]

Ambassador Gordón, distressed by what he regarded as unfair treatment of the Spanish story, sent many irate letters to the paper. *Excelsior* published and answered them, referring in its replies to "the Valencia faction" and to "the Ambassador of that Little Republic." The editors emphatically denied libeling Gordón and the Republic; what they *were* printing, they noted sarcastically, were the ambassador's news bulletins, "despite their almost never being in accordance with the facts." Shortly after the war started, *Excelsior's* owners took advantage of the demand for war news in Mexico City and created an afternoon paper called *Las Últimas Noticias.* This tabloid was unfair to the Republic and to almost everyone and everything that its editors found censurable. It relied on cheap sensationalism rather than on journalistic quality for its sales. The Mexican government disappointed Gordón by permitting *Excelsior* to publish what it pleased about the war. It made few exceptions to this lack of censorship, but one did occur in December 1937 when the paper printed a rumor, which turned out to be factual, about an impending secret shipment to Spain of airplanes purchased in the United States. As noted in the previous chapter, the Ministry of National Defense ordered *Excelsior* to print nothing further on this subject.[92]

Although many newspapers in the capital and in the states enthusiastically joined General Franco's crusade, others defended the Republic, often in an extremely partisan manner. Some papers promoted no particular line on Spain and maintained fairness to both sides in the conflict. In addition to those already mentioned, Mexico City newspapers taking a pro-Franco position included *El Hombre Libre, La Prensa, Novedades, Omega,* and *El Tornillo.*[93] *El Hombre Libre's* campaigns against Calles and its disenchantment with the Republic have already been described. Predictably it displayed a blatantly pro-Nationalist attitude throughout the war.

So many of the writers featured by the paper were peninsular Falangists or monarchists, and so partisan were its continual imprecations against the Republic and its glorifications of the military insurgents, that the political stance of the paper was indistinguishable from a right-wing Spanish publication. On January 3, 1938, the lead article on page one consisted of the text of a monarchist speech headlined "A Magnificent Talk by Don Antonio Goicoechea, Dedicated to Evoking the Work and the Sacrifice of the Glorious Precursor of the Crusade, Calvo Sotelo." Several months later another page-one article described "The Miracles of Franco, Mussolini, and Hitler." Lumped together by the paper as enemies of Mexico and Western civilization were President Cárdenas, the Jews, and the Spanish Republicans. On January 5, 1938, *El Hombre Libre* headlined its top story on the front page "Cárdenas is Defeated in Teruel," and regular attacks against the Jews depicted them as a "grave threat" to the country.[94]

To some extent offsetting this press support for the Franquista rebellion, *El Nacional* and *El Popular* relentlessly opposed what they saw as Spanish fascism. Initially run by an anti-Communist faction of the CTM, *El Popular* was eventually brought into harmony with the Comintern line by Lombardo. Progressive intellectuals wrote articles for its editorial pages; they included Octavio Paz, Andrés Iduarte, and Daniel Cosío Villegas. More doctrinaire contributions came from Víctor M. Villaseñor and Enrique Ramírez y Ramírez.[95] *El Nacional* presented official PNR views of the Civil War and served as a vehicle for information and opinion emanating from Loyalist Spain and from the Spanish embassy in Mexico City. Also in the capital, the weekly *Hoy* stood close enough to the political center to provide some help for the Republican cause. The paper often criticized Cárdenas and the PNR, yet it contained articles praising Mexico's Spanish policy and attacking General Franco. Mexicans thus read in *Hoy* Salvador Novo's tribute to the pro-Republican diplomacy of Bassols and de Negri in 1937 and José Vasconcelos's 1938 denunciation of Franco for reviving militarism in Spain. Bassols himself published articles in *Hoy*.[96]

The conservative organ of Mexico's Spanish colony, *El Diario Español*, hailed the military rebellion from the outset and during the war gave the Spanish Falange much favorable publicity. Its prudent editors rarely mentioned Mexican politics, but they vigorously attacked the Republic, Ambassador Gordón, and resident Spaniards who expressed support for the Popular Front. Initially the paper printed both the Loyalist and Franquista versions of the war news, but by August 1936 it was rebutting allegedly false information about the conflict issued daily by Ambassador Gordón. As the war progressed, *El Diario Español* became increasingly partisan. It began printing old speeches of Calvo Sotelo and Gil Robles, laudatory feature articles on the military leaders of the rebellion, and many pictures of pro-Franco Spaniards giving the fascist salute. It portrayed the Republican government as subservient to the Soviet Union and charged its members with fomenting brutality, barbarism, and hatred among brothers. One editorial asserted that despite the war's horrors, Spain would be much better off after the Nationalist army had rescued the country from Azaña and other so-called Communist tyrants. Propagandists had deceived Spanish workers, inducing them to bring ruin to themselves and to their country. Co-editor Braulio Suárez wrote that "When I was a miner in Asturias we worked twenty-five days a month and had food all thirty days; today the miners work eight days a month and have food six days." He added: "I want a government for my country that teaches the people to work," rather than a regime that "teaches them to hate . . . and to play politics."[97]

Among the provincial papers taking a pro-Franco line, three of the most important were *El Porvenir* (Monterrey), *El Diario de Yucatán* (Mérida), and *El Dictamen* (Veracruz). Spanish Civil War news and editorial comment were plentiful in all of them. *El Porvenir* featured the familiar galaxy of right-wing columnists found in most Mexican newspapers, and these writers were joined by such Franquista Spaniards as Manuel Aznar and José M. Pemán. Its pages repeatedly treated northern readers to such polemical articles as "The Anarchists and the Communist Terror of Red Spain."[98] Carlos R. Menéndez's *El Diario de Yucatán* also made no pretense of fairness when dealing with the war, and indeed the paper stumped for Franco day after day. Mexican exile Rodolfo Reyes, Franquista Spaniard Eduardo Quiñones, and Cuban conservative José I. Rivero eulogized Nationalist Spain in their regular columns. Typical of Menéndez's partisan style was his paper's treatment of an Associated Press story from Spain in April 1939. Headlined by Menéndez "The Reds are Paying with Their Lives for Their Terrible Crimes," the AP dispatch made no mention whatever of "Reds" or "terrible crimes."[99] Juan Malpica Silva, owner and editor of *El Dictamen*, printed pro-Franco publicity in almost every issue of his paper during the civil war, yet wrote few editorials himself on Spain. Glorification of the Nationalist cause he left to well-known Spanish and Mexican columnists. He even brought into the fray French rightist George Oudard, who depicted the Republicans as barbarians and the Franquistas as virtual saints.[100] In other ways, however, Malpica was willing to lend a more active hand to the Nationalists. With some justification apparently, Ambassador Gordón accused him of pro-Franco espionage. An investigation in the spring of 1937 revealed that the editor had assisted the Italian consul in Veracruz in photographing some airplanes stored for future shipment to Loyalist Spain.[101]

Other provincial newspapers, some of them controlled by the PNR, countered pro-Franco bias exhibited by large dailies in the state capitals by backing the Popular Front and Mexican foreign policy. Some of these papers were: *El Jalisciense*, Guadalajara's PNR paper, *El Diario de Puebla*, owned by federal deputy Julián Cacho; and *La Opinión*, a quasi-Marxist daily also published in Puebla.[102] *La Opinión* generally showed more sympathy for the Spanish and Mexican workers than it did for the Cárdenas regime, which it nonetheless endorsed. Although ardently for the Republicans, *La Opinión* seldom accurately informed its readers about events in the peninsula. The paper's staff rewrote wire service stories (without giving the wire services any credit for their material), inserting into them substantial editorial comment. During the battle for Madrid in November 1936, for example, the paper credited workers' militias with complete defense of the city, making no mention whatever of the Loyalist Spanish army. Editorials in *La Opinión* at this time described the Spanish conflict as a war waged by international fascism against the working class. Fascist forces led by Germany and Italy "were trying to crush the Spanish proletariat, trying to drown it in its own blood, and with it the proletariat of all nations." Because England and France were afraid to help the Republic, "criminal Legionnaires . . . and dirty Moors . . . are now washing their filthy feet in the noble blood . . . of Spanish militiamen in the ravaged streets of glorious Madrid." A serious fascist threat, moreover, still existed in Mexico, even though

President Cárdenas had thwarted a major plot by exiling former strongman Calles. Fascists remained hidden in the Mexican congress, in the Supreme Court, and in the various government ministries. To meet this danger the newspaper advised that "each day we must strengthen proletarian union and thus give, everywhere in the country, the same example as that given in Madrid by the Spanish militiamen."[103]

El Diario de Puebla made few references to glorious proletarian militiamen in its advocacy of the Spanish Republic. Its line on Spain more closely approximated that of President Cárdenas and the PNR: democracy, legality, and the Spanish people's liberty (rather than the working class) were under assault in the Iberian peninsula. For much of its editorial commentary on Spain, in fact, the paper turned to *El Nacional.* Quoting Isidro Fabela, *El Diario de Puebla* reproached the Western democracies for permitting such blatant violations of international legal principles as were occurring in the Spanish war. After praise of Fabela's speeches to the League of Nations, and a pious reference to Benito Juárez and his ideas about morality among nations, the Puebla paper continued: "In these chilling moments of international politics, it is well that Mexico persists in pointing out errors and condemning injustices so that the truth historically sustained by this nation endures in the world; yet still better is it that Mexico does this in attempting to make the great powers respond with generous impulses to this truth, thus assuring future peace, but also saving today's victims [of injustice]."[104] On another occasion the paper deplored political extremism, observing that one result of such fanaticism could be seen in Spain, as well as in the general European situation. "In Europe, Communism and fascism have made of Spain a testing ground, where they prepare for a mad war of extermination and annihilation."[105] In the Mexican provinces, then, as in the national capital, Republican sympathizers promoted two different versions of the issues behind the Spanish Civil War, and these ideological variations were reflected in the press. That they had more to do with political expediency than with an objective analysis of the peninsular tragedy seems fairly certain. Those Mexicans interested in Spain interpreted events of the Civil War in terms of the problems of Mexico uppermost in their own minds.

Partisan accusations notwithstanding, literate Mexicans had ample opportunity to keep themselves well and accurately informed about the progress of the Spanish war by reading their country's newspapers. There was no "fascist conspiracy" to prevent them from learning the "truth" about Spain. With few exceptions, neither the owners nor the editors of newspapers acted irresponsibly in reporting and commenting on Spain's terrifying drama. Coverage of the Spanish story was consistently extensive, and it was drawn from the best news sources available. If conservative editors slanted headlines against the Republic, they at least refrained from altering the wire service copy itself in order to change or distort its import. Few left-wing editors showed such professional scruples when they dealt with the Nationalists or Civil War news in general. One might fault Mexican newspapermen for deliberately oversimplifying their interpretations of the war and its underlying causes, but this particular shortcoming was not unique either to international press coverage of the Civil War or to journalistic coverage of any complex issue. The average Mexican newspaper reader from 1936 to 1939 had as much sound data to work with in searching for the significance of Spain's upheaval as did the average person anywhere else in the world. Quite possibly he or she had considerably more meaningful data upon which to make sound judgments than did the inhabitants of countries where even the journalistic oversimplifications themselves had their bases in hopeless incomprehension of Spain itself.

5

Politics, the Republican Refugee Question, and Evolution of a National Myth

Mexican Politics and the Refugees

Ambassador Tejeda and the Mexican embassy moved, along with the Republican government, from town to town in northeastern Spain during the Civil War's last months and then followed its members into France, finally stopping at Perpignan. Cárdenas called Tejeda home to report on March 1, 1939. In April Ambassador Gordón closed the Spanish embassy in Mexico City; he left the building and its archives in charge of the Cuban ambassador. Republican consuls closed their offices, too. In those foreign countries where the Republic still had diplomatic representation, Spanish officials entrusted buildings, archives, and funds to their Mexican friends for safekeeping. Cárdenas refused to recognize Franco's regime, but in July 1939 he turned over the Spanish embassy building to the Portuguese when they relayed to him the

145

general's desire for such a move. The Mexican president did permit some indirect trade with the peninsula to continue after the war, shipments being routed through such third countries as Cuba and Portugal. Yet he would not yield to Mexican commercial interests who called for resumption of full-scale trade with Spain. While permitting this small amount of private contact, Cárdenas nonetheless refrained from communicating in any way with the Franquista authorities. This made it impossible for Mexico to intercede directly on behalf of those Mexican civilians and volunteer soldiers held prisoner in Spain. It also forced Cárdenas to decline invitations from other Latin American countries to join with them in collective appeals to Franco to release all the Latin Americans taken prisoner by Nationalists during the war.[1] Mexico's lonely Civil War alliance with the Republicans thus ended on an exceedingly dismal note. Still ahead for the Mexicans lay the melancholy task of trying to rescue as many Spaniards as possible from the miseries and uncertainties of internment camps in France.

In sharp contrast to its depressing effect in government, labor, and left-wing circles, Franco's triumph prompted exuberant celebrations by his Mexican and Spanish sympathizers. In Mexico City, local Spanish Falangists came to a victory party at the Casino Español on April 2, 1939, praised Germany, Italy, and Japan, and urged adherence to Falangism in Mexico and elsewhere in the Americas. An audience largely made up of affluent Spanish families, but also including the German and Italian ministers, applauded speeches by Spaniards Alejandro Villanueva and Jenaro Riestra.[2] This event and newspaper jubilation over the Popular Front's demise in Spain provoked Mexican leftists into prompt retaliation. Even President Cárdenas could not control his anger. He ordered the Secretary of Government to begin suppression of the Spanish Falange in Mexico, and in private meetings with some of his extremist friends he encouraged their irresponsible plans for "street action" against major newspapers.

CTM leader Lombardo got countermeasures started with a speech on April 3. Labeling Mexico's Falange "an armed militia," he accused it of conspiring to restore the country to Spanish colonial rule. Lombardo expressed confidence that Cárdenas would move quickly to outlaw the organization; if not, he said, the CTM itself would be able to dissolve it "in a few minutes." The CTM had been especially offended by the Casino Español meeting, for when it ended some Falangists, "in a drunken state" Lombardo charged, committed insulting acts at the doors of several union offices. That same day Secretary of Government Ignacio García Téllez rejected the Falange's claim to be a legitimate political party. He announced that its members would be kept under surveillance to prevent them from furthering Franquista Spain's imperialistic designs. The secretary added that the Falange was also unwelcome because it had allied itself "with individuals and political groups opposed to the principles of our social reforms." Mexico had to protect its sovereignty and democracy; and the nation would go about its business without foreign interference of the sort contemplated by Spanish Falangists.[3]

On April 4 Cárdenas deported as undesirable aliens Villanueva, Riestra, and José Celorio Ortega, another Falangist. He accused them of flagrantly violating certain Mexican laws. Late that afternoon a mob of about five hundred anti-Falangists (CTM bakers, taxi drivers, and pro-Republic Spaniards) converged on the elegant old Casino Español downtown where they heard leftist speakers link the Falange to such domestic evils as a 1938 rebellion against Cárdenas by conservative Gen. Saturnino Cedillo. (At the time of Cedillo's abortive revolt, these same orators had blamed it on the foreign oil companies.) After the speeches the mob stormed the Casino and did considerable damage.[4]

An even bigger left-wing riot followed this disturbance. Narciso Bassols and David Siqueiros went to Cárdenas, who still fumed over the Republican debacle. They persuaded him to permit them to lead a demonstration against the capital's conservative newspapers: *Excelsior, El Universal,* and *Novedades.* Mobilized by the frenetic painter and his cohorts, a large crowd described as being workers and students assembled near the newspaper offices and listened to Siqueiros "explain the economic origin of those periodicals and the concrete capitalist interests found behind them." Then the crowd attacked the newspaper buildings, smashing everything that they could. Police arrived and eventually drove away the rioters after a wild battle.[5]

Far from being intimidated, however, conservative journalists intensified their attacks on Cárdenas, effectively exploiting his obvious blunder in unleashing Siqueiros. Columnist Rubén Salazar Mallén characterized the two violent incidents as beginning an "era of terror" that the PRM regime had been preparing for some

time. He accused the president of turning public power over to a
group of demagogues, thus "killing the principle of legitimate
authority." Communists such as Siqueiros attacked newspapers
because they feared the truth, their greatest enemy; and they had
rioted in hopes of precipitating "the destruction of Mexico" so that
"Asiatic barbarism" could be erected atop the nation's ruins.[6]
Siqueiros also failed to frighten right-wing Spaniards. Whenever
they encountered him in Mexico City they insulted him to his face,
and one of them, an editor who worked for *Las Últimas Noticias,*
derisively nicknamed him *"El Coronelazo,"* an allusion to the
painter's dubious claim to military distinction as a civil war
volunteer.[7]

Months before the Popular Front government asked Cárdenas in
late 1937 if Mexico would accept thousands of Republican
immigrants, Daniel Cosío Villegas (from Portugal) and Alfonso
Reyes (from Argentina) had already proposed to the Mexican
president that he bring the dispersed Spanish intellectuals to
Mexico and help them find useful employment. Cosío made his
initial plans on a small scale, suggesting that Cárdenas invite to
Mexico about thirty prominent Spaniards. While waiting for official
approval of the project, Reyes did what he could to aid personally
some of his old friends hurt by the war and certain to be among
those invited: José Ortega y Gasset, Juan Ramón Jiménez and his
wife, and Ramón Gómez de la Serna. Reyes also raised money for
the widow of his late friend, Ramón del Valle-Inclán. Important
support for the idea came immediately from other Mexican
intellectuals and politicians.[8] From these roots grew a plan that
culminated in July 1938 with a presidential decree creating the
Casa de España, an institute of research, higher learning, and
literary production in which exiled intellectuals would be em-
ployed. Conceived initially as a temporary facility, the Casa began
operations that same year. Cosío and Reyes served on its board of
directors. Included in the first group of Spanish staff members to
arrive were José Gaos, Adolfo Salazar, Juan de la Encina, and Jesús
Bal y Gay. When a Spanish club in Mexico City, also called the
Casa de España, protested use of its name, Cosío and the board
redesignated their creation El Colegio de México. Under that name
the institution has developed into the country's finest graduate
school for humanities and social sciences. Picturesquely located
near volcanic mountains south of Mexico City, it stands as a living

memorial not only to the humanism and love of Spain of Reyes and Cosío, but also to the one historical moment since its independence in 1821 when Mexico drew genuinely close to the former metropolis.[9]

Young Mexican writers and artists who had empathized with the Republicans and who had seen the Spanish conflict as their own struggle, too, joined with an older generation of liberals like Cosío and Reyes in welcoming the exiles into Mexico and in helping them to do productive work. Especially prominent in this regard were various left-wing personalities associated with *Taller,* a literary journal. Some of them like Communist José Revueltas may have been less than totally sincere in their displays of emotional attachment to Republican exile writers. Others, such as poet Octavio Paz, a nominal but far from conventional Marxist at the time, seemed powerfully moved by a real sense of kinship with his peninsular counterparts. Paz and the *Taller* staff did more than pay tribute to the patriotism of Republican writers who, "faithful to the people's cause," had remained in Spain until the very end; they also published their works and added several of them to the journal's editorial board.[10]

Origin of massive Republican emigration to Mexico can be traced to the secret mission in late 1937 of Juan-Simeón Vidarte, a Spanish socialist politician. Spain's non-Communist left passively accepted rather than truly supported Juan Negrín's Communist-dominated government that had been formed in the spring of that year. Thus Spanish Socialists such as Vidarte had begun to think seriously of defeat and exile. This was especially true after the Republican military failure at Brunete in the summer of 1937 and the subsequent fall of northern Spain to General Franco. As Gabriel Jackson has written in regard to the replacement of Largo Caballero by Negrín as prime minister, the former's forced resignation badly divided Loyalist Spain and signalled growing disunity within the Republic.[11] According to Vidarte, when he asked Cárdenas in 1937 how he would respond to such an appeal, the president without hesitation replied that Mexico would welcome an indefinite number of exiles. Cárdenas further assured his guest that the immigrants would discover what he termed a "second fatherland" when they arrived.[12] Late in 1938, with the war's end in sight, Cárdenas indicated that Mexico would take in about fifty thousand of the Republicans already interned (under

appalling conditions) in French camps.[13] Yet he made no immediate move to implement this offer or to fulfill his pledge to
Vidarte. Knowing that his decision would be resented and opposed
by many Mexicans, including some of his supporters, the president
had no desire to bring on that crisis any sooner than necessary. In
addition, Mexico had just accumulated enormous debts by nationalizing foreign oil companies; the expensive Republican immigration project would be another burden on the federal treasury.

Several Mexicans in Europe, however, sensed impending catastrophe for the growing number of Loyalist exiles in France. Three
of them successfully appealed to Cárdenas to begin a rescue
operation at once: Isidro Fabela, Adalberto Tejeda, and Narciso
Bassols. Fabela toured the dreadful camps in France and wrote
directly to Cárdenas. Bassols came back to Mexico from his
diplomatic post in France in spring 1939 to confront the president
in person. Tejeda wrote to Cárdenas through dispatches to the
Ministry of Foreign Relations from Perpignan, where he and the
Mexican embassy had come to rest along with the itinerant,
virtually defunct Popular Front government. Fearing that France
would send the refugees back to prison or certain death in Spain,
Tejeda urged that Cárdenas "initiate international action" on
behalf of all of them and that he bring to Mexico as rapidly as
possible a selection of the "talented poeple" among them: intellectuals, writers, teachers, and other professionals.[14] Moved by these
entreaties, in April 1939 the president authorized Minister Bassols
in France to announce that Mexico "would accept an unlimited
number of refugees if the Republican authorities would arrange to
finance their transportation and settlement in Mexico." A subsequent presidential decree enabled Loyalist Spaniards to acquire
Mexican citizenship quickly and simply.[15]

Initially the Mexican legation in Paris and the Evacuation
Service for Spanish Refugees (SERE) handled the emigration
process. Republican Prime Minister Juan Negrín nominally controlled SERE, which owed its existence to Mexico's official
sponsorship. The organization took its character from Minister
Bassols and the Spanish Communist leaders. Their idea was to save
as many PCE members as possible, while leaving behind to a grim
fate in France the non-Communist exiles, most of whom by then
could be considered anti-Communists as well. Mexican Communists Federico and Susana Gamboa helped Bassols administer the

SERE operation. In late 1939 and early 1940 SERE suffered several fatal reverses: it ran out of money, and the French government suppressed it as a Communist organization. Cárdenas, moreover, removed Bassols from Paris because of the scandalous uproar that his sectarian partisanship had been creating, not only in the press and among Mexican conservatives, but also among the refugees, many of whom had already reached Mexico. With the demise of SERE, the Aid Committee for Spanish Refugees (JARE) took over emigration responsibility. JARE was funded, ironically, by money from the Republican Treasury that Negrín had left at the Mexican legation in Paris. President Cárdenas, either by design or whimsy, had turned this money over to Indalecio Prieto, the socialist rival of Negrín, who created JARE. Under such auspices and accompanied by much controversy, the huge Loyalist emigration to Mexico began. The first few shiploads of refugees reached Veracruz in the summer of 1939; subsequent departures from France continued throughout the years of World War II. By 1945, as many as forty thousand Spanish exiles may have entered Mexico.[16]

As evacuation of Republicans from France proceeded, the Mexicans constantly had to pressure French authorities to prevent them from acquiescing to the Franco regime's many requests for extradition of people back to Spain. The problem became especially critical after the fall of France in 1940 and the establishment of the Vichy government. Although some Loyalists were sent back to their deaths in Spain, Mexico generally succeeded in protecting their wards from Franquista vengeance.[17] In this matter, representations from Mexican diplomats in France were supplemented by an international publicity campaign on behalf of the refugees that had its base in Mexico. Carried out by the Federation of Groups to Aid Spanish Republicans (FOARE), these concerted efforts probably had more effect on the spineless French regime—by shaming it before an increasingly antifascist world—than did official protests by the Mexican government. FOARE enjoyed the backing and nominal membership of almost every PRM, CTM, and left-wing organization and affiliate in the country. Two of the four women composing its "Honorary Presidency" were the wives of President Cárdenas and PRM presidential candidate, Manuel Avila Camacho. Yet José Mancisidor, the Communist who had manipulated LEAR to make it serve Stalinist interests in Spain during the civil war, ran FOARE's daily operations as its president. Working with leftists and other Republican sympathizers throughout the Americas, FOARE kept the welfare, protection, and prospect of evacuation of the refugees in France a major issue throughout World War II. It also regularly denounced Nationalist executions of Loyalist prisoners in Spain. The organization sponsored what were described as conventions of solidarity with the Spanish people, published a bulletin and special propaganda items, put up posters, organized protest demonstrations at the French legation in Mexico City, and sent countless petitions to diplomats accredited to the Mexican government. One of its officers observed in 1943, in the course of reviewing three years of FOARE activity, that since 1940 in Mexico there had been "no congress, assembly, meeting, or any kind of mass political gathering in which the question of the Spanish Republicans and international volunteers remaining in France had not been raised." Other FOARE projects in the 1940s included sponsorship of a sanatorium for ailing Republicans who had no money for medical bills and presentation of scholarships to some of the Spanish children who had arrived in Mexico in 1937.[18]

Mexican efforts to facilitate Republican emigration from France, begun officially in the spring of 1939, thus continued well into the 1940s and involved Mexico in negotiations with the Vichy regime after the Germans occupied the country during World War II. In addition to enabling Spaniards to come to Mexico, Cárdenas also sought homes elsewhere in the Americas for those still stranded in France, and he authorized substantial payments from the Mexican treasury to care for the needy exiles who probably never would leave that country. Mexico's diplomatic personnel in France continued to assist the Loyalists in countless acts of humanitarian service.

On various occasions the legation in Paris turned over to Negrín's government-in-exile money for refugee relief that had been given to Mexican diplomats in Spanish America by pro-Republican groups. From Buenos Aires, for example, Ambassador Félix F. Palavicini sent to the Mexican minister in France in early 1939 two large checks contributed by the Committee to Aid the Spanish Proletariat and by the Federation of Collective Cab Lines. The money had been raised to pay for refugee travel from France to Mexico. Bassols gave the checks to Republican officials.[19] Mexican consuls, such as Gilberto Bosques in Marseilles, extended their good offices on behalf of thousands of Spaniards in the post-Civil War years, helping them deal with the French bureau-cracy to obtain work permits or exit visas. Some politicians (Negrín, for example) eventually left France by means of Mexican passports that gave them false identities, and former Spanish president Manuel Azaña received protection and money during a long illness and, after his death in 1940, a state funeral from the Mexican government. Mexican Minister Luis I. Rodríguez took charge of the Republican government's archives and remaining treasury deposits and saw that the latter were shipped to Mexico from France for safekeeping.[20] Mexico maintained two big refugee centers in rural France in 1940–41 that cared for 2,500 people. Another facility financed by the Mexicans looked after 1,300 disabled war veterans and their families. In Marseilles alone, Mexican money supported nineteen welfare centers where Spanish exiles could get food, lodging, medical care, and if they were artisans, tools and raw materials so that they could work.[21]

Mexican support for refugees in France waned, however, and after 1946, the Revolutionary Party wearied of the continuing refugee burden. When the League of Amputees and Invalids of the Spanish War appealed from Paris to President Miguel Alemán in 1949 for economic assistance, he turned them down. The League had reported that there were still approximately two thousand disabled veterans suffering from hunger and cold in France and that the former Popular Front leaders, despite having "appro-priated the national patrimony" prior to their departure from Spain, had totally abandoned them. Alemán instructed Foreign Relations to tell them to address their petitions to the Spanish Republican government, a rather callous reply given the largely fictional character of that regime.[22]

After unsuccessfully making private appeals in early 1939 to several Latin American countries for help in relocating the Loyalist refugees, Cárdenas publicly asked all of them in June 1940 to accept Spanish exiles and thus relieve them from the threat of being turned over to the Germans or sent back to Spain. He hoped that each country would admit at least some Republicans as immigrants. Only Ecuador and Cuba, however, responded favor-ably to the Mexican president's request. Ecuador promised to ac-cept five thousand families, but the Cuban regime attached very restrictive conditions to its affirmative answer. Cuba would only take in Spaniards "willing to dedicate themselves to agricultural labor" or who "could create new industries by means of capital investment." Petty merchants would not be admitted under any circumstances. Other Latin American countries either made excuses, declined without comment, or offered only moral support for Mexico's project. Uruguay claimed that domestic politics prevented any humanitarian move on its part. El Salvador pointed to a coffee crisis as the reason it could not help. Bolivia claimed to be too poor to take in any Spaniards. Peru reminded Cárdenas of its 1940 law that prohibited any immigrants from entering the country. Panama wanted to take in several thousand Republican immigrants (allegedly to "whiten" its predominantly Black or mixed population), but the country's foreign secretary informed Mexico that U.S. President Roosevelt had specifically proscribed this because "Spanish radicals would threaten the Canal's security."[23]

Both 1939 and 1940 were very political years in Mexico, for during that time the PRM chose and elected an official candidate to succeed Cárdenas. The president's decision to admit thousands of Republican refugees inevitably became a much-discussed topic and a major issue in the election campaign. One anti-PRM pamphleteer charged that the Loyalist exiles "bring with them . . . a desire to transplant to our soil the germs of the desolation that provoked the Spanish catastrophe."[24] The nation generally seethed with discontent, organized movements opposed to the PRM steadily increased in number, many sectors of the population remained alienated from the Revolution, and civil war still seemed possible.[25] Cárdenas nevertheless refused to renege on his promise and admitted the refugees despite the almost universal unpopularity of his action. To counter adverse reactions to this and other PRM policies, the president made major efforts to reassure Catholics, middle-sector people, and political moderates that they had nothing to fear from him and that there would be no sovietization of the country. He also bypassed several obvious candidates considered as radicals for the PRM presidential nomination in favor of General Manuel Avila Camacho, a moderate Revolutionary with conciliatory skills. During the campaign, Avila Camacho even proclaimed himself to be a Catholic![26]

Emotions aroused by the Spanish war served opposition interests in various ways at this time. Anti-PRM Mexicans repeatedly exploited links between Republican Communism and both Cárdenas and candidate Avila Camacho, whose enthusiasm for the Popular Front regime as defense secretary had never waned. Some of the sharpest attacks came from people formerly associated with the Loyalist cause. Blanca L. Trejo, disillusioned by her wartime experiences, produced *Lo que vi en España* in time for the political debates of 1940. In this book she accused the PRM of planning to Bolshevize the country; and her account of wartime observations searingly condemned what she regarded as betrayal of the Spanish people by a corrupt, tyrannical Communist party. She linked Spanish and Mexican Communists directly to Cárdenas and the PRM: Mexican propaganda activities in Spain had been directed by Stalinist José Mancisidor; Ambassador de Negri had made himself a willing tool of the Spanish Communist party; Bassols and two other so-called Russian agents, Federico and Susana Gamboa, had conspired to pack Republican emigration to Mexico with Spanish Communists. Some of the Popular Front's worst offenders, moreover, had been among those exiles receiving warmest welcomes from the administration. Margarita Nelkin was being treated as a heroine when in fact her irresponsibility had done the Republic incalculable harm. Trejo penned moving descriptions of hardships endured by rank and file Republicans, which she said stemmed as much from Communist corruption and incompetence as from the war itself. She urged her readers to avoid a similar fate: "Mexican women, I would hate to see that which Spain's noble people have suffered come to Mexico. But this seems to be exactly what our demagogic and venal 'leaders' are preparing."[27]

A good index of the limits that widespread opposition imposed on even so powerful a figure as Mexico's president can be found in the collapse of Cárdenas's January 1939 project to save members of the International Brigades. He proposed to admit into Mexico as immigrants all of them who for political reasons could not return to their own countries. Most of these men had been interned in France, although some still fought in Spain. Cárdenas explained his decision as a move to assist what he called the noble cause of Azaña's government by helping it show the world that it relied on no foreign soldiers. Evidently he still faintly hoped that the League of Nations might decide to help the Republic. His announcement, however, provoked among Mexicans such violent demonstrations against entry of these soldiers that he had to move quickly to restore peace by publicly canceling his plan. He also decided to delay further the exodus of Loyalists from France to Mexico.[28]

In 1939–40 the PRM's major opponent in the presidential election was Gen. Juan Andreu Almazán, a wealthy, personable man who attracted a large following. Thirty-four army generals took leave from active duty to stump for him. Even the fledgling National Action Party (PAN), a Catholic organization led by Manuel Gómez Morín, ex-Revolutionary and ex-rector of the National University, urged its members to vote for Almazán. Not surprisingly, Gómez attacked the PRM's Spanish policy in his speeches. He charged that the administration "had aligned itself with the lowest of international interests in the affair of Spain." PRM candidate Avila Camacho handled himself astutely amidst the controversy and tension. He spoke in conciliatory fashion, obviously courting political moderates; yet he also allowed Lombardo and the Communists to play upon popular fears of fascist aggression by linking Almazán to alleged German and Falangist plots to seize Mexico. Avila Camacho did not, however, yield to renewed leftist demands that workers and peasants be organized into armed militias. Certain of army support, he knew that Almazán had no desire to die trying to become a Mexican version of Franco. Such a fate had befallen rebellious General Cedillo in 1938. The official candidate found it sufficient that pro-PRM leftists air these preposterous charges regularly during the campaign, sow some hysteria, and thus effectively smear his rival. Although Almazán's supporters claimed that he had received a majority of the votes cast, returns published by the government after the balloting predictably showed that Avila Camacho had scored a landslide victory.[29]

The many outstanding contributions of Spanish Loyalists to Mexican life and culture, and meanings of the immigration for both Mexicans and Spaniards, have been excellently detailed by Patricia Fagen in *Exiles and Citizens: The Spanish Republicans in Mexico* (1973); the subject need not be treated at length here. As Professor Fagen has written, Spanish refugees brought to the country at a decisive moment in its history skills that Mexico's small cultural elite often lacked. Although their settlement concentrated heavily in Mexico City, they at least gave Mexicans "the critical means necessary to create in their capital a cultural, an intellectual, and an artistic center of world importance."[30] They also stimulated the nation's economic growth by excelling in commerce, industry, and business in general. Many of these new Spanish-Mexican entrepreneurs, incidentally, had to go into business because local conditions made practice of their original professions impossible.[31]

Few Mexicans in 1939 perceived beneficial aspects in the Republican immigration; initially most of them vigorously opposed it, years passing before public opinion reconciled itself with the presence of so many exiles. Nativist reactions, especially intense during the first year, were not confined to conservatives. Right-wing nationalists and Mexican newspapers did indeed show xenophobic reactions by denouncing the refugees and their Mexican benefactors. But they were joined by many workers and peasants who feared loss of jobs or land and by elements in the Revolutionary bureaucracy. Even the teachers unions, usually enthusiastic supporters of PRM policy, found arrival of the Loyalists disturbing.[32] Alfonso Reyes, back in Mexico after a diplomatic assignment in Argentina, failed to find newspaper work for his Republican friend Ramón Gómez de la Serna, who remained without employment in Buenos Aires. Reyes himself could obtain no journalistic commissions. Writing to Gómez in 1942, Reyes observed that:

> On my return, and for no less than three years, newspapers not only closed their doors to me but attacked me every day, moved by stupid "nationalistic" motives, to make me pay for a grave sin, that of dedicating my efforts to finding a place for the many Spaniards, companions in letters, whom political currents had carried to Mexico.[33]

Inside the federal government some opposition to the immigration surfaced in the Secretariat of Public Education. Irked by personality clashes with several of the Spanish intellectuals who had received professorships at the National University and at the Colegio de México, and vexed by his lack of authority over the Colegio, Education Secretary Octavio Véjar Vázquez allegedly began in the early 1940s to intrigue against the latter institution. According to Daniel Cosío Villegas, only when he and other Colegio board members took the problem directly to President Avila Camacho did Secretary Véjar stop harassing the Spaniards.[34]

In contrast to such Revolutionary nativists, some of the PRM's staunchest foes—critics of both Loyalist Spain and Cárdenas's Spanish policy—welcomed the Republican immigration in 1939 when it was under heavy fire. Ranging ideologically from center to far right, they nevertheless shared a Hispanism that caused them to forgive any political sins that the new Spanish arrivals may have committed. Moderate journalist Salvador Novo answered attacks on the Republican intellectuals and scholars that portrayed them as foreigners unworthy of the preferential treatment they believed was afforded them by the Cárdenas administration. Novo observed that such distinguished professors as Juan de la Encina, Adolfo Salazar, and José Gaos would honor any institution of higher learning; universities all over the hemisphere would pay highly to get them; and Mexicans should feel themselves lucky to have them.[35] Ultraconservative José Vasconcelos also advocated a generous reception of the Spanish exiles. Although he had come to loathe the Republic well in advance of the Civil War, Vasconcelos never forgot that the Loyalists were still Spaniards and hence to be considered superior people despite their political follies. In 1939 he entered the controversy clearly on the side of the immigrants. Years later he reminisced:

> When the Spanish Republican refugees arrived in Mexico, there were organs of the press which condemned them as Communists. . . . I wrote an article for . . . *Hoy* asking my countrymen not to take into account, when the refugees arrived, whether they were Communists, Socialists, or whatever, but to receive them as Spaniards, that is to say, as the heirs of those who created our nationality. . . . Experience has justified all of us who looked with enthusiasm on the arrival of these Spanish families. . . .[36]

Liberal Luis Cabrera, although profoundly suspicious of the PRM's objective in bringing Spanish Republicans to Mexico, supplied additional prestigious support for the immigration. Cabrera could only attribute base motives to Cárdenas, so great was his aversion to the Mexican president; he accused him of either planning to use the Spaniards for some evil political purpose or admitting them merely to spite those people who had favored Franco. Yet Cabrera proudly noted, in contrast to official motivation,

> We Mexicans who see in Spain's afflictions nothing more than

the misfortune of our brothers receive the immigrants with good will *because they are Spaniards,* without ostentatious enthusiasm, but also without asking them about their political creed; [we welcome them] simply because they are people who share our customs . . . [and] our race.[37]

Most of the arrivals, Cabrera said, were not Communists or extremists, but rather "liberty-loving individuals." Only tragedy would result if the Mexican government forced them to serve Cárdenas's policy objectives. The administration should treat the Spaniards as guests, not as servants, and no guest should be welcomed, as the PRM was greeting the Loyalists, "with a megaphone." This suggested false hospitality. According to Cabrera, "we disinterested Mexicans" could set a much better example by shunning fanfare and saying quietly to the immigrants: "Come in, this is your house."[38]

The Republican exiles remained objects of popular hostility and suspicion for some time after the campaigns against them in 1939, and nativist resentment among all social classes lingered on, but gradually their presence ceased to be an issue in Mexican life. Over the years it became increasingly evident that these Spaniards played no role in national politics, but they were making valuable contributions to the country's development. As more "Spanish radicals" turned into successful "Mexican businessmen," it became harder for enemies of the immigration to exploit it politically by raising spectres of social upheaval and collectivism.[39] By the 1960s and 1970s, Mexican criticism of Spanish exiles came mainly from certain leftists who charged them with "selling out" ideologically by transforming themselves into wealthy *gachupines* who economically "exploited" the Mexican people. David A. Siqueiros, for example, complained in his memoirs that

. . . with excessive frequency Spanish Republicans have joined themselves to the new oligarchy that exploits the country and that is facilitating ever greater penetration by imperialism. All Mexico knows that behind every new Mexican plutocrat stands a new Spanish plutocrat. . . .[40]

The Spanish Republican Government-in-Exile

Internecine political divisions and the German occupation of France during World War II temporarily reduced the effectiveness and viability of Spain's Republican government-in-exile, which had been established in Paris in 1939. Azaña died in France in 1940; Negrín fled to England; socialist leader Indalecio Prieto settled in Mexico. Individually, however, Loyalist refugees contributed to Allied war efforts in various ways. Some of them joined one or another of the Allied armies and continued their fight against fascism. Others raised money and participated in propaganda activities on behalf of the United Nations. Republican exiles in Mexico worked closely with the PRM in advocating popular support for the war effort. Margarita Nelkin and other leftists appeared on the government radio program "For a Free World" to attack fascism and to present visions of a Marxist utopia that the postwar era presumably would enjoy.[41]

Although surviving Loyalist leaders remained dispersed throughout Europe and the Americas during World War II, and continued to be politically divided, those living in Mexico put ideological differences and personal antagonisms aside and formed Spanish Republican Action, an organization that spoke officially for the exile community. One of its chief wartime activities was keeping the issues of Franco's dictatorship and the Falangist threat to the Americas before the Allied powers. These same people later formed the Spanish Liberation Committee in an effort to get the victorious United Nations to move against Nationalist Spain. Armed with assurances from President Avila Camacho that at the United Nations Organization meeting in 1945 Mexico would speak for them in demanding exclusion of Franquista Spain, representatives of the Committee went to San Francisco. Once again Spanish Loyalists discovered that the Mexican secretary of foreign relations viewed their cause less enthusiastically than the president. Ezequiel Padilla (who had replaced General Hay) did not even intend to introduce a resolution on Spain, allegedly from fear that it would be defeated and thus embarrass Mexico. Only after heated confrontations with the Republicans, who threatened to telephone Avila Camacho, did Padilla reluctantly permit Mexico's delegation to call for exclusion of Spain from the United Nations on grounds that Franco had been imposed on the country by the Axis powers.[42]

Luis Quintanilla introduced the Mexican resolution. He told the UN delegates that by excluding Nationalist Spain they could decisively affirm nonintervention. Mexico and other small nations, he said, considered the principle "so essential to preservation of a decent world order that we believe even one exception to it at this time would gravely jeopardize the entire structure of collective security and of international law." Quintanilla also urged the UN to remember its moral obligation to the Republicans:

> Spain was one of the first victims of international fascism. Hundreds of thousands of heroes who struggled and fought there for the cause of democracy were, in reality, the first allies of the United Nations. Millions of surviving Spaniards have the right to share our victory, for it is their victory, too.[43]

After various seconding speeches (three of them made by representatives from Uruguay, Guatemala, and Chile, countries where political turnabouts had brought anti-Franco governments to power), the UN adopted Mexico's proposal by acclamation.[44] Despite additional Mexican efforts from 1946 to 1950 to prompt more effective sanctions against Franco, the UN lost interest in the issue, no doubt largely due to the Cold War and to fears of Soviet expansionism. Over Mexican objections, the UN even admitted Spain to UNESCO in 1952.[45]

In August 1945 the last obstacles to restoration of a Republican government-in-exile disappeared: Juan Negrín and Julio Álvarez del Vayo journeyed to Mexico City where they negotiated an accord with other Spanish exile leaders. The Loyalists then reconstituted the Spanish Cortes in the Mexican capital and formed an administration headed by President Diego Martínez Barrio and Prime Minister José Giral. When Avila Camacho recognized this "government," the Portuguese vacated the old Spanish embassy building that they had been holding for Franco and the Republicans moved back in. The Mexican president also returned to the Spaniards several million pesos that had been held in trust for them since 1939.[46] Spanish Republicans and their government-in-exile continued, however, to be as badly divided ideologically in Mexico as they had been during the Civil War. Spanish Communists, for example, remained militant and kept their ties with the Central Committee of the Spanish Communist Party in Europe. For their part, many non-Communist leftists still hated the Spanish Communists and shunned them.[47]

In contrast to their important cultural and economic influence the Spanish exiles had virtually no political impact on Mexican life. The largely ceremonial activities of Republican politicians provided at best regular opportunities for the Mexican government to reinforce a growing national myth about "democratic Mexico" helping "democratic Spain" (the legendary Republic) during the Civil War. As years passed, however, the rest of the world largely forgot about the Republicans and made its peace with Franco's Spain. Millions of European and North American tourists came to view Spain as an extraordinarily delightful place. Even Ernest Hemingway went back. What the Republican government-in-exile did or said became increasingly irrelevant. Mexican administrations treated internal exile politics as "cafe talk," which indeed it almost invariably was. Spain remained the country and people ruled by General Franco, and Mexico had certain specific business with the peninsula that had to be transacted: some trade existed; Spaniards and Mexicans traveled to each other's countries; airline service directly linked Mexico City to Madrid; and the two nations maintained postal, cable, and telephone connections. To deal with these and other matters the Mexican government in the 1950s authorized the opening of an Office of Spain, a thinly disguised Franquista embassy in Mexico City run by career diplomat Justo Bermejo.[48]

The Legendary Republic

During the post-Civil War decades, Mexicans continued to be interested in peninsular phenomena, but oftentimes it was limited to ephemeral contacts and was vastly overshadowed by things North American. Spanish entertainers and bullfighters came to Mexico in the 1960s, generated much excitement, and received cheers or jeers depending on the tastes and prejudices of Mexican audiences. But the diplomatic rift between their two countries kept Spaniards and Mexicans rather distant from and generally ignorant about each other.[49] By the late 1960s this remoteness contrasted sharply with the intimate knowledge that most urban and even many rural Mexicans had about life in the USA and with the massive volume of North American tourist traffic to its southern neighbor. Such a situation facilitated Mexico's ever-increasing cultural gravitation toward the United States. To take Mexican television fare as an example, by the late 1970s U.S. sports programs alone far outnumbered programs of all types emanating from Spain. (In addition to Saturday afternoon baseball and college football, Sunday NFL football, and Monday Night Football, covered by several channels, one Mexico City TV station specialized in showing all games played by the Dallas Cowboys.)

Despite these changes, the national myth about Mexico and Spain during the Civil War, a myth that is based on a largely fictional or legendary version of the Republic, and which dates from the 1930s, continues to play a central role in Mexican life. The myth of a legendary Spanish Republic, which had been defended by Mexico in the name of democracy and international justice, has considerable importance for the Mexican people's growing self-esteem and national pride, but it has perhaps even more significance as a feature of the myth of the Mexican Revolution itself. Briefly stated, this latter myth depicts the Revolution as having achieved such objectives as political democracy, social and economic reforms designed to benefit and to protect the lower classes, and national economic independence.

The Revolutionary party continues today, as it did in the 1930s, to claim legitimacy and to justify its control of the nation on the basis of these arguments. By stressing the historic solidarity of Mexico with the Spanish Republicans, Mexican leaders lend an appearance of reality to what they say is an outstanding record of social and political progress. Regular references by these leaders to Mexico's support for the Spanish Republic, portrayed by them as an innocent victim of foreign aggression, also bolster the Revolutionary party's carefully cultivated image of itself as an organization with an unbroken record of commitment to vigorous anti-imperialism in the political and economic spheres. This image reinforcement is especially important considering the Mexican nation's extensive economic ties to the United States, a country perceived by many observers as exercising undue influence, if not virtual control, over the Mexican economy. In short, the Civil War myth has more than mere symbolic importance in Mexico today. It is a political necessity for the ruling party, and it remains crucial to the party's reputation both at home and abroad.

The roots of the legendary Republic phenomenon, of course, go back to the Civil War itself and to the early 1940s, a propitious time for self-serving Mexican versions of the Spanish story as democracy battled fascism during World War II. Several post-mortems on Spain in the spring of 1939 by young writers associated with *Taller* established the tone for decades of myth-making in

artistic and literary circles about the meaning of the Republic's rise
and fall. PCM member José Revueltas claimed that "history" had
picked the Spaniards to serve as oracles of an imminent worldwide
conflict between freedom-loving "people" and the evil "forces" of
fascism. In their struggle, the Loyalists had constituted the "voice
of man" uttering a message of monumental importance. The
Western democracies had been too stupid or criminally negligent
to listen, yet the battle would continue; and the world would
witness "a transformation without precedent" after the fight had
been won.[50] For José Alvarado the Republicans had stood for
preservation of the nation rather than any partisan cause; thus one
of the peninsula's greatest patriots had been the late poet Antonio
Machado, whose wretched, lonely death in a French village at the
end of the war had been an unpardonable outrage. Machado
himself had been too old to fight, but he had put all of his art and
emotion "at the service of Spain's defense," and in doing this
inspired many young Spanish poets to go into battle in his name.[51]
Efraín Huerta called literary critic José Bergamín "an authentic
Spaniard" whose loyalty to the Republic had made of him "a
distinguished champion of liberty and democracy."[52]

The Mexican government was understandably quick to reinforce
an interpretation of Mexican support for Spain that presented it as
a steadfast defense of democratic principles. One of its most curious
efforts came when Foreign Relations brought out in 1940 a
collection of speeches by Eduardo Hay. As has been noted,
Secretary Hay never showed much feeling for the Spanish Republic. In the published volume, his remarks made only passing
references to Spain; he discussed in neutral terms that country's
tragedy and never once defended the Republicans. Yet the
government editors titled his Pan American Day address of April
14, 1937 (which did not deal with Spain) "The Spanish War:
Prologue to the War in Europe." Evidently Secretary Hay despite
himself was going to be made into a witness of the rectitude and
prophetic vision of the Revolutionary regime in supporting so
faithfully the Loyalist cause.[53]

Isidro Fabela, who had played a major role in elaborating
Mexico's official line on Spain, emphatically restated the thesis in
subsequent decades. As a widely respected figure, his pronounce-
ments carried considerable weight and always had the stamp of
genuinely Revolutionary dicta. Like young Efraín Huerta in 1939,

Fabela in the 1940s and 1950s characterized the Republicans as representing authentic Spain. Azaña's Popular Front regime in 1936 had been "democratic," and it had been supported by "the real Spanish people." The Loyalists had fought for "liberty" and for "legality." Their defeat had left the nation "trampled under foot by foreign hosts." Azaña himself had been a great patriot, a romantic yet noble idealist; he represented "the modern, comprehensive Spaniard who fought for . . . a Spain internally free and independent abroad."[54]

A counterpart to the adoration of the Republic was the denial of the Spanishness and even the humanity of General Franco and his supporters. Some Mexican accounts of the conflict give the impression that automated machinery rather than people carried out the Nationalist uprising. Republicans had dubbed their opponents "the anti-Spain." Pro-Loyalist Mexicans adopted this term and were still using it pejoratively against Franco's dictatorship in the 1970s. Concentration on the idealistic principles of Azaña and other Spanish liberals when writing or speaking about the Republic has been another common ploy in sustaining the myth. Such a tactic leaves unmentioned irresponsible left-wing violence and extremism during the Republican years, and it avoids the whole question of the extent to which, if at all, Spanish liberals ever actually governed the country or exercised control over the radicals who were nominally on their side.

During the 1950s and 1960s depiction of Mexico's civil war role as the mutual struggle of two democratic governments for justice and liberty became an entrenched national fantasy. The myth also took root in North American academic and political circles where liberals in the 1940s and 1950s persisted in characterizing the Spanish Republican and Mexican PNR/PRM governments as "democratic" regimes.[55] In 1954 Roberto Vega González, who had been a young Mexican volunteer in Spain, published his story and reflected on the war. Like so many of his countrymen, Vega recalled a pristine Republic unsullied by political vice. The Popular Front innocents had been cruelly victimized by heartless generals and Falangists in league with Mussolini and Hitler "to slaughter the Spanish people" and annihilate their democratic principles. Loyalists had waged an unsuccessful battle against the "enemies of democracy."[56] Two major Mexican writers also gave impetus to the myth in the 1950s: Andrés Iduarte and Octavio Paz restated, with the prestige that their endorsement ensured, certain of its premises. Commenting on Mexico's perennial identity problem, they linked their country and its culture to "the other Spain," that is to the liberal side of peninsular life that they saw manifested in the Republic. Iduarte, who was in Spain when the war started, praised the "Spanish spirit" that fought in 1936 "against the same feudal, clerical, and military privileges which were fought against in 1810 by the founders of the Spanish American republics."[57] Paz claimed to have made an identical perception. Mexicans were "part of the universal tradition of Spain, the only one that Spanish Americans can accept and carry on." But that tradition linked Mexico to the liberating ideals represented by the Republic and not to the repressive negations of General Franco. In his famous *Labyrinth of Solitude* (1959) he wrote: "There are two Spains: the Spain that is closed to the outside world, and the open, heterodox Spain that breaks out of its prison to breathe the free air of the spirit. Ours is the latter."[58]

In the 1960s the gap between fact and fiction in regard to the Spanish Republic and Mexico's role in supporting it grew wider. For his 1962 thesis in international relations at the National University, Omar Martínez Legorreta wrote *Actuación de México en la Liga de la Naciones (Mexico's Record in the League of Nations)*. This Disneyesque fable portrayed the Republic as a political Cinderella abused from the start by wicked relatives: professional soldiers, monarchists, and Falangists. Martínez erroneously claimed that in the 1931 elections the monarchists had suffered defeat "in almost all the voting places" and that "almost all" of Spain's military officers had been immediately disloyal. He made no mention of anticlericalism or of Spain's radical left, and in fact gave the impression of a Republic without faults or weaknesses. To explain the outbreak of the Civil War, therefore, Martínez had to invoke a plot whose only apparent motivation was the conspirators' evil nature. He included Mussolini in the cabal as early as 1931, "the Spanish officers seeing in [Italy's] fascist system the full realization of their most cherished dreams." Mexico's Spanish policy had been totally altruistic. Cárdenas had helped the Republic in 1936 because of his devotion to the principles of the League of Nations and international law. No ulterior motives were involved. "In its Spanish policy, Mexico was not defending any private economic or political interest; the interest it defended was the pure cause of Legality."[59]

Although one might be tempted to dismiss Martínez as willfully obtuse and hence not representative of the Mexican mind, it is clear that for most members of his generation myth had indeed become reality. Young José Emilio Pacheco, for example, would appear to have little in common with Martínez but age. He admitted to a strong liking for the writings of Salvador Novo, a moderate journalist who had been sarcastically hostile to Cárdenas and often cruelly satirical about Republican Spain. Yet in Pacheco's foreword to a 1964 collection of Novo's old newspaper columns, he presented a version of the Spanish war that would have stunned Novo had he still been alive to read it: "The [Spanish] generals aided by Hitler and Mussolini rose up in arms against the defenseless . . . Republic while the whole world indifferently contemplated the tragic struggle of a people against its army." President Cárdenas, however, by helping the Loyalists and through his overall foreign policy "maintained Mexican dignity."[60]

By the 1960s it was clear that Mexicans in general had come to see the Spanish experience in terms of national greatness. The country had acted selflessly to champion a just cause. Committed to liberty at home and abroad, the Mexican nation had helped Spaniards fight for their freedom while other countries, from stupidity or cowardice, did nothing. The Revolutionary Party had given Mexico one of its finest historical moments. There would never be recognition of the odious Franco regime, for justice demanded continued relations with the legal Spanish government-in-exile—which the Mexicans maintained rather meagerly in the dilapidated old building on Londres Street. Eventually many moderates and conservatives began to echo official thought, an increasingly easier thing to do as the Revolutionary Party itself moved to the right and as Franquism became more obviously anachronistic in the contemporary world. The myth not only survived the test of time, it grew ever stronger as years passed.

The Myth in the 1970s

With few exceptions, ideological lines on the question of Spain and Mexico became even more blurred in the 1970s than they had been in the previous decades. Contributors to such allegedly innovative journals as *Nueva Política* were uttering the same clichés about the Civil War as old leftists who had played a role in implementing Cárdenas's Spanish policy. Joining them in similar rhetorical exercises were the moderate columnists and editorialists on *Excelsior*, for years a leading source of journalistic opposition to Mexico's official party and one of the Spanish Republic's principal Mexican antagonists throughout the 1930s. In 1973, for example, Gilberto Bosques lectured to a Mexico City gathering on "Cárdenas and the Spanish Republic." Bosques had been a Mexican consul in Europe during the years of Republican emigration to Mexico. He said that for Mexican leftists the Spanish theme had never lost its relevance. Spain's experience had taught them that "legitimate, just causes," based on such principles as "freedom and the rights of man" must be defended. Mexican presidents subsequent to Cárdenas had maintained a "foreign policy of principle." Thus Mexico had continued to defend just causes throughout the world; and on such issues as the Cuban Revolution, admission of China to the United Nations, and the 1973 military revolt in Chile, the nation's diplomatic stand had been correct. Mexico believed in what Cárdenas had called the necessary "evolution of Law into a sense of justice for nations." Its people still hoped to see high ethical standards adopted everywhere as the basis for all international relations; and they agreed with the late president who had aided the Loyalists that "it is always the right time to work for a future where the association of nations morally linked together by justice will be possible."[61] During his talk, Bosques had used the old Civil War image of Franquism as "the anti-Spain." Writing on "Spanish Fascism as Seen from Mexico" in a 1976 issue of *Nueva Política*, Emilio Uranga also resurrected this concept when he denied Spanishness and humanity to the Nationalists. Interpretation of the Civil War presented no moral complexities to Uranga. Since it had pitted the "antihuman and antisocial" doctrines of fascism against "the Spanish people," justice had obviously been on on the latter's side.[62]

Franco died in November 1975. After an initial period of uncertainty and struggle for power, King Juan Carlos and Prime Minister Adolfo Suárez moved to dismantle oppressive institutions created by the dictator. Spain moved warily toward political freedom, and by early 1977 Spaniards were experimenting with representative government. Mexican politicians reacted by rejoicing at what they termed Spain's return to democracy. At long last justice had triumphed, and Mexican diplomacy had been vindicated. As the Spanish process developed in 1975–76, the Revolutionary Party added another flight of fancy to the old Civil War myth. Official commentary on Spanish events included depiction of democratic Mexico leading a fascistic, imperialistic world toward discovery of an international order where human rights and dignity would be respected, and weak nations no longer fell prey to the strong. President Luis Echeverría (1970–1976) made this idea one of his favorite oratorical themes. All of these notions characterized the words and deeds of Mexican leaders from 1975 to 1977 as they first attacked moribund Franco, then proceeded toward reunion with Spain after the caudillo's death.[63]

One of General Franco's last acts had been to order the execution of five antigovernment terrorists in September 1975. Following these executions, President Echeverría on September 28, 1975, sent to the United Nations a note in which he urged all member countries to suspend diplomatic and economic relations with Spain, thus isolating the Franquista regime as a "threat to world peace," as provided by Article 41 of the UN charter. Echeverría himself had already terminated Mexico's few commercial ties with the peninsula. Some unfriendly observers promptly pointed out that the Mexican note came from the man who seven years earlier as Minister of Government had been partially if not chiefly responsible for the October 1968 "Tlatelolco massacre," which had resulted in about four hundred young political dissidents being shot to death by the army as they peacefully assembled in Mexico City. Although the United Nations took no action against the Spanish government, Echeverría used his public appearances in Mexico as occasions to repeat his demands for isolation of Franco; and when he visited the UN in New York in October, he tried once again to get sanctions against Spain.[64]

The day after dispatching his note, Echeverría spoke in the capital to an audience of Spanish Loyalists from the Centro Republicano Español. He denounced the executions of five "heroes of liberty" by a regime that on the eve of its disappearance still did not understand the Spanish people and had to suppress them by such extreme measures. He alleged that current UN policy toward Franco resembled that of the League of Nations toward the Spanish Civil War forty years earlier. Making references to Chamberlain and appeasement, the Mexican president strongly implied the existence in 1975 of a real fascist threat to world peace and to the "liberties" of people living in Mexico and other "democratic" countries. This was why he wanted Article 41 invoked and why Mexico would continue to raise the Spanish question now as it had done before. According to Echeverría, the Spanish war had originated in a "nazi-fascist plot"; it had been an element in the Axis's general strategy for worldwide aggression. This was another reason why Mexico would never recognize Franco's government. "At the same time that nazi-fascism was destroying the Spanish Republic, it was attacking Mexico, too; in Mexico City and in many of our states, as in other Latin American countries, nazi-fascist groups were formed to undermine democratic, republican governments. . . ." Although it would never establish relations with a regime imposed by fascism, Mexico would recognize the Spanish government that followed Franco, even if it was less than fully democratic. This would be done to make use of the opportunity to foster peaceful change in Spain and thus lessen the chance of another civil war there. The friendship of other nations toward a new Spanish administration would be crucially important for the evolution of a true democratic process in Spain.[65]

On October 22 Echeverría again addressed members of the Centro and repeated his call for international sanctions against Franco. He said that the Spanish Republic had represented "an effort to overcome many centuries of undemocratic tradition, equal to the struggles launched by all the young democracies, struggles that are going on now throughout the world, in Latin America, in Mexico." The international conspiracy against the Spanish Republic in the 1930s was today paralleled by the current international conspiracy against Third World countries. Unfortunately, even the socialist powers refused to support his position on Spain, an attitude on their part that had serious implications for Mexico, the Third World, and peace. They, too, were selfishly playing politics at the expense of semideveloped countries like Mexico and Spain. Echeverría took a position similar to Cárdenas in the 1930s when he warned that if the great powers drew back from what obviously needed to be done concerning Franco, then "the errors that have caused international arguments, that have led to war, to interventions, and to the sacrifice of small and weak nations will continue." He then gathered into his arms the flags of Mexico and the Republic, theatrically telling his Spanish audience: "I will return the flags to you one day soon in Madrid."[66]

At this time José López Portillo, presidential candidate of the

Institutional Revolutionary Party (PRM had become PRI), was already campaigning for an uncontested election in 1976. He echoed Echeverría's sentiments about the Franco government and seconded the president's pledge to recognize any nondictatorial administration that succeeded it. In October 1975 he observed that: "We profoundly lament that [Spain] . . . has been unable to free itself from fascism and its infamous garrot. This is painful for us. But we know that the Spanish people will once again recover their dignity and pride from the dark forces [that oppress them]. At that moment, Mexico will be present."[67] Shortly after Franco's death in November, López Portillo indicated to an audience of Spanish Republicans under what circumstances Mexico would resume relations with Spain.[68] He began by recalling that as a pro-Cárdenas youth the first thing that had stirred his political conscience was "the drama of Spain; the Civil War, the nullification of liberty and democracy." Later he had belonged to a student generation "in large measure formed by remarkable Spanish teachers voluntarily exiled in Mexico," a generation that had "learned to love Spain by means of its best men: the intellectuals who came here to accompany us in our own achievements."

López Portillo noted that no doubt existed that the Spanish people loved both liberty and democracy, because they had made so many contributions to Western democracy and culture. Inexplicably, however, neither virtue had flourished in the country that had produced so many precursors of such great causes as freedom, equality, and human dignity. López Portillo assured the old Loyalists that "this causes me as much pain as it undoubtedly causes you, because my background and my career have given me the same values that sustain you in a life that is only worth living in liberty." PRI's candidate went on to relate the forty-year ostracism of Franco to Mexico's general foreign policy, which he said was based on an unshakeable determination to bring democracy to "the savage international world in which we are living." Mexico would continually work for the establishment of a world order based on respect for human rights and other Western democratic values. It would end the long struggle it had waged in concert with "the Spanish people" against Franco only when "there is full compliance with the values that historically explain it." Absence of relations with Spain for so long had been "a great and painful price" for Mexico to pay for remaining faithful to its principles, yet

Mexican affection for the Spaniards had been an important factor in maintaining the separation. López Portillo told of an aged Republican in 1939 who when asked, "Why are you going into exile?" had answered: "To die with dignity." He then added: "If aged men came here to die with dignity, we have to desire that our two peoples live together with dignity." That could only happen when "Spanish democracy and Mexican democracy are newly joined together by the coexistence of principles that they have shared for centuries." Out of loyalty to the Spanish people, Mexico could only normalize relations with the peninsula "when the Spaniards who fled persecuted from Spain can say: 'We are returning to Spain with dignity!' "[69]

Many of the Loyalists present, however, thought that such a dignified return could only be made to a "republican" Spain. (The Bourbon monarchy had been restored.) Speaking for them, Francisco Varea Rodríguez, president of the Centro Republicano, issued a warning: the antidemocratic, internal enemies of Mexico and Spain were now seeking foreign help, just as they had done in the 1930s. Then the assistance had come from totalitarian dictators; "today those same enemies solicit aid from the multinational corporations, which are always willing to protect their markets by helping anyone who will guarantee their interests. . . ." Democracy in Spain would threaten these foreign beneficiaries of the Franquista system that had turned the country into a colony, "an interminable series of Gibralters." For that reason the multinationals conspired against democracy. Varea doubted that the present post-Franco political arrangement could ever bring liberty to the people since it had been cynically prepared as a method of continuing Franquism. He urged López Portillo to reject the monarchy as unacceptable and to postpone Mexico's reconciliation with Spain until it had returned to a republican form of government.[70] His request went unheeded.

Early in 1977, after Spain had moved shakily but inexorably toward representative government under the aegis of a king, Mexico resumed diplomatic relations with the *madre patria*. President López Portillo then visited Spain in October, the first such trip by a Mexican chief of state. PRI spokesman Guillermo Cosío Vidaurri explained to the press that the president's journey "represented an opportunity to establish propitious conditions that would permit the Mexican and Spanish economies to complement each other in the task of advancing democracy through social justice." *El Nacional* emphasized the president's desire to obtain results economically favorable for the country. More than a routine visit, his trip was part of Mexico's general plan of development, and "during his stay various commercial agreements will be negotiated that along with many other benefits will enable [this country] to balance its trade with the peninsula. . . ."[71] Spanish capitalists made it obvious that they looked eagerly to Mexico as a promising recipient of their investments. Andrés Ribera Rovira, president of Barcelona's Chamber of Commerce, told a Mexican journalist that Chamber members had studied Mexico and regarded it as the best foreign country in which to invest. Ribera said that Catalan businessmen desired a greater volume of trade with Mexico, and he pictured each country as helping the other commercially: Mexico could be "the door" through which Spanish trade passed to Latin America, just as Spain could serve as "a bridge" for Mexican trade with Europe. López Portillo told the Catalans that his country would welcome their capital, although he emphasized the need for "responsible investment" in developing nations such as Mexico. Speaking to the Chamber of Commerce in Barcelona, he said: "We wish to benefit from your industrial expertise and your genius for organization, and place at your disposal Mexican resources for their development."[72]

The Mexican president received many courtesies in official circles during his stay in Spain. King Juan Carlos bestowed on him the Order of Isabella the Catholic, the highest honor accorded to foreigners. Seville's municipal government named him an "adopted son." The people of Caparroso, Navarre, home town of one of the president's ancestors, welcomed him as honorary alcalde. The Spanish Cortes invited him to speak.[73] A Mexican newspaper, however, observed that López Portillo's presence "was passing unnoticed by the Spanish public" and that various functions and receptions associated with his trip attracted few guests. There did seem to be more popular interest in such ancillary events as a Mexican book fair, the "Mexico 77" industrial exhibit, the Ballet Folklórico de México, a display of Mexican paintings, and concerts of Mexican music.[74]

Leaders of Spain's left-wing opposition, many of them recently returned from decades of exile, warmly welcomed López Portillo and praised "Mexican democracy," but most Spanish leftists saved their greatest tributes for Lázaro Cárdenas. Even Communist octogenarian Dolores Ibarruri, who had turned furiously on Mexico over the Trotsky issue, praised the late president. López Portillo publicly returned these compliments. Following a speech to the Spanish Cortes, for example, he vigorously applauded *La Pasionaria* and blew her kisses with his fingers in what he evidently intended to be another manifestation of Mexico's long-standing devotion to peninsular democracy as well as an indication of his esteem for the old woman. That a conservative Mexican president would risk offending his equally conservative hosts by such a demagogic gesture cannot be related exclusively to his need to placate left-wing opinion at home. His behavior in the Cortes also reinforces one's impression that the Civil War myth continues to play a major role in sustaining PRI's self-image as a popularly approved, hence legitimate, political regime.[75]

Much of the rhetoric of the Mexico-Spain rapproachement struck a strongly Hispanist note. Writers and political leaders called attention to the "common destinies" of Mexico and Spain and placed special emphasis on hispanidad as a basis for lasting union between the peninsula, Mexico, and all Spanish-speaking countries. Yet López Portillo, shortly before going to Spain, observed that "economic imperialism" still constituted an insuperable obstacle to unity among the American republics.[76] The Spanish king himself used the occasion of "Day of Hispanidad" ceremonies, over which he and the Mexican leader jointly presided on October 12, to lament the "poverty, ignorance, and emigration" that was eroding the sense of identity of so many Spanish-speaking people.[77]

In Mexican government circles, the degree of Hispanism manifested in 1977 was unprecedented. Predictably in a country where Spaniards and the Spanish record have always been controversial subjects, journalistic reaction to this phenomenon ranged from approbation to derision, and some critics even questioned PRI's optimism about Mexico's new relationship with Spain. Hispanist Iñigo Laviada found it encouraging that so many administration members, "who until recently denied their Iberian blood," now admitted not only that they had Spanish parents but also that they were full-fledged Hispanophiles. Planeloads of these bureaucrats had accompanied the president on his journey, and Laviada thought that the "returns" to Mexico were worth all the public money it took to pay their expenses. Were he there with them, "I would be convinced that Spain, Hispanism, and the reconciliation merit these expenses . . . and that López Portillo and the . . . Mexicans accompanying him have taken an important step toward the rediscovery of our identity."[78] Fellow journalist Antolín Martínez, however, laughed at the way each bureaucrat suddenly sought to appear more Spanish than any of his colleagues. Their Hispanism, he predicted, would expire with López Portillo's term of office, for each Mexican president seemed to spark a particular fad that died as abruptly as it had been born. Martínez recalled that the same individuals who had been "frantic socialists" under Cárdenas spent the six years of Avila Camacho's presidency as "fervid believers" [Catholics]. Observing that in Madrid López Portillo had proudly pointed out those members of his cabinet who had Spanish parents, Martínez suggested that other cabinet officials were now "ready to swear that their father is also a *gachupín,* even at the risk of being eliminated as possible presidential candidates."[79] Pedro Gringoire, veteran of half a century of political journalism, also had reservations about the euphoria accompanying Mexico's reunion with the *madre patria.* He wondered how anyone could take completely seriously the government's present "honeymoon" with monarchical Spain when the PRI had plunged into so many contradictory love affairs in the recent past—with Castro's Cuba, Allende's Chile, Mao's China, and even "with the Arab band led by Yaser Arafat."[80]

López Portillo's visit to Spain naturally prompted much press comment on the Spanish Civil War and its significance for the nation. By this time, however, the noble heroism of the democratic Republicans and the propriety and courage of Mexican policy had the status of truisms among most journalists. Even *Excelsior* took positions indistinguishable from those of *El Nacional.* In the former paper, both an anonymous editorial writer and columnist Jorge Calvimontes recalled the "necessity" of Mexico's long alienation from Spain due to "the triumph of Franquism." Cavimontes added that all Mexican governments had spurned Franco after 1939 because they refused to legitimize with diplomatic recognition his "spoliation of democracy." It had been "morally essential" for Mexicans to await the demise of Franco's "unjust regime of repression" before re-establishing relations with Spain. Mexico's present role in the peninsula was to provide external approval and hence moral stimulation for the "new democracy and liberty of the nation of García Lorca and [Antonio] Machado."[81]

Perhaps the best journalistic analysis of the Mexico-Spain question came from Iñigo Laviada on the eve of the presidential trip.[82] Not a subscriber to official mythology, Laviada remained intellectually free to consider historical developments with detachment; he thus stood in sharp contrast to most of his colleagues, who wrote articles indistinguishable from PRI public relations handouts. Laviada observed that since 1939 Mexico and Spain had continued modernization using the same model: capitalistic economic development directed by an authoritarian government. Despite differences in political rhetoric, paternalism marked both processes and had been greater in "revolutionary" Mexico than in "dictatorial" Spain. Paradoxically, this coincidental development was initiated in Spain by a ruler associated with the traditional agrarian social structure and in Mexico by a bureaucratic regime said to be heir to a victorious peasant revolution. Evaluating results, Laviada concluded that although both the Franco and PRI regimes failed to keep their promises of developmental benefits to rural areas (hence mass exodus from the countryside to cities and to neighboring countries), the Spanish government had achieved more than PRI in trying to solve this problem. By the 1970s rural Spain had moved well ahead of rural Mexico in agricultural productivity, living standards, general modernization and prosperity, order, and security. The Mexican countryside continued to be a violent, insecure place, and, far from showing the signs of progress evident in Spain, most Mexican villages remained "exactly as they were a century ago."

Laviada found Mexico and Spain similar in regard to the political aspects of their development. The modernizing, pragmatic governments of both countries were "linked to the bourgeoisie, but interested in the social and economic advancement of the neediest people." Despite Franco's right-wing rhetoric, "Spain's social circumstances led the Spanish regime to formulas not very different from the Mexican ones." The Mexican political system permitted greater popular involvement in decision-making, but Mexican presidents received far more adulation than did Franco. The Spanish general had presided over a "mild dictatorship," and the peninsular state consistently wielded less power than its

Mexican counterpart. Despite the absence of popular participation in government, Franco's Spain had much more freedom than did East European or most Latin American countries. Without the least trace of democracy, Spaniards had an "acceptable degree of liberty." Laviada also saw parallels between Mexico and Spain in their economic evolution since the Civil War. In both countries wealth had greatly increased; yet in both of them "the price paid for this had been an excessive increase in foreign investment and in technological dependence, as well as a process of transculturation through introduction of foreign ideas and customs, and through appearance of the consumer society in large cities." Fortunately, resumption of diplomatic relations would draw Mexico and Spain closer together by means of "a growing volume of cultural, technological, commercial, financial, and tourist exchanges." President López Portillo's "Hispanic figure" and his love for Spain, moreover, boded well for concord and cooperation between the two countries.

Laviada's final opinions notwithstanding, PRI's 1977 decision to go along with Spain (for the record at least) and back a revival of Hispanism in Mexico that could be used for defensive purposes against North American "imperialism" and U.S. cultural influence seemed destined to fail. Mexicans did not appear to be finding their "lost identity" by embracing their Spanish roots. Just the opposite, in fact, was happening: day by day the country and its people came under increasing United States influence. In the peninsula, moreover, Spaniards (despite what they told Mexicans and other Latin Americans) showed much more interest in union with their European neighbors than with their former colonies in the western hemisphere. Still, the Mexicans would always have their special relationship with Republican Spain in the 1930s. It had contributed importantly to their self-esteem and to a rediscovery of "the other Spain" that many of them had forgotten. Through their Civil War role Mexicans obtained another national myth to justify their Revolution and their government; and they could relish their country's admirable diplomatic stand at a time when ignoble cowardice and appeasement were the prevailing norms. Especially in regard to their rescue of the Loyalist refugees stranded in France, Mexicans can forever point with pride to what they did when the rest of the world remained indifferent to human suffering. In reality Mexico's defense of the often-exasperating Spanish

Republic cast little glory on the country, but it has come to have great importance today. Legendary versions of that story, now accepted as dogma by an overwhelming majority of the people, contribute to a growing national pride for which Mexicans have long and painfully searched.

Notes

Chapter 1

1. Richard A. Sinkin, "Modernization and Reform in Mexico, 1855-1876" (Ph.D. diss., University of Michigan, 1972); T. G. Powell, *El liberalismo y el campesinado en el centro de México (1850 a 1876)* (México, 1974); Friedrich Katz, "Labor Conditions on Haciendas in Porfirian Mexico: Some Trends and Tendencies," *Hispanic American Historical Review* (hereafter *HAHR*) 54 no. 1 (1974): 1–47; Jan Bazant, *Cinco haciendas mexicanas* (México, 1976).

2. Rodney D. Anderson, *Outcasts in Their Own Land: Mexican Industrial Workers, 1906–1911* (Dekalb, 1976); John M. Hart, *Los anarquistas mexicanos, 1860–1900* (México, 1974).

3. Fernando Rosenzweig *et al.*, *Historia moderna de México. El Porfiriato: La vida económica,* 2 vols. (México, 1965); Charles C. Cumberland, *Mexican Revolution: Gensis Under Madero* (Austin, 1952); Stanley R. Ross, *Francisco I. Madero, Apostle of Mexican Democracy* (New York, 1955).

4. Robert E. Quirk, *The Mexican Revolution and the Catholic Church, 1910–1929* (Bloomington, 1973).

5. Charles C. Cumberland, *Mexican Revolution: The Constitutionalist Years* (Austin, 1972); Michael C. Meyer, *Huerta, a Political Portrait* (Lincoln, 1972); John Womack, Jr., *Zapata and the Mexican Revolution* (New York, 1969); Martin Luis Guzmán, *El águila y la serpiente* (México, 1928).

6. Robert E. Quirk, *An Affair of Honor: Woodrow Wilson and the Occupation of Veracruz* (New York, 1962) and *The Mexican Revolution, 1914–1915: The Convention of Aguascalientes* (Bloomington, 1960); Howard F. Cline, *The United States and Mexico,* rev. ed. (Cambridge, Mass., 1963); Kenneth J. Grieb, *The United States and Huerta* (Lincoln, 1969).

7. John W. F. Dulles, *Yesterday in Mexico: A Chronicle of the Revolution, 1919–1936* (Austin, 1961).

8. Fredrick B. Pike, *Spanish America, 1900–1970. Tradition and Social Innovation* (New York, 1973), 46–55.

9. Gabriel Jackson, *The Spanish Republic and the Civil War, 1931–1939* (Princeton, 1965).

10. For discussion of Spanish politics, see Jackson, *Spanish Republic and the Civil War,* passim; also see: Stanley G. Payne, *Falange: A History of Spanish Fascism* (Stanford, 1961) and *The Spanish Revolution* (New York, 1970).

11. Dulles, *Yesterday in Mexico,* passim.

12. James W. Wilkie and Edna Monzón de Wilkie, *México visto en el siglo XX: Entrevistas de historia oral* (México, 1969), 662.

13. Juan-Simeón Vidarte, *Todos fuimos culpables* (México, 1973), 790.

14. Jean A. Meyer, *The Cristero Rebellion: The Mexican People Between Church and State, 1926–1929,* trans. Richard Southern (Cambridge, Eng., 1976); James W. Wilkie, "The Meaning of the Cristero Religious War Against the Mexican Revolution," *Journal of Church and State,* 13 (1966): 214–33.

15. Mark Falcoff, unpublished biography of José Vasconcelos in manuscript. The author thanks Professor Falcoff for making this material available to him.

16. *El Hombre Libre,* June 9, 1931, p. 1; June 11, 1931, p. 2. Unless otherwise noted, all newspapers cited were published in Mexico City.

17. Víctor Alba, *The Mexicans: The Making of a Nation* (New York, 1967), 180; *La Antorcha* 1 no. 7 (1931): 27; ibid., 1 no. 11–12 (1932), 31. The author thanks Professor Mark Falcoff for making microfilm copies of *La Antorcha* available to him.

18. Eugenia Meyer, *Luis Cabrera* (México, 1972), 19, 54–56.

19. Samuel Ramos, *Profile of Man and Culture in Mexico,* trans. Peter G. Earle (New York, 1962), 143.

20. Meyer, *Luis Cabrera,* 155–59.

21. *El Universal,* July 28, 1936, p. 3.

22. Quoted in Salvador Novo, *La vida en México en el periodo presidencial de Lázaro Cárdenas* (México, 1964), 77.

23. Wilkie and Wilkie, *México visto en el siglo XX,* 280; Albert L. Michaels, "Mexican Politics and Nationalism from Calles to Cárdenas" (Ph.D. diss., University of Pennsylvania, 1966), 1–25. The author thanks Professor Michaels for making a copy of this work available to him.

24. Michaels, "Mexican Politics and Nationalism," 27.

25. Ibid., 27–28; Alan M. Kirschner, *Tomás Garrido Canabal y el movimiento de las camisas rojas* (México, 1976), 7–50; Graham Greene, *The Lawless Roads* (London, 1950).

26. Dulles, *Yesterday in Mexico,* 529–30; Michaels, "Mexican Politics and Nationalism," 148–49.

27. *La Antorcha* 1 no. 7 (1931): 29–30.

28. Quirk, *Mexican Revolution and the Catholic Church,* 120–26, 165.

29. *Revista eclesiástica de la diócesis de Zamora* (hereafter *REDZ*) 4 no. 5 (1937): 104. Words quoted are those of Piux XI, paraphrasing his 1931 encyclical.

30. Ibid., 4 no. 4 (1937): 74.

31. Josefina Vázquez de Knauth, *Nacionalismo y educación en México* (México, 1975), 166.

32. Alberto M. Carreño, ed., *Pastorales, edictos y otros documentos del Excmo. y Rvmo. Sr. Dr. D. Pascual Díaz, Arzobispo de México* (México, 1938), 207–23; Michaels, "Mexican Politics and Nationalism," 111–14.

33. *REDZ* 4 no. 2 (1936): 41–42.

34. Ibid., 4 no. 7 (1936): 175.

35. Octavio Paz, *The Other Mexico: Critique of the Pyramid,* trans. Lysander Kemp (New York, 1972), 120–21; Michaels, "Mexican Politics and Nationalism," 33.

36. Wilkie and Wilkie, *México visto en el siglo XX,* 662; Michaels, "Mexican Politics and Nationalism," 50–52.

37. Interview with Spanish Republican source who wishes to remain anonymous.

38. Dulles, *Yesterday in Mexico,* passim; William C. Townsend, *Lázaro Cárdenas, Mexican Democrat* (Ann Arbor, 1952).

39. Interview, Francesca Linares de Vidarte, in Buffalo, N.Y., April 24, 1978. Hereafter, Linares de Vidarte interview.

40. Cárdenas quoted in Vidarte, *Todos fuimos culpables,* 805.

41. See Jackson, *Spanish Republic and the Civil War,* passim.

42. Radio broadcast to the nation, December 8, 1938, printed in Lázaro Cárdenas, *Ideario político* (México, 1972), 27–28.

43. Kirshner, *Tomás Garrido,* 63–66.

44. Ibid., 66.

45. Dulles, *Yesterday in Mexico,* passim.

46. Kirshner, *Tomás Garrido,* 79–84, 116; Michaels, "Mexican Politics and Nationalism," 60.

47. Kirshner, *Tomás Garrido,* 72, 79–84, 91, 116; Michaels, "Mexican Politics and Nationalism," 60, 151–52.

48. Kirshner, *Tomás Garrido,* 87–90, 112.

49. Ibid.

50. Ibid., 91; *REDZ* 4 no. 2 (1936), 39–40.

51. Kirshner, *Tomás Garrido,* 72; Michaels, "Mexican Politics and Nationalism," 151–52; Quirk, *Mexican Revolution and the Catholic Church,* 90–91; Dulles, *Yesterday in Mexico,* 626–27.

52. Michaels, "Mexican Politics and Nationalism," 153–55, 161–62; Kirshner, *Tomás Garrido,* 92.

53. For biographical information on Bassols see Jesús Silva Herzog, "Introducción," in Narciso Bassols, *Obras* (México, 1964), vii–xxxvii. For a discussion of the Spanish education controversy see Jackson, *Spanish Republic and the Civil War,* 48–51, 62–65.

54. John A. Britton, *Educación y radicalismo en México,* 2 vols. (México, 1976), I: 12–15, 35–37, 40–42.

55. Ibid., 127–36, 154–59; II: 120–21; Michaels, "Mexican Politics and Nationalism," 114–15.

56. *Excelsior,* October 5, 1934, pp. 1, 8; October 6, 1934, p. 3; October 7, 1934, pp. 3–4; October 14, 1934, second section, pp. 1, 5; October 19, 1934, p. 10; October 15, 1934, p. 1; Michaels, "Mexican Politics and Nationalism," 142.

57. *Excelsior,* October 20, 1934, pp. 1, 3–4.

58. Donald L. Herman, *Comintern in Mexico* (New York, 1974), 115–17.

59. *Excelsior,* October 5, 1934, pp. 1, 3; October 7, 1934, p. 10.

60. Ibid., October 6, 1934, pp. 1, 10.

61. Ibid., October 14, 1934, second section, p. 10.

62. Britton, *Educación y radicalismo en México,* II: 22–32.

63. *El Universal,* July 31, 1936, p. 1.

64. Kenneth Prager, "The Mexican Sinarquistas, 1937–1945" (Ph.D. diss., Indiana University, 1975), 2–3, 129.

65. Ibid., 23, 113; Allan Chase, *Falange: The Axis Secret Army in the Americas* (New York, 1943), 168.

66. Prager, "Mexican Sinarquistas," 10–17; Jean Meyer, "Campesinos reaccionarios," *Vuelta* 1 no. 9 (1977): 16–21.

67. Prager, "Mexican Sinarquistas," 21, 164–66, 170; *El Universal,* April 5, 1939, p. 3; Albert L. Michaels, "The Crisis of Cardenismo," *Journal of Latin American Studies* 2 no. 1 (1970): 74; Wilkie and Wilkie, *México visto en el siglo XX,* 179.

68. Prager, "Mexican Sinarquistas," 21–22.

69. Robert P. Millon, *Mexican Marxist: Vicente Lombardo Toledano* (Chapel Hill, 1966); Novo, *La vida en México,* 109–10; Wilkie and Wilkie, *México visto en el siglo XX,* 307; Karl M. Schmitt, *Communism in Mexico: A Study in Political Frustration* (Austin, 1965), 17–18; *Excelsior,* November 2, 1933; pp. 1, 10.

70. Michaels, "Mexican Politics and Nationalism," 245–47.

71. Herman, *Comintern in Mexico,* 118–20; Schmitt, *Communism in Mexico,* 18.

72. Michaels, "Mexican Politics and Nationalism," 203–4.

73. *El Dictamen* (Veracruz), January 7, 1938, p. 1.

74. Miguel A. Velasco, "El partido comunista durante el período de Cárdenas," in Gilberto Bosques *et al.*, *Cárdenas* (México, 1975), 38; *Excelsior,* October 5, 1934, p. 3; Michaels, "Mexican Politics and Nationalism," 275; Schmitt, *Communism in Mexico,* 14–19; Herman, *Comintern in Mexico,* 112–14; Wilkie and Wilkie, *México visto en el siglo XX,* 308, 323, 653–56, 666.

75. Dulles, *Yesterday in Mexico,* 640–46, 659–81; Michaels, "Mexican Politics and Nationalism," 70.

76. Michaels, "Mexican Politics and Nationalism," 73.

77. Ibid., 57, 67, 144–45; Pike, *Spanish America,* 46–52.

78. Novo, *La vida en México,* 115–16.

79. Ibid., 169–76.

80. Paz, *The Other Mexico,* 26.

81. Wilkie and Wilkie, *México visto en el siglo XX,* 319–20.

82. Heather F. Salamini, *Agrarian Radicalism in Veracruz, 1920-1938* (Lincoln, 1978), passim.

83. Michaels, "The Crisis of Cardenismo," passim.

Chapter 2

1. Juan de D. Gojórquez, *La inmigración española de México* (México, 1932), 1–13.

2. Daniel Cosío Villegas, *Memorias* (México, 1976), 144; Lois E. Smith, *Mexico and the Spanish Republicans* (Berkeley, 1955), 175, fn. 37.

3. *Boletín Oficial de la Secretaría de Relaciones Exteriores* (hereafter *BOSRE*) 56 no. 1 (1931), 12–24.

4. Andrés Fernández, "Carta abierta al negro agachupinado Diego Arenas Guzmán," printed flyer, Nov. 25, 1933, Archivo Histórico de la Secretaría de Relaciones Exteriores (hereafter AHSRE), III/243(46)/9, III–231–13.

5. Barbara B. Aponte, *Alfonso Reyes and Spain* (Austin, 1972), 81–85.

6. Bojórquez, *Inmigración española en México,* 6–7.

7. *La Antorcha,* 1 no. 3 (1931): 3–9; Cosío Villegas, *Memorias,* 144; Félix Gordón Ordás, *Mi política fuera de España,* 2 vols. (México, 1965–1967), I: 491.

8. For references to the conservatism and monarchism of Mexico's Spanish colony, see: *El Universal,* April 14, 1931, p. 1; Roberto Núñez y Domínguez, *Como vi la república española (Película impresionista)* (México, 1933), 7–8.

9. Aponte, *Reyes and Spain,* 187–88.

10. *Excelsior,* April 14, 1931, p. 3; ibid., April 15, 1931, p. 3; *El Universal,* July 27, 1936, p. 1; Gordón Ordás, *Mi política,* I: 135–46.

11. Bojórquez, *Inmigración española en México,* 8; Smith, *Mexico and the Spanish Republicans,* 218.

12. José Elguero, *España en los destinos de México* (México, 1929), 9–11.

13. Jesús Guisa y Azevedo, "No hay crítica donde hay decadencia," *Lectura* 1 no. 3 (1937): 193–96.

14. Fernando Robles, "La religión y la hispanidad," ibid., 1 no. 4 (1937): 345–349.

15. *La Antorcha* 1 no. 3 (1931): 3–9.

16. Aponte, *Reyes and Spain,* 193.

17. Alfonso Reyes, *Momentos de España. Memorias políticas, 1920–1923* (México, 1947), 11, 35–36, 60.

18. José Vasconcelos and Miguel Alessio Robles, *México y España,* 2nd ed. (México, 1929). The first edition appeared in 1919.

19. Falcoff, Vasconcelos biography in manuscript, 112–21.

20. Vasconcelos and Alessio, *México y España*, 7–12, 16–23.

21. Ibid., 3–6, 13–17.

22. Abel Paz, *Durruti: The People Armed*, trans. Nancy Macdonald (New York, 1977), 74–76; John M. Hart, *Anarchism and the Mexican Working Class, 1860–1931* (Austin, 1978), 159–83.

23. *Excelsior*, October 9, 1934, p. 5; October 11, 1934, pp. 3, 9; October 12, 1934, p. 5; October 17, 1934, pp. 1, 3.

24. Mary K. Vaughn, *History Textbooks in Mexico in the 1920s* (Buffalo, 1974).

25. Ibid., 37.

26. *Excelsior*, November 14, 1935, p. 5; Emiliano Iglesias to Eduardo Hay, Mexico City, December 3, 1935, AHSRE, III/243(46–72), III–315–13.

27. *Excelsior*, October 12, 1934, p. 5.

28. "La Embajada de España se queja de las calumnias e injurias a españoles por la Agrupación Reintegración Económica Mexicana de Veracruz," 1935; Fernández, "Carta abierta," AHSRE, III/243(46)9, III–231–13.

29. "La obra española en México," flyer, January 1935, ibid.

30. Amador E. Vélez, "Esclavos Hermanos de Indo-America," flyer, June 28, 1935, ibid.

31. Alejandro Gómez Maganda, *España sangra* (Barcelona, n.d.), 44.

32. *BOSRE* 60 no. 1–2 (1933): 73; ibid., 61 no. 8–9 (1933): 7.

33. Payne, *The Spanish Revolution*, 136.

34. *Excelsior*, April 17, 1931, p. 1; Núñez y Domínguez, *Como vi la república española*, 77, 80; *BOSRE* 56 no. 5 (1931): 9.

35. Smith, *Mexico and the Spanish Republicans*, 165–67.

36. *BOSRE* 56 no. 6 (1931): 36; Mexico, Embajada en España, *Relaciones internacionales iberoamericanas. Discursos pronunciados con motivo de la presentación de credenciales del primer embajador de los Estados Unidos Mexicanos ante el gobierno de la República Española* (Madrid, 1931), 11–13.

37. *BOSRE* 60 no. 4 (1933): 16–18.

38. Ibid., 57 no. 11 (1931): 27–32; ibid., 60 no. 5 (1933): 12–13; ibid., 61 no. 8–9 (1833): 40–42.

39. Ibid., 60 no. 6 (1933): 20–23; ibid., 61 no. 7 (1933): 28.

40. Ibid., 61 no. 8–9 (1933): 19; ibid., 61 no. 7 (1933): 26–30.

41. See, for example, Félix F. Palavicini, *México: Historia de su evolución constructiva*, 4 vols. (México, 1945), IV: 256–57.

42. Aponte, *Reyes and Spain*, 188.

43. *Excelsior*, April 20, 1931, pp. 5–6; Linares de Vidarte interview.

44. Núñez y Domínguez, *Como vi la república española*, 81–83.

45. *Excelsior*, November 5, 1933, pp. 1, 9.

46. Ibid.

47. José Vasconcelos, *Que es el comunismo* (México, 1936), 9–23.

48. *Excelsior*, April 14, 1931, pp. 1, 3; ibid., April 17, 1931, pp. 3–4.

49. Ibid., April 16, 1931, pp. 2, 5–6; ibid., April 17, 1931, p. 3; ibid., April 21, 1931, p. 3.

50. Ibid., April 16, 1931, pp. 2–3.

51. Ibid., November 5, 1933, pp. 1, 9.

52. *El Hombre Libre*, May 14, 1931, p. 1.

53. Ibid., April 18, 1931, p. 1.

54. Ibid., April 21, 1931, pp. 1–4.

55. Ibid., April 18, 1931, pp. 1–2.

56. Material from *El Sol* reprinted in Mexico, Embajada en España, *Relaciones internacionales iberoamericanas*. Passages quoted appeared in the paper on July 24 and August 6, 1931.

57. Ibid., 21–22; for a detailed study of Hispanism in the twentieth century, see, Fredrick B. Pike, *Hispanismo, 1898–1936: Spanish Conservatives and Liberals and Their Relations with Latin America* (Notre Dame, 1971).

58. Vasconcelos, *Que es el comunismo*, 18–23; *El Hombre Libre*, June 11, 1931, pp. 1, 4. See also *La Antorcha* 1 no. 1 (1931): 16.

59. Rodolfo Reyes, *Cuatro discursos* (Madrid, 1933), 6–22.

60. *El Hombre Libre*, May 16, 1931, pp. 1, 4.

61. Novo, *La vida en México*, 348; *BOSRE* 61 no. 7 (1933): 28.

62. Núñez y Domínguez, *Como vi la república española*, 58–59.

63. *El Hombre Libre*, June 11, 1931, pp. 1–2.

64. Núñez y Domínguez, *Como vi la república española*, 80.

65. Aponte, *Reyes and Spain*, 73–86.

66. Linares de Vidarte interview.

67. *La Antorcha* 1 no. 3 (1931): 3–9; ibid., 1 no. 8 (1931): 12; ibid., 1 no. 11–12 (1932): 10.

68. Vasconcelos, *Que es el comunismo*, 10–11.

69. Ibid., 32–33, 39–43, 49–54, 95–98.

70. *El Hombre Libre*, May 5, 1931, pp. 1–2.

71. Ibid., June 13, 1931, pp. 1–3.

72. *El Universal*, April 15, 1931, p. 3.

73. *Excelsior*, April 15, 1931, p. 3.

74. Gordón Ordás, *Mi política*, I: 148.

75. *El Diario Español*, August 6, 1936, p. 1.

76. Pedro Serrano, *Política española. España en 1920* (México, 1921).

77. *Excelsior*, April 16, 1931, pp. 5, 10; ibid., September 8, 1932, p. 5.

78. Ibid., April 16, 1931, p. 1; ibid., April 17, 1931, p. 3.

79. Ibid., April 18, 1931, p. 5.

80. Ibid., September 13, 1932, pp. 5–6; September 28, 1932, p. 5; Gordón Ordás, *Mi política*, I: 135–37, 144–46; Mateo Solano y Gutiérrez, *La raíz mística del comunismo, del socialismo, del Catalanismo y el sindicalismo español* (Oaxaca, 1933), 58–81.

81. *Excelsior*, November 24, 1933, pp. 5, 7.

82. Ibid., October 18, 1934, pp. 5, 10.

83. Gordón Ordás, *Mi política*, I: 137–38, 168–69.

84. *El Diario Español*, July 9, 1936, p. 1; ibid., July 13, 1936, pp. 1–2; ibid., July 16, 1936, p. 1.

85. Gordón Ordás, *Mi política*, I: 368–69.

86. José G. Moreno de la Torre to Claudio Sánchez Albornoz, Madrid, November 14, 1933; P. de M. Aguirre y de Cárcer to José G. Moreno de la Torre, Madrid, November 20, 1933; Ambassador of Mexico to Secretary of Foreign Relations, Madrid, November 22, 1933, AHSRE, III/243(72–46)/2, III–125–42.

87. "Informes sobre la cuestión religiosa mexicana en España, 1935,"; Manuel Pérez Treviño to Secretary of Foreign Relations, Madrid, February 17, 1936; Luis Garrido to Secretary of Government, Mexico City, March 16, 1936; Honorary Consul to Chargé d'affaires of Mexico, Málaga, December 22 and 27, 1934, ibid., III/514(46)(04)/1, III–307–31.

88. Palavicini, *México*, IV: 259; "La Embajada de España se queja," AHSRE, III/243(46)/9, III–231–13.

89. Emiliano Iglesias to Eduardo Hay, Mexico City, December 3, 1935, AHSRE, III/243(46–72)/5, III–315–13.

90. *Excelsior*, November 14, 1935, p. 5.

91. Ibid., November 21, 1933, p. 5.

92. Ibid., October 8, 1934, p. 5; ibid., October 11, 1934, p. 5.

93. Jackson, *Spanish Republic and Civil War*, passim.

94. Gordón Ordás, *Mi política*, I: 153–54.

95. Ibid., 154.
96. Ibid., passim.
97. Ibid., 164.
98. Ibid., 351.
99. Ibid., 141–47.

Chapter 3

1. Patricia Fagen, *Exiles and Citizens: Spanish Republicans in Mexico* (Austin, 1973), 38–39.
2. Lázaro Cárdenas, *Apuntes, 1913–1940* (México, 1972), 355.
3. Joseph P. Lash, *Eleanor and Franklin,* Signet edition (New York, 1973), 856.
4. *Memoria de la Secretaría de Relaciones Exteriores. Períodos 1934–35 y 1935–36,* 2 vols. (México, 1939), II: 89–117.
5. See, for example, Isidro Fabela's remarks to the League, September 20, 1937, quoted in Omar Martínez Legorreta, *Actuación de México en la Liga de las Naciones: El caso de España* (México, 1962), 203.
6. Alba, *The Mexicans,* 182–83.
7. Interview, Spanish Republican who wishes to remain anonymous.
8. Smith, *Mexico and the Spanish Republicans,* 171–72, 177.
9. Vidarte, *Todos fuimos culpables,* 768; Linares de Vidarte interview.
10. Gordón Ordás, *Mi política,* I: passim; *El Diario Español,* August 27, 1936, p. 3; ibid., August 29, 1936, p. 2; ibid., September 7, 1936, p. 3; and ibid., passim, July-September 1936; Leobardo Ruiz to Secretary of Foreign Relations, Valencia, November 2, 1937, AHSRE, III/510(46)"37"/1, III–770–3; Spanish Office of Information, *The International Brigades: Foreign Assistants of the Spanish Reds* (Madrid, 1952), p. 20; Linares de Vidarte interview.
11. Alfonso Reyes to Secretary of Foreign Relations, Buenos Aires, August 7, 1937, AHSRE, III/510 (46)"37"/1, III–769–3, part 1. See also other documents in this file.
12. David A. Siqueiros, *Me llamaban el coronelazo* (México, 1977), 341–42.
13. President of Euzkadi Government to Lázaro Cárdenas, Bilbao, June 13, 1937; Lázaro Cárdenas to President of Euzkadi Government (draft telegram), Mexico City, June 19, 1937; Eduardo Hay to Ramón P. de Negri, Mexico City, June 19, 1937; Ramón P. de Negri to Secretary of Foreign Relations, Valencia, June 21, 1937, AHSRE III/510(46)"37"/1, III–764–1, part. 2.
14. Miguel Cabanellas to Minister of Foreign Relations (Mexico), Burgos, July 28, 1936; Ramón M. de Pujadas to Secretary of Foreign Relations, Mexico City, July 29, 1936, August 13 and 23, 1936, ibid., parts 1 and 2; *El Universal,* July 30, 1936, pp. 1–2; Gordón Ordás, *Mi política,* I: 430–31.
15. Cárdenas, *Apuntes,* 370.
16. Ibid., 390, 397, 409; *El Universal,* Feb. 25, 1938, pp. 1–4; Francisco Castillo Nájera to Secretary of Foreign Relations, Washington, April 25, 1938, AHSRE, III/510(46)"37"/1, III–767–11.
17. Ignacio García Téllez to Ernesto Hidalgo, Mexico City, November 5, 1937, AHSRE, III/510(46)"37"/1, III–767–11.
18. "Acta de la sesión celebrada por el cuerpo diplomático en la embajada de Chile, el día 13 de Agosto de 1936," ibid., III/510(46)"37"/1, III–764–1, part 1.
19. Lázaro Cárdenas to Leobardo Ruiz, Mexico City, October 22, 1937, ibid., part 2.
20. A. Serrano-Victori to Adalberto Tejeda, Paris, December 26, 1936; Adalberto Tejeda to Secretary of Foreign Relations, Paris, January 6, 1937; Ramón Beteta to Adalberto Tejeda, Mexico City, February 1, 1937, ibid., III/510(46)"37"/1, III–767–13.
21. Cienfuegos to Secretary of Foreign Relations, Guatemala City, June 23, 1937;

Eduardo Hay to Cienfuegos, Mexico City, June 24, 1937, ibid., III/510(46)"37"/1, III–764–1, part 2.

22. Manuel Avila Camacho to Eduardo Hay, Mexico City, August 12, 1937, ibid., III/510(46)"36"/1, III–766–3.

23. Rafael de la Colina to Ambassador of Mexico, New York, November 25, 1936; Luis Quintanilla to Rafael de la Colina, Washington, December 2, 1936; Arturo Beteta to Chargé d'affaires, St. Louis, November 21, 1936, ibid., III/510(46)"37"/1, III–767–11.

24. Cárdenas, *Apuntes*, 354; Copy of contract signed by Efraín Buenrostro and Félix Gordón Ordás, Mexico City, October 9, 1936; Gordón Ordás to Eduardo Hay, Mexico City, November 18, 1936; J. Rendón y Ponce to Anthony Eden, London, August 20, 1936; H. J. Seymour to J. Rendón y Ponce, August 28, 1936, AHSRE, III/146(46)/1, III–1325–5.

25. *New York Times*, August 21, 1936, no page number, clipping in file; Ramón P. de Negri to Secretary of Foreign Relations, Santiago, Chile, September 2, 1936; Luis Quintanilla to Secretary of Foreign Relations, Washington, August 24, 1936; Daniel Cosío Villegas to Secretary of Foreign Relations, Lisbon, November 8, 1936, AHSRE, III/146(46)/1, III–1325–5.

26. Eduardo Espinosa y Prieto to Secretary of Foreign Relations, Tegucigalpa, January 8, 1938; clipping from *Renacimiento* dated November 30, 1937 (appeared in Tegucigalpa on January 7, 1938), ibid.

27. Solórzano to Secretary of Foreign Relations, Guatemala City, November 6, 1937; Eduardo Hay to Solórzano, Mexico City, November 16, 1937, ibid., III/510(46)"37"/1, III–770–3.

28. "Venta de armas y municiones a España, 1936," ibid., III/146(46)/1, III–1325–5; *Washington Herald*, January 3, 1937 and *New York Times*, January 3 and 4, 1937, no page numbers, clippings in ibid.; F. Jay Taylor, *The United States and the Spanish Civil War* (New York, 1956), 67–68.

29. Lázaro Cárdenas to Ramón P. de Negri, Oaxaca City, March 22, 1937, AHSRE, III/510(46)"37"/1, III–764–1, part 2; Narciso Bassols to Secretary of Foreign Relations, Paris, Dec. 8, 1938; Eduardo Hay to Bassols, Mexico City, January 19, 1939, ibid., III/146(46)/1, III–1325–5.

30. Gordón Ordás, *Mi política*, I: 763–68; Novo, *La vida en México*, 372–73.

31. Smith, *Mexico and the Spanish Republicans*, 190–95; Félix Gordón Ordás to Eduardo Hay, Mexico City, March 15, 1937, AHSRE, III/510(46)"37"/1, III–764–1, part 3; Ramón P. de Negri to Secretary of Foreign Relations, Valencia, February 8, 1937; Hay to de Negri, Mexico City, February 16, 1937, ibid., part 2; Pascual Gutiérrez Roldán to Eduardo Hay, Mexico City, March 4, 1937, ibid., III/146(46)/1, III–1325–5; Leobardo Ruiz to Secretary of Foreign Relations, Valencia, November 9, 1937; Luis Bobadilla to Eduardo Hay, Mexico City, November 16, 1937, ibid., III/510(46)"36"/1, III–766–1, part 6; *Renacimiento* (Tegucigalpa), November 30, 1937, p. 13.

32. For other security lapses, see: Félix Gordón Ordás to Eduardo Hay, Mexico City, March 15, 1937; Ramón Beteta to Secretary of Government, Mexico City, March 18, 1937; Ernesto Hidalgo to Secretary of Communications and Public Works, Mexico City, April 19, 1937; Silvestre Guerrero to Eduardo Hay, Mexico City, April 13, 1937, AHSRE, III/510(46)"37"/1, III–764–1, part 3; *Washington Herald*, August 22, 1937, no page number, clipping in file, ibid., III/146(46)/1, III–1325–5.

33. *El Mundo* (Havana), April 2, 1937, no page number, clipping in ibid., III/510(46)"37"/1, III–769–3, part 1; *Washington Post*, May 10, 1937, p. 1; Jaime Torres Bodet to Francisco Castillo Nájera, Mexico City, May 21, 1937, ibid., III/510(46)"37"/1, III–767–11.

34. Adalberto Tejeda to Secretary of Foreign Relations, Paris, July 28, 1936; Hay to Tejeda, Mexico City, July 29, 1936; Tejeda to Hay, Paris, October 10, 1936, ibid.,

III/510(46)"37"/1, III–764–1, part 2; Tejeda to Hay, Paris, December 27, 1937; Jaime Torres Bodet to Eduardo Hay, Brussels, February 3, 1938, ibid., III/146(46)/1, III–1325–5.

35. Martínez Legorreta, *Actuación de México*, 104–5, 199–202.

36. Novo, *La vida en México*, 37; Luis Echeverría Álvarez, *Posición de México ante el franquismo* (México, 1975), 3–4; Linares de Vidarte interview.

37. Isidro Fabela, "La política internacional del presidente Cárdenas," *Problemas Agrícolas e Industriales de México* 7 no. 4 (1955): 3–10.

38. Ibid.

39. Martínez Legorreta, *Actuación de México*, 203–13; Fedro Guillén, *Isidro Fabela, defensor de España y de otros países agredidos* (México, n. d.), 77–78.

40. See correspondence between Secretary Hay and Ramón P. de Negri, Daniel Cosío Villegas, and Leobardo Ruiz, AHSRE, III/510(46)"37"/1, III–764–1, part 2; and III/510(46)"37"/1, III–770–3; Gravioto to Secretary of Foreign Relations, Havana, October 22, 1937; Hay to Gravioto, Mexico City, October 26, 1937; Hay to Primo Villa Michel, Mexico City, September 27, 1937; Villa Michel to Hay, London, September 29, 1937, ibid., III/510(46)"37"/1, III–770–3.

41. Dulles, *Yesterday in Mexico*, 392–93, 409–10, 430–32, 469, 494–95, 519, 524, 541–43, 574–77. Interview, María Luisa Tejeda Chardí, Coyoacán, D. F., September 20, 1977 (hereafter Tejeda Chardí interview).

42. Manuel Pérez Treviño to Secretary of Foreign Relations, Madrid, September 16, 1936, AHSRE, III/510(46)"37"/1, III–764–1; part 1; Blanca L. Trejo, *Lo que vi en España* (México, 1940), 112–13.

43. *La Prensa* (New York), October 21, 1936, pp. 1, 6.

44. Manuel Pérez Treviño, "La situación española," October 10, 1936, AHSRE, III/510(46)"37"/1, III–764–1, part 1.

45. Ibid.

46. Ibid.

47. Ibid.

48. Several documents signed by Manuel Pérez Treviño, November 1936; Adalberto Tejeda to President Lázaro Cárdenas, Paris, January 8, 1937, ibid.

49. Manuel Pérez Treviño to Secretary of Foreign Relations, Madrid, December 10, 1936, ibid., part 2.

50. Francisco Navarro to Secretary of Foreign Relations, Madrid, August 10 and 17, 1936, ibid., part 1.

51. Francisco Navarro, "La sovietización del territorio español controlado por el gobierno," October 13, 1936, ibid., part 3.

52. J. Rubén Romero to Ramón Beteta, Barcelona, August 30, 1936, ibid., part 1.

53. Ibid.

54. Alfonso Reyes to Secretary of Foreign Relations, Buenos Aires, October 18, 21, 23 and 24, 1936, ibid., III/516(46–0)/2, III–1246–6.

55. Daniel Cosío Villegas to Secretary of Foreign Relations, Lisbon, October 28, 1936, ibid.

56. Daniel Cosío Villegas to Secretary of Foreign Relations, Lisbon, November 7, 1936, ibid.

57. Alfonso Reyes, "Memorandum," Buenos Aires, October 22, 1936, ibid., III/510(46)"36"/1, III–766–3.

58. *Las Últimas Noticias*, January 14, 1937, no page number, clipping in file, ibid., III/510(46)"37"/1, III–770–5.

59. Manuel Pérez Treviño to Secretary of Foreign Relations, Madrid, July 27 and 28, 1936, ibid., III/510(46)"37"/1, III–764–1, part 1; Ramón P. de Negri to Secretary of Foreign Relations, Valencia, April 2, 1937, ibid., III/516(46–0)/2, III–1246–6; Smith, *Mexico and the Spanish Republicans*, 183–84.

60. Francisco A. Ursúa to Secretary of Foreign Relations, Santiago, Chile, November 13, 1936, AHSRE, III/146(46)/1, III–1325–5; Interviews with Mexican and Spanish Republican sources who wish to remain anonymous.

61. Ramón P. de Negri, *Panorama social, político y militar de España desde la rebelión de Julio hasta la fecha* (México, 1937); Siqueiros, *Me llamaban el coronelazo*, 360.

62. Ramón P. de Negri to Secretary of Foreign Relations, Santiago, Chile, September 2, 1936; Eduardo Hay to de Negri, Mexico City, September 25, 1936; Francisco A. Ursúa to Secretary of Foreign Relations, Santiago, Chile, November 13, 1936, AHSRE, III/146(46)/1, III–1325–5; de Negri to Hay, Santiago, Chile, October 7, 1936, ibid., III/510(46)"36"/1, III–767–7.

63. "Memorandum confidencial para el C. Presidente de la República," unsigned, undated; Ramón P. de Negri to Secretary of Foreign Relations, Valencia, January 25, 1937; Eduardo Hay to de Negri, Mexico City, February 11, 1937, ibid., III/510(46)"37"/1, III–764–1, part 2; Tejeda Chardí interview.

64. Adalberto Tejeda to Lázaro Cárdenas, Paris, January 8, 1937; Cárdenas to de Negri, Mexico City, January 10, 1937, AHSRE, III/510(46)"37"/1, III–764–1, part 2.

65. Ramón P. de Negri to Secretary of Foreign Relations, Valencia, April 2, 1937, ibid., III/516(46–0)/2, III–1246–6; *Memoria de la Secretaría de Relaciones Exteriores: 1936–1937* (México, 1938), 35–36.

66. "Memorandum confidencial"; Eduardo Hay to Ramón P. de Negri, Mexico City, February 15, 1937; Juan B. Arriaga, "Informe sobre la actuación del señor embajador en ésta," and "Continuación del informe confidential al Sr. Secretario de Relaciones Exteriores," undated; Hay to de Negri, Mexico City, July 21, 1937; Hay to Leobardo Ruiz, Mexico City, July 21, 1937, AHSRE, III/510(46)"37"/1, III–764–1, part 2; Ruiz to Hay, Valencia, September 20 and November 10, 1937, ibid., III/510(46)"36"/1, part 6; Interview with Spanish Republican source who wishes to remain anonymous.

67. *El Mercantil Valenciano* (Valencia), October 13, 1937, no page number, clipping in file; Leobardo Ruiz to Secretary of Foreign Relations, Madrid, November 21, 1937, AHSRE, III/510(46)"36"/1, III–766–1, part 6; Ruiz to Secretary of Foreign Relations, Valencia, October 1 and November 19, 1937, ibid., III/510(46)"37"/1, III–770–3.

68. Dulles, *Yesterday in Mexico*, 579, 585–86, 641–42; Tejeda Chardí interview; interview with Spanish Republican source who wishes to remain anonymous.

69. Novo, *La vida en México*, 144.

70. Alfonso Reyes to Secretary of Foreign Relations, Buenos Aires, November 4, 1936, AHSRE, III/510(46)"36"/1, III–766–3.

71. Ramón P. de Negri to Secretary of Foreign Relations, Santiago, Chile, August 12, 1936, ibid., III/510(46)"36"/1, III–767–7.

72. Ramón P. de Negri to Secretary of Foreign Relations, Santiago, Chile, September 8, 1936, ibid.

73. Alfonso Reyes to Secretary of Foreign Relations, Buenos Aires, October 10, 1936, ibid., III/510(46)"36"/1, III–766–3.

74. Salvador Pardo Bolland to Secretary of Foreign Relations, Asunción, August 20, 1937, ibid., III/510(46)"37"/1, III–769–3, part 1.

75. Alfonso Reyes to Secretary of Foreign Relations, Buenos Aires, February 11, 1937 and July 3, 1937, ibid., III/510(46)"37"/1, III–766–3.

76. Moisés Sáenz to Secretary of Foreign Relations, Lima, August 11, 1936 and December 8, 1936; Bernardo Reyes to Secretary of Foreign Relations, Lima, April 15 and May 31, 1937, ibid., III/510(46)"36"/1, III–768–8.

77. Ramón P. de Negri to Secretary of Foreign Relations, Santiago, Chile, October 7, 1936, ibid., III/510(46)"36"/1, III–767–7. Attached to this document are clippings from *El Diario Ilustrado*, October 4, 1936, and *El Imparcial*, October 6, 1936; Francisco A. Ursúa to Secretary of Foreign Relations, Santiago, Chile, November 13, 1936, ibid., III/146(46)/1,

III–1325–5; Ezequiel Burguete F. to Secretary of Foreign Relations, Mexico City, January 11, 1939, ibid., III/545.2/23, III–694–8.

78. Eduardo Hay to Ramón P. de Negri, Mexico City, February 11, 1937; de Negri to Hay, Valencia, February 14, 1937; Hay to Francisco A. Ursúa, Mexico City, February 15, 1937, ibid., III/510(46)"37"/1, III–764–1, part 2; Bassols, *Obras,* 395–404.

79. Jaime Torres Bodet to Moisés Sáenz, Mexico City, August 20, 1936; Bernardo Reyes to Luis Careaga, Lima, May 31, 1937; Eduardo Hay to Moisés Sáenz, Mexico City, July 2 and 8, 1937, AHSRE, III/510(46)"36"/1, III–768–8.

80. See *La Vanguardia* (Buenos Aires), October 31, 1936, no page number, clipping in ibid., III/510(46)"36"/1, III–766–3.

81. An extensive file of correspondence from Reyes describing these activities can be found in ibid.

82. Alfonso Rosenzweig Díaz to Secretary of Foreign Relations, La Paz, May 26, 1937, ibid., III/510(46)"37"/1, III–770–5; typescript, undated (but April 1937), ibid., III/510(46)"37"/1, III–769–3, part 1.

83. Adolfo Cienfuegos y Camús to Secretary of Foreign Relations, Guatemala City, June 9, 1937; Enrique Solórzano to Secretary of Foreign Relations, Guatemala City, July 31, 1937, ibid., III/510(46)"37"/1, III–767–14.

84. "Sesión solemne, Cámara de Diputados, Febrero 17, 1939," *Revolución* 2 no. 2 (1939): 47; Fernando Lagarde y Vigil to Secretary of Foreign Relations, Havana, May 27, 1939 AHSRE, III/510(46)"37"/1, III–767–6; Romero to Secretary of Foreign Relations, Havana, June 22, 1940, ibid., III/553.1(46)/1205, III–2394–15.

85. J. D. Ramírez Garrido to Secretary of Foreign Relations, Bogotá, June 11, July 21, and September 7, 1937, AHSRE, III/510(46)"36"/1, III–767–4.

86. *Memoria de la Secretaría de Relaciones Exteriores: 1936–1937,* pp. 29–30; "Gestiones del gobierno mexicano ante los demás países del mundo para poner fin a la guerra civil en España, 1937"; typed copy of A.N.T.A. news story, Geneva, April 3, 1937, AHSRE, III/510(46)"37"/1, III–770–5.

87. Carlos Peón del Valle y Verona to Secretary of Foreign Relations, Stockholm, May 21, 1937; Primo Villa Michel to Secretary of Foreign Relations, London, April 13, 1937, AHSRE, III/510(46)"37"/1, III–770–5; Tejeda Chardíi interview.

88. Carlos Darío Ojeda to Secretary of Foreign Relations, Brussels, April 5, 1937, AHSRE, III/510(46)"37"/1, III–770–5.

89. Manuel Maples Arce to Secretary of Foreign Relations, Brussels, September 2, 1937, ibid., III/510(46)"37"/1, III–769–3, part 1. Press clippings attached.

90. Luciano Joublanc Rivas to Secretary of Foreign Relations, Bogotá, September 7, 1937, ibid., III/510(46)"36"/1, III–767–4.

92. Typed copy of A.N.T.A. news story, Geneva, April 5, 1937, ibid., III/510(46)"37"/1, III–770–5; *Avance* (Havana), April 6, 1937, pp. 1, 4.

93. Carlos A. Baumbach to Secretary of Foreign Relations, Managua, April 17, 1937; Adolfo Cienfuegos y Camús to Secretary of Foreign Relations, Guatemala City, April 8, 1937, AHSRE, III/510(46)"37"/1, III–770–5.

94. Manuel Y. de Negri to Secretary of Foreign Relations, San Salvador, April 3, 1937, ibid.

95. Salvador Martínez de Alva to Secretary of Foreign Relations, San José, April 16, 1937, ibid.; Martínez de Alva to Secretary of Foreign Relations, San José, May 19, 1937, ibid., III/510(46)"37"/1, III–769–3, part 1; *Excelsior,* August 20, 1937, p. 11.

96. M. Alonzo-Romero to Secretary of Foreign Relations, Caracas, April 15, 1937, AHSRE, III/510(46)"37"/1, III–770–5; Salvador Navarro Aceves to Secretary of Foreign Relations, Caracas, August 9, 1937, ibid., III/510(46)"37"/1, III–769–3, part 1.

97. *La Crónica* (Lima), April 1, 1937, no page number, clipping in ibid.

98. Alfonso Rosenzweig Díaz to Secretary of Foreign Relations, La Paz, May 26, 1937, ibid., III/510(46)"37"/1, III–770–5.

99. The following AHSRE files have material on press reaction to Mexico's 1937 note on Spain: III/510(46)"37"/1, III–770–5 and III/510(46)"37"/1, III–769–3, part 1.

100. Vidarte, *Todos fuimos culpables*, 601.

101. Cosío Villegas, *Memorias*, 167–68.

102. Trejo, *Lo que vi en España*, 61, 67, 81.

103. CONSULMEX to Secretary of Foreign Relations, Barcelona, January 8, 1937, AHSRE, III/510(46)"37"/1, III–764–1, part 2; Eduardo Hay to Leobardo Ruiz, Mexico City, November 27, 1937; Ruiz to Hay, Barcelona, December 8, 1937, ibid., III/510(46)"37"/1, III–770–3.

104. See the correspondence from Luis Padilla Nervo in ibid., III/323.4(46)/1, III–344–1.

105. Bernardo Reyes to Luis Careaga, Lima, May 31, 1937, ibid., III/510(46)"36"/1, III–768–8.

106. Alfonso Reyes to Eduardo Hay, Buenos Aires, September 7 and 17, 1936, ibid., III/510(46)"36"/1, III–766–3.

107. Raimundo Cuervo Sánchez to Secretary of Foreign Relations, Bogotá, September 25, 1936, ibid., III/510(46)"36"/1, III–767–4.

108. Ibid.

109. Félix Gordón Ordás to Eduardo Hay, Mexico City, February 23, 1937; Hay to Gordón Ordás, Mexico City, Febuary 24, 1937; Luis Padilla Nervo to Secretary of Foreign Relations, Montevideo, March 11 and 17, 1937, April 29, 1937, May 21 and 25, 1937, ibid., III/323.4(46)/1, III–344–1; Bernardo Reyes to Secretary of Foreign Relations, Lima, May 23, 1937; Bernardo Reyes to Señor Ministro de Estado (at Valencia), Lima, May 29, 1937, ibid., III/510(46)"36"/1, III–768–8; Smith, *Mexico and the Spanish Republicans*, 189, fn. 54.

110. F. A. de Icaza to Secretary of Foreign Relations, Berlin, November 9, 1936, AHSRE, III/510(46)"37"/1, III–764–1, part 1.

111. Cosío Villegas, *Memorias*, 163–66; Eduardo Hay to Daniel Cosío Villegas, Mexico City, February 8, 1937; Cosío Villegas to Hay, Lisbon, February 10, 1937, AHSRE, III/510(46)"37"/1, III–764–1, part 2.

112. Jaime Torres Bodet to Ministro Plenipotenciario de México (at San Salvador), Mexico City, September 17, 1937, AHSRE, III/510(46)"36"/1, III–766–1, part 6; Antonio L. Schmidt to Secretary of Foreign Relations, Chicago, May 7, 1937, ibid., III/510(46)"37"/1, III–770–5.

113. Luis Padilla Nervo to Secretary of Foreign Relations, Montevideo, July 5, 1937; Jaime Torres Bodet to Luis Padilla Nervo, Mexico City, July 16, 1937, ibid., III/323.4(46)/1, III–344–1.

114. Navarro, "Sovietización del territorio español," ibid., III/510(46)"37"/1, III–764–1, part 3.

115. Roberto Vega González, *Cadetes mexicanos en la guerra de España* (México, 1954), 39–50.

116. Gómez Maganda, *España sangra*, 76–77. The Spanish text reads: ¡España no te amilanes/aunque te echen italianos!/contigo está la justicia/y todos los mexicanos.

117. Ramón P. de Negri to Secretary of Foreign Relations, Valencia, February 14 and 15, 1937, AHSRE, III/510(46)"37"/1, III–764–1, part 3; Leobardo Ruiz to Secretary of Foreign Relations, Valencia, August 16, 1937, ibid., III/510(46)"36"/1, III–766–1, part 6.

118. J. Rubén Romero to Secretary of Foreign Relations, Barcelona, December 8, 1936, and February 10 and 18, 1937; Eduardo Hay to Romero, Mexico City, February 16, 1937; Ramón P. de Negri to Secretary of Foreign Relations, Valencia, February 13, 1937, ibid., III/510(46)"37"/1, III–764–1, parts 1–3.

119. Ramón P. de Negri to Secretary of Foreign Relations, Valencia, March 1, 1937, ibid., III/510(46)"37"/1, III–764–1, part 3.

120. Leobardo Ruiz to Federación Provincial de Trabajadores Municipales (Albacete), Valencia, August 31, 1937; Ruiz to Comisión Ejecutiva del Congreso Provincial Socialista

(Castuera, Badajoz), Valencia, August 31, 1937, ibid., III/110(46–0)"37"/1, III–69–6; Ruiz to Secretary of Foreign Relations, Valencia, November 4, 1937, ibid., III/510(46)"37"/1, III–770–3; Ruiz to Secretary of Foreign Relations, Barcelona, December 2, 1937, ibid., III/510(46)"36"/1, III–766–1, part 6.

121. *El Diario de Puebla* (Puebla), September 23, 1937, p. 1.

122. Leobardo Ruiz to Secretary of Foreign Relations, Madrid, November 21, 1937, AHSRE, III/510(46)"36"/1, III–766–1, part 6.

123. Leobardo Ruiz to Secretary of Foreign Relations, Madrid, November 23, 1937, ibid., Adalberto Tejeda to Secretary of Foreign Relations, Barcelona, May 11, 1938; "Efemerides de la prensa de hoy martes 3 de mayo de 1938," (Barcelona), ibid., III/510(46–0)/1, III–770–2.

124. Comité Antifascista Español to President Lázaro Cárdenas, Los Angeles, September 16, 1936, ibid., III/146(46)/1, III–1325–5; Rafael de la Colina to Secretary of Foreign Relations, New York, October 25, 1937, ibid., III/510(46)"37"/1, III–767–11; Luis Padilla Nervo to Secretary of Foreign Relations, Montevideo, May 31, 1937, ibid., III/323.4(46)/1, III–344–1; Alfonso Reyes, correspondence with Foreign Relations, ibid., III/510(46)"36"/1, III–766–3; Gómez Maganda, *España sangra*, 57.

125. Guillén, *Isidro Fabela*, 72, 77; Estrella Morales, "Romance a Don Isidro Fabela," typescript dated 1962, Museo Fabela, San Ángel, D. F.; Linares de Vidarte interview.

126. Aponte, *Reyes and Spain*, 116–18.

Chapter 4

1. Smith, *Mexico and the Spanish Republicans*, 196–97; Vidarte, *Todos fuimos culpables*, 546, 807; *El Universal*, November 24, 1938, p. 2.

2. Siqueiros, *Me llamaban el coronelazo*, 348; Vega González, *Cadetes mexicanos*, 201–17.

3. Gordón Ordás, *Mi política*, I: 350; Leobardo Ruiz to Secretary of Foreign Relations, Valencia, November 2, 1937, AHSRE, III/510(46)"37"/1, III–770–3.

4. *Excelsior* August 22, 1937, p. 1; Vega González, *Cadetes mexicanos*, 39–40.

5. Ramón P. de Negri to Secretary of Foreign Relations, Valencia, August 7, 1937, AHSRE, III/510(46)"37"/1, III–764–1, part 2.

6. Leobardo Ruiz to Secretary of Foreign Relations, Valencia, November 2, 1937, ibid., III/510(46)"37"/1, III–770–3; Siqueiros, *Me llamaban el coronelazo*, 337.

7. Siqueiros, *Me llamaban el coronelazo*, 332, 358–63; Smith, *Mexico and the Spanish Republicans*, 196–97; "Memorandum," unsigned, undated (but evidently October 1937), AHSRE, III/510(46)"37"/1, III–764–1, part 2; Tejeda Chardí interview.

8. Siqueiros, *Me llamaban el coronelazo*, 317, 322–23.

9. Interview with Spanish Republican source who wishes to remain anonymous.

10. Velasco, "El partido comunista," 37, 47 fn. 33; *Excelsior*, August 21, 1937, pp. 1, 8; Herman, *Comintern in Mexico*, 127.

11. Vega González, *Cadetes mexicanos*, 14–30, 62, 66, 75; *Excelsior*, August 3, 1937, pp. 1, 10; August 4, 1937, p. 5.

12. Vega González, *Cadetes mexicanos*, 14–16.

13. *Excelsior*, August 3, 1937, pp. 1, 10.

14. Trejo, *Lo que vi en España*, 49 and passim.

15. Leobardo Ruiz to Secretary of Foreign Relations, Valencia, September 28, 1937, AHSRE, III/110(46–0)"37"/a, III–69–6.

16. Rita Guibert, *Seven Voices: Seven Latin American Writers Talk to Rita Guibert* (New York, 1973), 212–13.

17. Trejo, *Lo que vi en España*, 63–81; 103–9; Siqueiros, *Me llamaban el coronelazo*, 333–36, 355–57.

18. Gómez Maganda, *España sangra*, 24–25.

19. *REDZ*, 1936 and 1937, passim; On Pius XI's instructions to the Mexicans, see, Elwood R. Gotshall, "Catholicism and Catholic Action in Mexico, 1929–1941: A Church's Response to a Revolutionary Society and the Politics of the Modern Age" (Ph.D. diss., University of Pittsburgh, 1970), 143.

20. Encyclical text printed in *REDZ* 4 no. 5 (1937): 91–126.

21. Ibid., 4 no. 9 (1936): 221; Smith, *Mexico and the Spanish Republicans*, 174.

22. Rubén Salazar Mallén, "La rebelión en España," *El Universal*, July 30, 1936, pp. 3, 8.

23. News coverage printed in Gordón Ordás, *Mi política*, I: 435–37.

24. Ibid.

25. *El Universal*, January 6, 1938, p. 3; January 29, 1938, p. 3.

26. Fernando Robles, "La hispanidad y nosotros los hispanoamericanos," *Lectura* 2 no. 4 (1937): 358–64.

27. See *Ábside*, 1937, passim.

28. Manuel de la Cueva, "Comprensión de nuestro momento histórico," *Ábside* 1 no. 6 (1937): 30–38.

29. Carlos Gómez Lomelí, "En torno a los problemas espirituales y temporales de una nueva cristianidad," *Ábside* 1 no. 9 (1937): 5–15.

30. *Lectura*, 1937, passim.

31. Michaels, "Mexican Politics and Nationalism," 288–91.

32. *Lectura* 1 no. 1 (1937): 95–96.

33. Efraín González Luna, "Pasión y destino de España," *Ábside* 4 no. 1 (1940): 3–16.

34. Alfonso Junco, *El difícil paraíso* (México, 1940), 7–18.

35. Ibid., 19–62, 79–93, 109–13, 239–61.

36. *El Diario Español*, August 22, 1936, p. 2; Gordón Ordás, *Mi política*, I: 370; Trejo, *Lo que vi en España*, 15; *La Opinión* (Puebla), November 29, 1936, p. 3; ibid., December 1, 1936, pp. 3, 5.

37. *El Porvenir* (Monterrey), January 2, 1938, p. 3.

38. Novo, *La vida en México*, 69.

39. For press commentary written by Spanish rightists see the articles reprinted in Gordón Ordás, *Mi política*, I: 179 and passim. Enrique Lumen, *Adanzas de un periodista revolucionario* (México, 1964), 187; Benito Menacho Ulibari to President Lázaro Cárdenas, Ixtacalco, D. F., August 17, 1936, AHSRE, III/510(46)"37"/1, III–770–5.

40. Manuel Barreiro González to Sr. Representante del Gobierno Nacionalista (at Rome), Tampico, June 12, 1937; Gustavo Villatoro to Secretary of Foreign Relations, Rome, September 18, 1937; Ramón Beteta to Secretary of Government, Mexico City, November 5, 1937, AHSRE, III/510(46)"37"/1, III–770–3; Smith, *Mexico and the Spanish Republicans*, 172–74, 205–6; *El Universal*, November 8, 1938, p. 1; *El Diario Español*, August 13, 1936, p. 1.

41. Novo, *La vida en México*, 235–38.

42. Gordón Ordás, *Mi política*, I: 472–73.

43. Ibid., 442, 445; Linares de Vidarte interview; *El Dictamen* (Veracruz), January 9, 1938, p. 3; *El Universal*, February 8, 1938, p. 11; Enrique Guardiola Cardellach, *La anti-España* (México, 1938), passim.

44. Quoted in Gordón Ordás, *Mi política*, I: 371–76.

45. *La Opinión* (Puebla), November 8, 1936, p. 1; ibid., November 29, 1936, pp. 1, 6; ibid., December 1, 1936, pp. 3, 5; Gómez Maganda, *España sangra*, 59–60; *Excelsior*, August 5, 1937, p. 3; Vidarte, *Todos fuimos culpables*, 805–6.

46. Félix Gordón Ordás to Secretary of Foreign Relations, Mexico City, March 8, 1937; "Memorandum confidencial," AHSRE, III/510(46)"37"/1, III–764–1, parts 2–3; Adalberto Tejeda to Yvon Delbos, Paris, May 8, 1937, ibid., III/110(44–0)"937"/1, III–69–4; Cárdenas, *Apuntes*, 369; Fagen, *Exiles and Citizens*, 26–27; *Crisol* (Guatemala City), November 13, 1937, p. 1; *El Universal*, November 1, 1938, pp. 1, 9.

47. *Memoria de la Secretaría de Relaciones Exteriores: 1936–1937,* pp. 41–46.

48. Gordón Ordás, *Mi política,* I: 481–82.

49. Ibid., 378, 482, 487; Albert L. Michaels, *The Mexican Election of 1940* (Buffalo, 1971), 9; *El Nacional,* June 13, 1937, p. 1; *Revolución* 2 no. 1 (1939): 59–61; ibid., 2 no. 4 (1939): 18–23.

50. *Excelsior,* August 3, 1937, p. 1; Gordón Ordás, *Mi política,* I: 351.

51. Reynaldo A. Híjar, "Informe sobre el Ejército Popular Republicano," November 1938, AHSRE, III/510(46)"37"/1, III–763–9, part 2.

52. Edwin Lieuwen, *Mexican Militarism: The Political Rise and Fall of the Revolutionary Army* (Albuquerque, 1968), 115–29.

53. Ibid., 127.

54. Ibid., 115–29.

55. Ibid., 115; Novo, *La vida en México,* 61, 195; *Revista del Ejército* 16 no. 11 (1936), 904–6; ibid., 16 no. 12 (1936): 1042–59; ibid., 17 no. 3 (1937): 177, 182; ibid., 17 no. 4 (1937): 287.

56. Novo, *La vida en México,* 229–35; Gordón Ordás, *Mi política,* I: 351–52; Smith, *Mexico and the Spanish Republicans,* 188; *Revolución* 2 no. 3 (1939): 6–7; *Excelsior,* August 3, 1937, pp. 1–2; ibid., August 21, 1937, pp. 1, 8.

57. Gordón Ordás, *Mi política,* I: 488.

58. Miguel Mendoza Schwerdtfeger, *La revolución y la rebelión militar en España* (México, 1937), passim.

59. *El Diario de Puebla* (Puebla), October 29, 1937, p. 3.

60. Ibid.

61. Gordón Ordás, *Mi política,* I: 477–79.

62. Vega González, *Cadetes mexicanos,* 37–39.

63. *El Diario Español,* August 27, 1936, p. 2; August 29, 1936, p. 2; September 5, 1936, p. 2.

64. José Ma. G. Garza and Luis Mata to Félix Gordón Ordáz (sic), Monterrey, January 6, 1937, AHSRE, III/510(46)"37"/1, III–770–5.

65. *Excelsior,* August 5, 1937, p. 1; *El Universal,* January 9, 1938, second section, p. 1; ibid., February 1, 1938, p. 1; *El Diario Español,* August 13, 1936, p. 2; *El Popular,* July 3, 1938, p. 6; Novo, *La vida en México,* 229; Gordón Ordás, *Mi política,* I: 483–84.

66. *El Universal,* November 30, 1938, pp. 1, 14.

67. Narciso Bassols, "México ante España," and "¿Adonde va el proletariado español?" reprinted in Bassols, *Obras,* 395–404.

68. *El Popular,* July 19, 1938, p. 4.

69. Interview with Spanish Republican source who wishes to remain anonymous.

70. *El Universal,* July 31, 1936, p. 1; February 14, 1938, p. 8; February 17, 1938, p. 2; February 18, 1938, p. 10; Herman, *Comintern in Mexico,* 115.

71. *La Opinión* (Puebla), November 6, 1936, p. 1; ibid., November 9, 1936, pp. 1, 6; ibid., November 11, 1936, p. 3.

72. Ibid., November 23, 1936, p. 1; November 25, 1936, p. 1; November 29, 1936, pp. 1, 6; December 1, 1936, pp. 3, 5.

73. Bosques *et al., Cárdenas,* 37, 44. fn. 34; Armando de María y Campos, *Por un mundo libre* (México, 1943), 16, 53–56, 338–95.

74. Rafael Abella, *La Vida cotidiana durante la guerra civil: la España republicana* (Barcelona, 1975), 316–17.

75. *El Popular,* July 17, 1938, pp. 5, 7; Guibert, *Seven Voices,* 212–13; Trejo, *Lo que vi en España,* 49 and passim; Bosques *et al., Cárdenas,* 12; Eutiquio Aragonés, *Blancos y rojos (España 1936)* (México, 1937); L. Hurlburt, "David Alfaro Siqueiros's 'Portrait of the Bourgeoisie'," *Art Forum* (February 1977).

76. Francisco A. Gómez to Félix Gordón Ordás, Santiago Tuxtla, December 22, 1936; Francisco A. Gómez to C. Presidente de la Reunión Conferencista de Paz Americana,

Santiago Tuxtla, November 4, 1936 (carbon copy), AHSRE, III/510(46)"37"/1, III–770–5; Gordón Ordás, *Mi política*, I: 488–89.

77. See, for example, Palavicini, *México*, IV: 262–63.

78. *La Opinión* (Puebla), November 22, 1936, p. 3.

79. *El Universal*, February 24, 1938, pp. 1, 11, prints some of these charges.

80. Lombardo quoted in Tzvi Medin, *Ideología y praxis política de Lázaro Cárdenas*, 4th ed. (México, 1976), 198.

81. Nathaniel and Sylvia Weyl, "La reconquista de México: Los años de Lázaro Cárdenas," *Problemas Agrícolas e Industriales de México* 7 no. 4 (1955): 321.

82. *Excelsior* and *El Universal*, 1936–1939, passim; for information about Mexican correspondents, see, Ian Gibson, *The Death of Lorca* (Chicago, 1973), 144–45, 200; and also see "Efemerides de la prensa de hoy martes 3 de Mayo de 1938," AHSRE, III/510(46)–0)/1, III–770–2.

83. Gordón Ordás, *Mi política*, I: 353–54; Junco, *El dificul paraiso*, 222; *El Universal*, 1936–1939, passim.

84. *El Universal*, July 1, 1936, p. 3; ibid., Janaury 12, 1938, p. 3, ibid., January 19, 1938, p. 3; ibid., January 25, 1938, p. 3; ibid., January 29, 1938, p. 3; ibid., February 1, 1938, p. 3; ibid., April 3, 1939, pp. 3, 12.

85. Ibid., July 6, 1936, pp. 3, 5; and ibid., 1936–1939, passim.

86. Ibid., July 1936, passim; ibid., January 12, 1938, p. 2; ibid., January 22, 1938, p. 2.

87. Ibid., January and February 1938, passim.

88. See, for example, ibid., January 3, 1938, p. 3.

89. Ibid., January 1, 1938, p. 3.

90. See *Excelsior*, August 1937, passim; and press coverage quoted in Gordón Ordás, *Mi política*, I: 141–43, 475–76.

91. *Excelsior*, August 4, 1937, p. 5; ibid., August 6, 1937, p. 5.

92. Gordón Ordás, *Mi política*, I: 370, 377, 448–49, 765.

93. Ibid., 365–70, 443.

94. *El Hombre Libre*, January 3, 1938, p. 1; ibid., January 5, 1938, p. 1; ibid., May 6, 1938, p. 1; ibid., May 27, 1938, pp. 1, 4; and ibid., 1938 passim.

95. Herman, *Comintern in Mexico*, 123; *El Popular*, July 1938, passim.

96.. Gordón Ordás, *Mi política*, I: 417–72; Novo, *La vida en México*, 34–38, 115.

97. *El Diario Español*, July 27, 1936, pp. 1–2, 10; ibid., July 30, 1936, p. 1; ibid., August 1, 1936, p. 2; ibid., August 8, 1936, p. 1; and ibid., July-September 1936, passim.

98. *El Porvenir* (Monterrey), January 10, 1938, p. 3; and ibid., January 1938, passim.

99. *El Diario de Yucatán* (Mérida), April 4, 1939, p. 1; and ibid., April 1939, passim.

100. *El Dictamen* (Veracruz), January 1938, passim.

101. Félix Gordón Ordás to Secretary of Foreign Relations, Mexico City, March 15, 1937, AHSRE, III/510(46)"37"/1, III–764–1, part 3.

102. Gordón Ordás, *Mi política*, I: 478–79; *El Diario de Puebla* (Puebla), October 1937, passim; *La Opinión* (Puebla), November 1936, passim.

103. *La Opinión* (Puebla), November 11, 1936, p. 3; ibid., November 22, 1936, p. 3, and November 1936, passim.

104. *El Diario de Puebla* (Puebla), September 22, 1937, p. 3.

105. Ibid., October 11, 1937, p. 3.

Chapter 5

1. Smith, *Mexico and the Spanish Republicans*, 198–206; Vega González, *Cadetes mexicanos*, 62–66, 187–92; Jorge Zawadzky (of Colombian Legation) to Eduardo Hay, Mexico City, March 19, 1940; Hay to Zawadzky, Mexico City, March 21, 1940, AHSRE, III/524.9/94, III–2398–10.

2. *El Universal,* April 3, 1939, pp. 1, 10.

3. Ibid., April 4, 1939, pp. 1, 7.

4. Ibid., April 5, 1939, pp. 1, 7.

5. Siqueiros, *Me llamaban el coronelazo,* 350–54.

6. *El Diario de Yucatán* (Mérida), April 15, 1939, p. 3.

7. Siqueiros, *Me llamaban el coronelazo,* 348–50.

8. Aponte, *Reyes and Spain,* 136–37, 188–92; Fagen, *Exiles and Citizens,* 28–29.

9. Aponte, *Reyes and Spain,* 188–92; Cosío Villegas, *Memorias,* 168–79.

10. See *Taller,* July-November 1939, passim.

11. Gabriel Jackson, *A Concise History of the Spanish Civil War* (New York, 1974), 121; Vidarte, *Todos fuimos culpables,* 649–765.

12. Vidarte, *Todos fuimos culpables,* 788–89.

13. Palavicini, *México,* IV: 272; Fagen, *Exiles and Citizens,* 32–33.

14. Fagen, *Exiles and Citizens,* 32–33, 40–41; Amaro del Rosal, *El oro del Banco de España y la historia del "Vita"* (México, 1976), 9–10; Adalberto Tejeda to Secretary of Foreign Relations, Perpignan, February 18, 1939 (message relayed by Narciso Bassols to Secretary of Foreign Relations, Paris, February 18, 1939), AHSRE, III/510(46)"37"/1, III–767–13; Tejeda Chardí interview.

15. Fagen, *Exiles and Citizens,* 31–33, 59.

16. Ibid., 34–39; Smith, *Mexico and the Spanish Republicans,* 231–37; Pablo de Azcárate, "Service pour L'Evacuation des Refugies Espagnols (S.E.R.E.). Memoire sur son origine, constitution et activities," February 1940, AHSRE, III/553.1(46)/1205, III–2394–15. For one version of the controversy between Negrín and Prieto over the Republican treasury funds, see, Del Rosal, *Oro del Banco de España.*

17. Smith, *Mexico and the Spanish Republicans,* 209–11; Bernardo Reyes to Secretary of Foreign Relations, Paris, March 15, 1940, AHSRE, III/553.1(46)/1205, III–2394–15.

18. FOARE, *Memoria de las actividades de ayuda a los Republicanos Españoles: Estados Unidos, Cuba, México* (México, 1943); FOARE, *Boletín,* numbers 10–11 (mimeographed, undated), AHSRE, III/524.9/94, III–2398–10; Octaviano Campos Salas to Secretary of Foreign Relations, Mexico City, June 23, 1940; Executive Committee of FOARE, "Al Pueblo de México. Imped que el pueblo francés entregue millares de españoles a sus verdugos," undated flyer (but February or March 1940), ibid., III/553.1(46)1205, III–2394–15.

19. Félix F. Palavicini to Narciso Bassols, Buenos Aires, April 12, 1939; Bassols to Palavicini, Paris, April 20, 1939; Ángel Álvarez to Félix F. Palavicini, Buenos Aires, April 22, 1939; Narciso Bassols to Secretary of Foreign Relations, Paris, May 26, 1939, AHSRE, III/510(46)"36"/1, III–766–3.

20. Smith, *Mexico and the Spanish Republicans,* 212–14.

21. Ibid., 214–15.

22. J. Jadraque and A. Trabal to President of the United States of Mexico, Paris, December 6, 1949; Alfonso Guerra to C. Secretario Particular de la Presidencia de la República, Mexico City, January 29, 1950; Vicente Sánchez Gavito to Chargé d'affaires (at Paris), Mexico City, February 6, 1950, AHSRE, III/553.1(46)/1205, III–2394–15.

23. Pablo Campos Ortiz to Secretary of Foreign Relations, Santiago, Chile, April 3, 1939, ibid., III/510(46)"36"/1, III–767–7; two unsigned, undated "Memoranda" (but post-June 1940); Romero to Secretary of Foreign Relations, Havana, June 22, 1940; Alfonso Rosenzweig Díaz to Secretary of Foreign Relations, Panamá, June 21, 1940, ibid., III/553.1(46)/1205, III–2394–15.

24. Quoted in Michaels, "The Crisis of Cardenismo," 75–76.

25. Lieuwen, *Mexican Militarism,* 129–35; Michaels, "The Crisis of Cardenismo," passim.

26. Fagen, *Exiles and Citizens,* 41–52; Michaels, *Mexican Election of 1940,* p. 34.

27. Trejo, *Lo que vi en España,* 128 and passim.

28. Smith, *Mexico and the Spanish Republicans,* 183, 219–20.

29. Lieuwen, *Mexican Militarism,* 129–35; Michaels, *Mexican Election of 1940,* passim; Lumen, *Andanzas,* 317–21.

30. Fagen, *Exiles and Citizens,* 58.

31. Linardes de Vidarte interview.

32. Fagen, *Exiles and Citizens,* 44.

33. Aponte, *Reyes and Spain,* 179.

34. Cosío Villegas, *Memorias,* 178–79.

35. Novo, *La vida en México,* 356–57.

36. Vasconcelos quoted in Smith, *Mexico and the Spanish Republicans,* 297–98.

37. Luis Cabrera, "Los refugiados españoles," *El Diario de Yucatán* (Mérida), June 23, 1939, pp. 3, 6.

38. Ibid.

39. Fagen, *Exiles and Citizens,* 41–52 and passim.

40. Siqueiros, *Me llamaban el coronelazo,* 350.

41. For transcripts of these programs, see, de María y Campos, *Por un mundo libre,* passim.

42. Gordón Ordás, *Mi política,* II: 521–29, 693–16, 730–33.

43. Ibid., 737–41.

44. Ibid.

45. Smith, *Mexico and the Spanish Republicans,* 291–94.

46. Ibid., 285–86, 289; Josephus Daniels, *Shirt-Sleeve Diplomat* (Chapel Hill, 1947), 332–33.

47. Schmitt, *Communism in Mexico,* 218; interview with a Spanish Republican source who prefers to remain anonymous.

48. Smith, *Mexico and the Spanish Republicans,* 299–301.

49. See, for example, the comments of Carlos A. Medina, *Las Últimas Noticias,* October 14, 1977, pp. 1, 10; and the remarks made by Spanish newspaperman Miguel Higueras, quoted in *El Nacional,* October 8, 1977, p. 1; see also *Excelsior,* October 8, 1977, pp. 1, 9.

50. José Revueltas, "Profecía de España," *Taller,* no. 2 (April 1939), 28–30.

51. José Alvarado, "Antonio Machado," ibid., no. 3 (May 1939), 23–29.

52. *Taller,* no. 4 (July 1959), 54–55.

53. Eduardo Hay, *Discursos pronunciados en su carácter de Secretario de Relaciones Exteriores (1936–1940)* (México, 1940), 3–7.

54. Isidro Fabela, *Azaña y la política de México hacia la República Española* (México, 1943); and "La política internacional," *Problemas Agrícolas e Industriales de México* 7 no. 4 (1955): 3–10.

55. See, for example, Townsend, *Lázaro Cárdenas;* Daniels, *Shirt-Sleeve Diplomat;* and Claude G. Bowers, *My Mission to Spain: Watching the Rehearsal for World War II* (New York, 1954).

56. Vega González, *Cadetes mexicanos,* 12–14, 28, 39.

57. Andrés Iduarte, *Pláticas hispanoamericanas* (México, 1951), 9–18.

58. Octavio Paz, *The Labryinth of Solitude: Life and Thought in Mexico,* trans. Lysander Kemp, 2nd ed. (New York, 1959), 154.

59. Martínez Legorreta, *Actuación de México,* 1–10, 159, 177.

60. José Emilio Pacheco, "Nota preliminar," in Novo, *La vida en México,* 11.

61. Gilberto Bosques, "Cárdenas y la República española," in Bosques *et al., Cárdenas,* 9–21.

62. Emilio Uranga, "El fascismo español desde México," *Nueva Política,* no. 1 (January-March 1976), 67.

63. Echeverría, *Posición de México ante el franquismo,* passim; José López Portillo, *Regresar a España con dignidad* (México, 1976).

64. Echeverría, *Posición de México ante el franquismo,* passim.

65. Ibid., 3–9.

66. Ibid., 11–15.

67. Speech of October 5, 1975, quoted in *El Nacional*, October 10, 1977, p. 4.

68. López Portillo, *Regresar a España*, passim.

69. Ibid., 15–20.

70. Speech of Francisco Varea Rodríguez printed in ibid., 4–6.

71. *El Nacional*, October 7, 1977, p. 5; ibid., October 8, 1977, p. 4.

72. *Excelsior*, October 13, 1977, pp. 1, 8; *The News* (Mexico City), October 14, 1977, p. 2.

73. "En Contacto Directo," news program, Channel 5 (Mexico City), October 8, 1977; "México en España," news program, Channel 13 (Mexico City), October 13, 1977.

74. *Las Últimas Noticias*, October 14, 1977, pp. 1, 10.

75. *El Nacional*, October 8, 1977, p. 1; ibid., October 10, 1977, pp. 1, 4; *Excelsior*, October 8, 1977, pp. 1, 9; ibid., October 13, 1977, pp. 1, 8; ibid., October 15, 1977, p. 1.

76. *El Universal*, October 2, 1977, pp. 1, 7.

77. *Excelsior*, October 13, 1977, pp. 1, 11.

78. Iñigo Laviada, "Reencuentro de la Identidad," ibid., October 15, 1977, p. 6.

79. *Las Últimas Noticias*, October 14, 1977, p. 4.

80. *Excelsior*, October 15, 1977, pp. 7–8.

81. Ibid., October 8, 1977, pp. 6–7.

82. Iñigo Laviada, "España y México," *Excelsior*, parts 1–10, September 21–30, 1977. The author thanks María Lourdes de Urbina for providing him with copies of this file of articles.

Bibliography

Primary Sources

Archives.

Archivo Histórico de la Secretaría de Relaciones Exteriores. Mexico City.

Published Materials.

Aragonés, Eutiquio. *Blancos y rojos (España 1936)*. México, 1937.
Azaña, Manuel. *Presente y futuro de la República Española*. México, 1932.
Bassols, Narciso. *Obras*. México, 1964.
Bojórquez, Juan de D. *La inmigración española en México*. México, 1932.
Cabrera, Luis. *La revolución de entonces (y la de ahora)*. México, 1936.
Cárdenas, Lázaro. *Apuntes, 1913–1940*. México, 1972.
———. *Ideario político*. México, 1972.
Carreño, Alberto M., ed. *Pastorales, edictos y otros documentos del Excmo. y Rvmo. Sr. Dr. D. Pascual Díaz, Arzobispo de México*. México, 1938.
Cosío Villegas, Daniel. *Memorias*. México, 1976.
Daniels, Josephus. *Shirt-Sleeve Diplomat*. Chapel Hill, 1947.
De Alcázar, Ricardo. *Unión fusión y confusión de las colonia española*. México, 1928.
———. *El gachupín, problema de México*. México, 1934.
De María y Campos, Armando. *Por un mundo libre: Un reportaje radiofónico*. México, 1943.
de Negri, Ramón P. *Panorama social, político y militar de España desde la rebelión de Julio hasta la fecha*. México, 1937.
Domingo, Marcelino. *México ejemplo: El mundo ante España*. Paris, 1938.
Echeverría Álvarez, Luis. *Posición de México ante el franquismo*. México, 1975.
Embajada de México en España. *Relaciones internacionales iberoamericanas. Discursos pronunciados con motivo de la presentación de credenciales del primer embajador de los Estados Unidos Mexicanos ante el gobierno de la República Española*. Madrid, 1931.
Fabela, Isidro. *Cartas al Presidente Cárdenas*. México, 1947.
Federación de Organismos para la Ayuda a los Republicanos Españoles. *Memoria de las*

198

actividades de ayuda a los Republicanos Españoles. Estados Unidos, Cuba, México. México, 1943.

Gómez Maganda, Alejandro. *España sangra.* Barcelona, n. d.

Gordón Ordás, Félix. *Mi política fuera de España.* 2 vols. México, 1965–1967.

Guardiola Cardellach, Enrique. *La anti-España.* México, 1938.

Guibert, Rita. *Seven Voices: Seven Latin American Writers Talk to Rita Guibert.* New York, 1973.

Hay, Eduardo. *Discursos pronunciados en su carácter de Secretario de Relaciones Exteriores (1936–1940).* México, 1940.

Iduarte, Andrés. *Pláticas hispanoamericanas.* México, 1951.

Junco, Alfonso. *El difícil paraíso.* México, 1940.

López Portillo, José. *Regresar a España con dignidad.* México, 1976.

Lumen, Enrique. *Andanzas de un periodista revolucionario.* México, 1964.

Madero, Luis O. *El octubre español.* México, 1935.

Manjárrez, Froylán C. *La España auténtica en el curso de la historia.* México, 1936.

Matesanz, José A., ed. *México y la República española: Antología de documentos, 1931–1977.* México, 1979.

Menacho, Benito. *Los pueblos crueles: Lectura para emigrantes españoles. Ensayos.* México, 1924.

Mendoza Schwerdtfeger, Miguel. *La revolución y la rebelión militar en España.* México, 1937.

Novo, Salvador. *La vida en México en el periodo presidencial de Lázaro Cárdenas.* México, 1964.

Núñez y Domínguez, Roberto. *Como vi la república española (película impresionista).* México, 1933.

Paz, Octavio. *The Labryinth of Solitude: Life and Thought in Mexico.* Trans. Lysander Kemp. 2nd. ed. New York, 1959.

———. *The Other Mexico: Critique of the Pyramid.* Trans. Lysander Kemp. New York, 1972.

Ramos, Samuel, *Profile of Man and Culture in Mexico.* Trans. Peter G. Earle. New York, 1962.

Reyes, Alfonso. *Momentos de España: Memorias políticas, 1920–1923.* México, 1947.

Reyes, Rodolfo. *Cuatro discursos.* Madrid, 1933.

Secretaría de Relaciones Exteriores. *Relaciones internacionales de México, 1935–1956, a través a los mensajes presidenciales.* México, 1957.

———. *Memoria, 1936–1937.* México, 1938.

———. *Memoria, 1934–1935 y 1935–1936.* México, 1939.

Serrano, Pedro. *Política española: España en 1920.* México, 1921.

Siqueiros, David A. *Me llamaban el coronelazo.* México, 1977.

Solano y Gutiérrez, Mateo. *La raíz mística del comunismo, del socialismo, del Catalanismo y el sindicalismo español.* Oaxaca, 1933.

Spanish Office of Information. *The International Brigades: Foreign Assistants of the Spanish Reds.* Madrid, 1952.

Trejo, Blanca L. *Lo que vi en España.* México, 1940.

Vasoncelos, José. *Que es el comunismo.* México, 1936.

Vasconcelos, José and Alessio Robles, Miguel. *México y España.* 2nd. ed. México, 1929.

Vega González, Roberto. *Cadetes mexicanos en la guerra de España.* México, 1954.

Vidarte, Juan-Simeón. *Todos fuimos culpables.* México, 1973.

Villaseñor, Victor M. *Los problemas del mundo contemporáneo.* México, 1937.

———. *Memorias de un hombre de izquierda.* 2 vols. México, 1976.

Wilkie, James W. and Edna Monzón de. *México visto en el siglo XX: Entrevistas de historia oral.* México, 1969.

Typescripts.

Morales, Estrella. "Romance a Don Isidro Fabela." Museo Fabela, San Ángel, D.F., 1962.
Tejeda, Adalberto. "Informe sobre la guerra de España." Archivo Histórico de la Secretaría
de Relaciones Exteriores, Mexico City, File III/510(46)"36"/1, III–770–4, 1939.

Newspapers.

El Diario Español
El Diario de Puebla
El Diario de Yucatán
El Dictamen
Excelsior
El Hombre Libre
El Nacional
La Opinión
El Popular
El Porvenir
Las Últimas Noticias
El Universal

Journals.

Ábside
La Antorcha
Boletín de la Federación de Organismos para la Ayuda a los Republicanos Españoles.
Boletín Oficial de la Secretaría de Relaciones Exteriores
Lectura
Revista del Ejército
Revista Eclesiástica de la Diócesis de Zamora
Revolución
Taller

Interviews.

Francesca Linares de Vidarte. Buffalo, N.Y., April 14 and April 24, 1978.
Maria Luisa Tejeda Chardí. Coyoacán, D.F., September 10, 1977.

Secondary Sources.

Abella, Rafael. *La vida cotidiana durante la guerra civil: la España republicana.* Barcelona,
1975.
Alba, Víctor. *The Mexicans: The Making of a Nation.* New York, 1967.
Anderson, Rodney D. *Outcasts in Their Own Land: Mexican Industrial Workers, 1906–1911.*
Dekalb, 1976.
Aponte, Barbara B. *Alfonso Reyes and Spain.* Austin, 1972.
Arrarás, Joaquín. *Historia de la segunda República Española.* 4 vols. Madrid, 1956–1968.
Bazant, Jan. *Cinco haciendas mexicanas.* México, 1976.
Bosques, Gilberto, *et al. Cárdenas.* Mexico, 1975.
Bowers, Claude G. *My Mission to Spain: Watching the Rehearsal for World War II.* New
York, 1954.
Britton, John A. *Educación y radicalismo en México.* 2 vols. México, 1976.
Carr, Raymond. *The Republic and the Civil War in Spain.* New York, 1971.

Chase, Allan. *Falange: The Axis Secret Army in the Americas.* New York, 1943.

Cline, Howard F. *The United States and Mexico.* Rev. ed. Cambridge, Mass., 1963.

Córdova, Arnaldo. *La política de masas del cardenismo.* México, 1974.

Cumberland, Charles C. *Mexican Revolution: Genesis Under Madero.* Austin, 1952.

———. *Mexican Revolution: The Constitutionalist Years.* Austin, 1972.

Del Rosal, Amaro. *El oro del Banco de España y la historia del "Vita."* México, 1976.

Dulles, John W. F. *Yesterday in Mexico: A Chronicle of the Revolution, 1919–1936.* Austin, 1961.

Fabela, Isidro. *Azaña y la política de México hacia la República Española.* México, 1943.

———. "La política internacional del Presidente Cárdenas." *Problemas Agrícolas e Industriales de México* 7 (October-December 1955): 3–10.

Fagen, Patricia. *Exiles and Citizens: Spanish Republicans in Mexico.* Austin, 1973.

Foix, Pere. *Cárdenas.* 2nd. ed. México, 1956.

Fresco, Mauricio. *La emigración republicana española: Una victoria de México.* México, 1950.

Gibson, Ian. *The Death of Lorca.* Chicago, 1973.

Gómez Cangas, José Antonio. *El caso México-España.* México, 1960.

Gotshall, Elwood R. "Catholicisim and Catholic Action in Mexico, 1929–1941: A Church's Response to a Revolutionary Society and the Politics of the Modern Age." Ph.D. dissertation, University of Pittsburgh, 1970.

Greene, Graham. *The Lawless Roads.* London, 1950.

Grieb, Kenneth J. *The United States and Huerta.* Lincoln, 1969.

Guillén, Fedro. *Isidro Fabela, defensor de España y de otros países agredidos.* México, n. d.

Guzmán, Martin Luis. *El águila y la serpiente.* México, 1928.

Hart, John M. *Los anarquistas mexicanos, 1860–1900.* México, 1974.

———. *Anarchism and the Mexican Working Class, 1860–1931.* Austin, 1978.

Herman, Donald L. *Comintern in Mexico.* New York, 1974.

Hurlburt, L. "David Alfaro Siqueiros's 'Portrait of the Bourgeoisie'." *Art Forum.* February 1977.

Jackson, Gabriel. *The Spanish Republic and the Civil War, 1931–1939.* Princeton, 1965.

———. *A Concise History of the Spanish Civil War.* New York, 1974.

Katz, Friedrich. "Labor Conditions on Haciendas in Porfirian Mexico: Some Trends and Tendencies." *Hispanic American Historical Review* 54 (February 1974): 1–47.

Kirshner, Alan M. *Tomás Garrido Canabal y el movimiento de las camisas rojas.* México, 1976.

Lash, Joseph P. *Eleanor and Franklin.* Signet edition. New York, 1973.

Lieuwen, Edwin. *Mexican Militarism: The Political Rise and Fall of the Revolutionary Army.* Albuquerque, 1968.

Martínez, Carlos. *Crónica de una emigración: la de los Republicanos españoles en 1939.* México, 1959.

Martínez Legorreta, Omar. *Actuación de México en la Liga de las Naciones: El caso de España.* México, 1962.

Medin, Tzvi. *Ideología y praxis política de Lázaro Cárdenas.* 4th ed. México, 1976.

Meyer, Eugenia. *Luis Cabrera.* México, 1972.

Meyer, Jean A. *The Cristero Rebellion: The Mexican People Between Church and State, 1926–1929.* Trans. Richard Southern. Cambridge, Eng., 1976.

———. "Campesinos reaccionarios." *Vuelta* 1 (August 1977): 16–21.

Meyer, Michael C. *Huerta, a Political Portrait.* Lincoln, 1972.

Michaels, Albert L. "Mexican Politics and Nationalism from Calles to Cárdenas." Ph.D. dissertation, University of Pennsylvania, 1966.

———. "The Crisis of Cardenismo." *Journal of Latin American Studies* 2 (May 1970): 51–79.

———. *The Mexican Election of 1940.* Buffalo, 1971.

Millon, Robert P. *Mexican Marxist: Vicente Lombardo Toledano.* Chapel Hill, 1966.

Padelford, Norman J. *International Law and Diplomacy in the Spanish Civil Strife.* New York, 1939.

Palavicini, Félix F. *México: Historia de su evolución constructiva.* 4 vols. México, 1945.

Payne, Stanely G. *Falange: A History of Spanish Fascism.* Stanford, 1961.

————. *The Spanish Revolution.* New York, 1970.

Pike, Fredrick B. *Spanish America, 1900–1970. Tradition and Social Innovation.* New York, 1973.

————. *Hispanismo, 1898–1936: Spanish Conservatives and Liberals and Their Relations with Latin America.* Notre Dame, 1971.

Powell, T. G. *El liberalismo y el campesinado en el centro de México (1850 a 1876).* México, 1974.

Prager, Kenneth. "The Mexican Sinarquistas, 1937–1945." Ph.D. dissertation, Indiana Univeristy, 1975.

Quirk, Robert E. *The Mexican Revolution, 1914–1915. The Convention of Aguascalientes.* Bloomington, 1960.

————. *An Affair of Honor: Woodrow Wilson and the Occupation of Veracruz.* New York, 1962.

————. *The Mexican Revolution and the Catholic Church, 1910–1929.* Bloomington, 1973.

Rosenzweig, Fernando, *et. al. Historia moderna de México. El Porfiriato: La vida económica.* 2 vols. México, 1965.

Ross, Stanley R. *Francisco I. Madero: Apostle of Mexican Democracy.* New York, 1955.

Salamini, Heather F. *Agrarian Radicalism in Veracruz, 1920–1938.* Lincoln, 1978.

Schmidt, Henry C. *The Roots of Lo Mexicano: Self and Society in Mexican Thought.* College Station, 1977.

Schmitt, Karl M. *Communism in Mexico. A Study in Political Frustration.* Austin, 1965.

Sinkin, Richard A. "Modernization and Reform in Mexico, 1855–1876." Ph.D. dissertation, University of Michigan, 1972.

Smith, Lois E. *Mexico and the Spanish Republicans.* Berkeley, 1955.

Taylor, F. Jay. *The United States and the Spanish Civil War.* New York, 1956.

Thomas, Hugh. *The Spanish Civil War.* New York, 1961.

Townsend, William C. *Lázaro Cárdenas, Mexican Democrat.* Ann Arbor, 1952.

Turner, Frederick C. *Dynamic of Mexican Nationalism.* Chapel Hill, 1968.

Uranga, Emilio. "El fascismo español desde México." *Nueva Política* No. 1 (January-March 1976).

Vaughn, Mary K. *History Textbooks in Mexico in the 1920s.* Buffalo, 1974.

Vázquez de Knauth, Josefina. *Nacionalismo y educación en México.* México, 1975.

Von Sauer, Franz A. *The Alienated Loyal Opposition: Mexico's Partido Acción Nacional.* Albuquerque, 1974.

Weyl, Nathaniel and Sylvia. "La reconquista de México: los años de Lázaro Cárdenas." *Problemas Agrícolas e Industriales de México* 7 (October-December 1955): 3–357.

Wilkie, James W. "The Meaning of the Cristero Religious War Against the Mexican Revolution." *Journal of Church and State* 13 (Spring 1966): 214–33.

Womack, John, Jr. *Zapata and the Mexican Revolution.* New York, 1969.

Index